Literature
and liberation

Arnold Kettle (1916–86)

Literature
and liberation
Selected essays
Arnold Kettle

edited by
Graham Martin *and* W. R. Owens
Introductory essay by Dipak Nandy

Manchester University Press
Manchester and New York
Distributed exclusively in the USA and Canada by
St. Martin's Press, New York

Copyright:
essays © The Estate of Arnold Kettle;
preface © Graham Martin and W. R. Owens 1988;
introductory essay © Dipak Nandy 1988.

Published by Manchester University Press
Oxford Road, Manchester M13 9PL, UK

Distributed exclusively in the USA and Canada
by St. Martin's Press, Inc.,
Room 400, 175 Fifth Avenue, New York, NY 10010, USA

British Library cataloguing in publication data
Kettle, Arnold
  Selected essays.
  1. English literature – History and
  criticism
  I. Title   II. Martin, Graham, 1927 –
  III. Owens, W. R.
  820.9   PR401

Library of Congress cataloging in publication data

Kettle, Arnold.
    Literature and liberation: selected essays/Arnold Kettle;
  edited by Graham Martin and W. R. Owens; introductory essay by Dipak
  Nandy.
    p.   cm.
    Bibliography: p. 225.
    Includes index.
    ISBN 0-7190-2541-9: $35.00 (U.S.: est.)
    1. English literature – History and criticism.   2. Marxist
  criticism.   I. Martin, Graham, 1927 –   .   II. Owens, W. R.
  III. Title.
  PR99.K434 1988
  820'.9 – dc19

BT app 1/24/89

ISBN 0–7190–2541–9 *hardback*

Typeset in Hong Kong
by Best-set Typesetter Ltd

Printed in Great Britain
by Billing & Sons Ltd., Worcester

Contents

Editors preface

Arnold Kettle's reputation as one of the best literary critics of his generation derived mainly from his well-known and widely translated *Introduction to the English Novel* (1951–3). The aim of the present book is to make available a selection of his other, occasional, writings from periodicals or essay collections, many of them long out of print. The onset of serious illness shortly after he retired as Professor of Literature in The Open University made it impossible for him to assemble the book himself. But as editors, we had his direct advice in choosing from the wealth of available material.

Arnold Kettle was a Marxist critic, but strikingly different in approach and style from either the tradition of European Marxist criticism with its preponderantly theoretical cast, or the more recent development of a similar body of English criticism. Perfectly aware of theoretical issues, he was reluctant to elaborate them in critical essays save briefly, and in passing. He was convinced that writing about literature should avoid a specialised 'professional' language. It should be accessible to the general reader, and concentrate less on its own subtleties and profundities than on directing attention to the novels, poems, or plays under discussion. The usual mistake of intellectuals, literary and otherwise, he would often say, was to suppose that by thinking, and yet more thinking, they would finally arrive at 'truth', whereas the prime task was 'not to understand the world, but to change it'. Literature had its own special contribution to make to that process of human liberation, and the critic's job was to help literature have that effect.

In method, he usually concentrated on single texts, yet not as 'autonomous', always with a complex sense of their genesis in a non-literary history. Text and context were inseparable, save for temporary pedagogic purposes. Evaluation was important, and especially praise, but in a questioning spirit. 'This is so, is it not?': Kettle's criticism achieves the effect of the famous Leavis question the more effectively for the genuine 'open-ness' of its tone. Rather than 'literary critic', he thought of himself as a teacher, and a teacher who eschewed didacticism.

The essays in Part I engage general issues never far from his mind: the responsibility of the writer and critic to the State, and the view to be taken today of the long history of bourgeois writing. In Part II, the range of his interests in poetry and drama are demonstrated, and the final part discusses a number of novels other than those discussed in his *Introduction to the Novel*. The introductory essay by Dipak Nandy proposes that in such writing lay the germ of an unwritten book about a novelistic tradition, drawing its sustenance from and speaking directly to the needs and interests of a popular readership.

As friends and colleagues of Arnold Kettle's, we feel it an honour to have edited these essays. We are confident that they will reveal to a new generation of readers the deeply-held convictions and variety of insight of a remarkable literary critic, as well as the compassion and wisdom of an impressive man. We would like to thank Mrs Margot Kettle for her help and encouragement in the preparation of the book; and also, for their assistance in tracking down the sources of quotations in some of the essays, Mrs Joan Bellamy, Professor P. N. Furbank, Professor G. Hosking, Mrs Helen Rapp, Mr Andrew Rothstein, and Mr Brian Stone.

Graham Martin
W. R. Owens

Arnold Kettle and English Marxist Literary Criticism

Dipak Nandy

Marxist literary criticism in Britain today is voluminous, flourishing and seriously regarded. It was not always thus. For at least two decades, from the end of the 1930s to the end of the 50s, there were perhaps only three figures recognised as serious Marxist literary critics – Georg Lukács, Alick West and Arnold Kettle. And it was only the third of the trio who won general acceptance, both amongst readers and academics, as a deeply serious Marxist critic who did not demand a prior allegiance to Marxism as a condition of access to his work. There is a clear sense in which Arnold Kettle's critical achievement is unique. It marks the first successful junction (I have not forgotten Douglas Garman and Edgell Rickword) between the Cambridge English School and English Marxism. As such it is by definition unrepeatable. But the claim of Arnold Kettle to our attention is not that of a critic of the Cambridge English School who just *happened* to be a Marxist. The concern of this essay is to indicate his place in the evolution of the tradition of English Marxist literary criticism, a place developed and strengthened in the body of work produced after the publication of his seminal *Introduction to the English Novel*.

I

The first volume of *An Introduction to the English Novel* was published in 1951, a second following in 1953. Reading it today, it is easy to forget that it was a young man's book. Very occasionally, in a sentence like: 'The subject of *Tess of the D'Urbervilles* is stated clearly by Hardy to be the fate of a "pure woman"; in fact it is the destruction of the English peasantry' (II. 49), one is reminded of the brashness and *élan* of Marxism in the 1930s.[1] But the main, the abiding impression is of a rare and sustained sureness of touch; and, for a man of thirty-five, an enviable and wholly unpretentious wisdom which manifests itself every so often in massively central judgements. I am thinking of simple, lucid and memorable remarks which have not only stood the test of time but whose effect, now as when one first read them, is to send one back to the writer or the work with fresh eyes, remarks like: 'Hence the paradox that though Richardson is sentimental *Clarissa*, by and large, is not' (I.68); or the gruffly magisterial rebuke to Jack Lindsay for facilely equating the Celestial City with the socialist dream of international fellowship: 'Bunyan believed in a life after death and there is no point in insinuating that, had he known better, he would have believed in something else' (I.44); or the explication of the passage in *Vanity Fair* in which Becky throws Dr Johnson's dictionary out of the coach window:

This is excellent; but there is one word in the passage that prevents the scene from being fully dramatic and stops it achieving its potential force – the word 'actually' in the sentence describing the flinging of the book. This one word colours the scene, investing it with a sense of scandalised amazement which ... weakens ... the objective force of the episode. It is Thackeray who steps in and in stepping in reduces the whole episode. The tone of that 'actually' is the tone that puts almost everything in *Vanity Fair* at a distance (I.158);

or the 'placing' of Graham Greene's too-knowing pessimism in *The Heart of the Matter*: 'The question arises as to whether the sentimentality involved in seeing life as better than it really is, is necessarily more offensive than an opposite kind of sentimentality which takes pleasure in seeing the world as worse than it happens to be' (II.174); or the comment on Henry James's heroines, his 'vessels' of fine consciousness, that: '. . . the more finely conscious they become of their situation the more unable are they to cope with it in positive terms' (II.32); or the observation in the middle of a finely appreciative account of E. M. Forster: '. . . that there is always a certain sense in an E. M. Forster novel of life's being rather more casual than it is, not flat, not mechanical, certainly not dull, but arbitrary somewhere deep down' (II.155). To quote these remarks simply as testimonies of a shrewd and alert critical mind at work might be sufficient. But one notices also how unobtrusive and transparent, in a word, how tactful, the critical presence is even when the critic speaks *in propria persona*, so that the reader's eye is never distracted from the work itself. This is criticism as criticism – the general observation solidly anchored in the particular text – and not philosophy or propaganda masquerading as criticism. Above all, one observes, particularly in the comment on *Vanity Fair*, the way in which the critic's attention fastens on some tangible feature of a specific passage and then, and only then, makes the transition from a commentary on the text to a comment on the author.

Of all the essays in the *Introduction* none is so remarkable as that on Richardson: so much that is acute and just about a novel of over 2,000 pages is compressed into a mere six pages of criticism. Having placed Richardson securely in his age, Kettle turns directly to the question of what gives *Clarissa* a trans-historical vitality:

Here we reach a point at which Richardson ceases to be merely of historical interest. For in his delving into the private feelings and secret motives of his characters he achieved something quite different from the mere evocation of the sentimental moment which he seems to have intended. He got deeper into the subtle, wayward and contradictory feelings of human beings than any previous novelist had managed, and he did so because, in his search for the easily pathetic, he stumbled on a situation fully tragic ...

Tragedy occurs when a situation arises which men, in the particular point of development that they have reached, are unable to solve. Such a situation in the eighteenth and nineteenth centuries – and the problem is not yet answered – was the growing consciousness of women of the necessity of their emancipation ... Clarissa *has* to fight her family and Lovelace; they for their part *cannot* let her win without undermining all that is to them necessary and even sacred. It is from the examination of such situations that the artist makes contact with the stuff and movement of life. The actual material of tragedy changes. Clarissa today could solve her problem, at any rate after a fashion. But we still respond to Richardson's novel because in the world of the novel the problem is not soluble and yet the direction of the solution is indicated in the quality of sympathy which Clarissa herself (silly as she often is) evokes. *Pamela*, in which there is no such insight, we throw aside. But by *Clarissa* our human sympathy and understanding is quickened. It is in this sense that works of art are timeless; they capture the tensions and movement of life which, though for ever altering in form, are nevertheless perpetually going on.

... We shall not enjoy *Clarissa* unless we approach it sympathetically, through history. But if we approach it *only* through history we shall not enjoy it either. The past and the present are at once different and inseparable. It is precisely because he stumbled on one of the real, contemporary dilemmas of his own time that Richardson achieved an art which has relevance to ours. (I.70–1).

And that truly bears the mark of the great critic. One notes, as one takes a final look at this enduring and rich *Introduction to the English Novel* that in it, as in that passage, all the judgements about life, politics and art (which one might wish to re-examine and, here and there, reformulate) are nonetheless securely bracketed between what this critic considers to be his proper business: a particular author, a specific work.

There is a sentence in the essay on George Eliot, in which Kettle asks: 'Can we perhaps . . . *put our finger on* a note in *Middlemarch* which may justly be described as a shade flat?' (I.174; my italics). It was a recurrent phrase in his conversation. 'Put our finger on': tact. And this sense of touch goes together with that other kind of tact, moral rather than technical, which respects each thing for being what it is and not another thing. It is the necessary tact of the good critic.

II

Remarkable as *An Introduction to the English Novel* is, it is Arnold Kettle's *Meisterstück* – the evidence of his mastery of his craft – not the crowning masterpiece of his career as a literary critic. Of that masterpiece, only an unfinished torso is visible, in a clutch of essays on novels and novelists reprinted in this volume. In these may be discerned the fragments of an original, magisterial Marxist revaluation of the English novel on a foundation historically more secure than Leavis's and culturally more concrete than Lukács's. What is of absorbing interest too is that in laying such a foundation Kettle had to jettison some of the fundamental conventions of novel criticism, stemming from Henry James, which had once come to assume the status of axioms. Nowhere is this more evident than in his robust and, in places, eloquent vindication of Defoe's achievement in *Moll Flanders* or in the account he gives of the sources of Dickens's strength as a novelist. In retrospect it is obvious that no Marxist critic of any standing could have failed to join issue with the inheritors and guardians of the Jamesian tradition, but what is conspicuous is the manner in which Kettle does so. The corrective issues not out of a theoretical debate (by itself a fairly easy task); it seeps, so to speak, out of the pores of a highly specific analysis of a particular novel, the distinctive achievement of a particular novelist.

In these essays the grasp of the specificities of the relevant historical and cultural milieu remind one that this critic was an historian by training and a literary critic by election. Consider the way in which the fairy-tale element in Dickens is elucidated:

> The novels are full of witches and wicked uncles and Cinderellas and babes in the wood. It is perhaps worth making the point that such traditional elements in folk culture do not have to be turned into 'archetypes' in order to gain significance and interest. The prevalence of the wicked uncle is quite easily explained in historical terms rather than as the manifestation of some abstract psychological pattern. In a society in which inheritance and primogeniture are important, it is naturally uncle, father's younger brother, who has a particular interest to do the babes out of their rights. Ralph Nickleby needs no Jungian pedigree. The little lost boys of Dickens are an all too natural product of a situation in which the maternity death rate was still something like 20 per cent.[2]

Such a sense of social context and historical development is of a different order from that of Leavis, whose social history was limited to (and fatally limited by) a postulated *Gemeinschaft*, the 'organic community', of which *The Wheelwright's Shop* was the last remaining trace and the early novels of D. H. Lawrence the last memorable growth. History, including literary history, then came to a stop.

Georg Lukács is a different proposition. *Studies in European Realism* derives its strength from one of Marx's central theses on European history – the pivotal place of the Revolution of 1848. Up to then, Marx had argued, the European bourgeoisie in their attempt to wrest power from the governing class, the landed aristrocracies, needed, sought and forged an alliance with the nascent proletariat. It was the heroic age of the bourgeoisie, speaking, in its historic role as the midwife of the new social order, the confident, unself-conscious language of universal human rights – the language not of liberties, but of liberty. But 1848 marks, in the Aristotelian sense, the moment of catastrophe in this European drama: the moment in which an abrupt change of fortune occurs in the hitherto triumphant rise of the hero. The break-up of the bourgeois–proletarian alliance now leaves on the one side a bourgeoisie in power, but bereft of the legitimacy of the universal appeal it had until then been able to claim, and, on the other, a rising proletariat laying claim with increasing confidence (as it transforms itself from a class *en soi* to a class *pour soi*) to that very language of universal human liberation. The mantle of the champion of liberty, not for a class but for mankind, passes from bourgeois to proletarian. Bourgeois economic and political theory now correspondingly turn from their explanatory, revelatory phase to their apologetic, justificatory phase. Science gives place to ideology, and bourgeois economists now turn, in Marx's celebrated phrase, into 'the hired prizefighters of capitalism'. It is this view which is the root from which all of Lukács's work (save only the early radical and heretical *History and Class Consciousness*) stems. But what might have been a supple tool of analysis[3] turned, under the relentless Stalinist pressure towards orthodoxy, into an arid, mechanical device for sorting out the elect from the damned: before 1848, *ergo* realist; after 1848, *ergo* decadent, a naturalist, a portrayer of surfaces, of appearances rather than objective reality; or, at best a 'critical realist,' essentially *of* as well as *in* his society, critical as he may be of aspects of it.

Despite the manifest drawbacks of his view of modern art, Lukács's strategic value to his successors cannot be facilely written down. His adumbration of the features of realism in the high noon of bourgeois realism was evidently useable for a critic of the English novel, and it provided an alternative to the Leavisite tradition. What was perhaps the most promising germ in Lukács was the conception of the great (realist) artist as one who had sunk his roots deep in the soil of popular struggle, whose capacity to penetrate beneath the surface was a function of his freedom from a dominating, constricting view of reality and his perception of a wider, richer reality as it took shape in popular experience. This was the germ out of which some of Kettle's most telling perceptions in the *Introduction*, and more particularly in the later essays grew.

The strategy of the essays is clear. The first, decisive move is the deferential but deft side-stepping of Lukács's iron embrace in the opening paragraphs of 'Dickens and the popular tradition', which opens up a space between the as yet unrealised promise of 'socialist realism' on the one hand and the undifferentiated portmanteau of 'critical realism' on the other. In this space the novels of Defoe, Dickens and Hardy come into their own.

The second, perhaps equally decisive move, is a rejection of the Jamesian dogma of what properly constituted a 'novel'. Leavis's dismissal of *Moll Flanders* was a scandal: '[Defoe] made no pretension to practising the novelist's art, and matters little as an influence.' Nor were matters much improved by Ian Watt's scrupulous, not unsympathetic, but ultimately dismissive verdict in *The Rise of the Novel*: a master of the brilliant episode, but incapable of narrative or psy-

chological coherence. It is with these verdicts – or rather the un-
examined assumptions behind them – that Arnold Kettle joined
issue. And the issue is at the bottom whether 'the novel' is to be
delimited to works which centre round consciousnesses, 'depositories of intelligence' of a certain kind – intelligences, to be plain,
endowed in their physical embodiments with a certain amount of
wealth (from whatever origin – not a matter necessarily for close
scrutiny by the novelist), thus with status and the liberties and
privileges of leisure, cultivation, 'culture' and congenial company,
which bring in their train at once the prospect of dense, stable, personal relationships and the socially granted space in which to be conscious of, absorbed in and perplexed by the matter of relationships.
Which then furnishes the novelist with endlessly ramifying veins to
quarry. But if the novelist's scope is to be thus arbitrarily circum-
scribed, then poor Moll Flanders has as little hope of being received
into *this* world as she had into the respectable world of the free
gentlewoman to which she aspired.

Crucial to Kettle's (and Watt's) analysis of *Moll Flanders* is the
episode in the meeting-house when Moll attempts to steal a gold
watch, fails, but escapes because the crowd seizes instead on a young
man:

At that very instant, a little farther in the crowd and very luckily too, they
cried out, 'A Pickpocket', again, and really seized a young fellow in the
very act. This, though unhappy for the wretch, was very opportunely for
my case, though I had carried it handsomely enough before; but now it was
out of doubt, and all the loose part of the crowd ran that way, and the poor
boy was delivered up to the rage of the street, which is a cruelty I need
not describe, and which, however, they are always glad of, rather than be
sent to Newgate, where they lie often a long time, till they are almost
perished, and sometimes they are hanged, and the best they can look for,
if they are convicted, is to be transported.

It is, of course, both possible and permissible to dwell on the in-
consistencies, both within that passage and between it and the rest
of the novel, though at the risk of missing the real effect of the
scene, an effect of moral and psychological rather than photographic
realism:

The phrase 'and very luckily too' leads us into it. What is lucky for Moll is
the lynching of the boy for whom she can afford no more fellow-feeling
than a single use of the adjective 'poor' and the dubious consolation that
lynching is better than hanging or transportation ... Moll's reactions to

the episode, humanly speaking, are quite inadequate ... The paragraph is a flat one, a disclaimer, a refusal to see what has happened.... But that last sentence is, objectively considered, all compassion. The phrase, 'and sometimes they are hanged', the whole rhythm of the sentence, the toneless forcing out of facet after facet of horror, all these contribute to a marvellous effect. Moll is playing it all down; she can't do anything else, she who has put herself beyond the possibility of looking at such a scene objectively.[5]

But, if not a string of brilliant episodes, where is the organising moral centre of *Moll Flanders*? In one of his characteristically perceptive observations of profound but unobserved details in fiction, Alick West, in his essay on Defoe, had pointed out the significance of the fears of the little girl Moll of being forced to become a servant and her contrasting aspiration to be a gentlewoman instead,[6] a point which, Kettle notes, 'illuminates the specific artistic pattern of the book':

What makes [Moll] splendid – a great heroine – is that she wants her independence, to work for herself in freedom. She is a woman who is determined to be a human being, not a servant, and the feeling of what it means to be a servant is what generates the impulses which carry her through most of the book, until she too has become a gentlewoman with servants, living on riches whose origins she likes to forget about or to confuse but which Defoe has only too clearly explained.[7]

It is this organising pattern of the novel – with all the necessary forgetfulness, all the self-deception, necessary and gratuitous – which accounts for the problem of Moll's fragmented relationships with the people in her life:

Moll's life is not an isolated life; she has as many personal relationships as anyone else. That she is unable to have full and satisfactory personal relationships is due not to her individualism but to the actual problems she is faced with. Moll is forced to be an individualist by her decision to try to be free in the man's world of eighteenth-century England; but her impulse to be free is due not to individualism but to a desire for better relationships with other people than life as a servant will permit.[8]

Ian Watt gives one account of *Moll Flanders*; Arnold Kettle another. Which of them we find more convincing will depend as much on the breadth and depth of the critic's knowledge of and empathy with people in vastly different circumstances from his own as well as on his analytical acuteness. A grasp of the psychology of poverty, the cynicism of the poor, especially about intentions and promises, the Schweik-like cunning essential for survival, the prejudices of the underprivileged – these are not by and large part of the prescribed equipment of academic critics. I have no doubt that Kettle accounts for the 'technical' problems of *Moll Flanders* in a way not only more plausible but also more humanly illuminating. And that because he has looked at life from the underside, as has his Defoe, from the point of view of an extraordinary 'ordinary' woman whose experiences throw into relief the condition of life of the vast majority of ordinary people for whom limits, frustrations, discontinuities of experience are as real as their mainly inarticulate aspiration to freedom as an essential condition of being human.

The irrelevance of the Jamesian canon is brought out explicitly in the essay on *Our Mutual Friend*, a novel which James had written off as 'the poorest of Mr Dickens's works'[9]:

> Clearly it is because [James] is unable to see the Boffins as the depositories of the kind of intelligence which he, Arnold-like, associates with those whose destiny it is to set standards for society and spread sweetness and light, that Henry James cannot even recognise their natural sense and natural feeling. James sees the Boffins as eccentrics. Whereas to Dickens it is they, above all, who are the representatives of the sort of nature he was most interested in – popular nature in the true nineteenth-century sense of popular, expressive of the worth and potentiality of the people as opposed to those who rule and exploit them.[10]

What is this 'popular nature' of the characters central to *Our Mutual Friend*, and what is it that is important and, to us, relevant about it? It is in describing this – in relation to the central theme of the novel (as of the prosperous Victorian world of the 1860s), the theme of 'rising' in the world – that the continuity of argument between this essay and that on *Moll Flanders* shows itself:

> The question that Bella and the Boffins have to face is whether, given the opportunity, they want to 'rise', i.e. emerge morally from the working-class world into the world of Podsnap the bourgeois . . . . The corrupting force in *Our Mutual Friend* is not money but bourgeois attitudes to it . . . . These people, despite their poverty, decline to 'rise' by grasping opportunities that will undermine their humanity.[11]

Moll grasps whatever opportunity presents itself – that is her world and that is how she is – and she 'rises', with consequences which Defoe not only describes but also enables us to assess. Dickens's characters do not, and that refusal (which says much about their well-formed working-class world) is an instantiation of ' . . . a moral embedded deep in the novel: that a genuine emancipation or even

amelioration involves the maintenance of their moral independence
by working-class people and that such independence is incompatible
either with "rising" or with the acceptance of the sort of charity
which has bourgeois strings attached.'[12] One need only add that by
the 'moral' of the novel Kettle means nothing so crass as moral precepts ('Honesty is the best policy'), but rather 'moral pattern', as he
habitually calls it, the organising structure of the novel as distinct
from its narrative plot.

The revaluation of the English novel in these essays was evidently
part of a larger design, and the outlines of that design are delineated
(as the context of a brilliant, dense, suggestive analysis of *Bleak
House*) in 'Dickens and the popular tradition'.

First, there is the essential marking out of a crucial distinction,
for what does it avail a critic to lump together as 'critical realists'
novelists as diverse in kind and stature as George Eliot and George
Gissing?

Within the general movement of Critical Realism ... there are certain
writers who — though certainly critical of bourgeois society — remain in
their overall sensibility essentially attached to the ways of thinking and
feeling of that society. They are honest writers, they have many insights
and attitudes highly inconvenient to the ruling class ... But their sensibility ... does not, even in the case of George Eliot (the best of them),
burst the buckles of bourgeois consciousness, though it certainly strains
them. Whereas, in a basic and essential way, Emily Brontë and Dickens
and Hardy *do* burst the buckles.

The metaphor of 'bursting the buckles' (adapted no doubt from the
language of *The Communist Manifesto*) is expressive enough as it is,
but not for Kettle's purpose. What precisely does it entail? '... the
essential difference between these two groups of critical realist
writers is that the latter write from a point of view which can be
described not merely in somewhat negative terms as critical but in
positive terms as popular ....'[13] What is now required is to give
body to the notion of 'popular', and here it is a splendid sentence in
one of Dickens's political speeches that Kettle uses with strategic
effect. His political creed, Dickens had said in 1869, was contained
in two articles: 'My faith in the people governing, is, on the whole,
infinitestimal; my faith in The People governed, is, on the whole,
illimitable.'

The faith is a grounded one, and it is grounded, to borrow Sir
Peter Medawar's phrase, in 'the hope of progress'; for in that respect

Dickens was always closer to his scientific rather than his literary contemporaries. It was in particular a faith in the potentialities of the mass of 'ordinary' people, 'the People governed'. But the distinctive feature of Dickens's conception of 'the people' is just that he does not see them as 'ordinary', 'people of no name', as the Earl of Clarendon had put it two centuries earlier: 'Dickens . . . sees the People not as a vague or all-inclusive term − an indiscriminate "everybody" − but as a specific force in contradistinction to those who rule. And he sees them hopefully, confidently.'[14] Here, too, a distinction is necessary. Dickens's contemporary, John Stuart Mill, was writing, at almost exactly the same time, that he had 'sympathized more or less ardently with most of the rebellions, successful and unsuccessful, which have taken place in my time.'[15] Mill's lifelong radical liberalism, which grew more radical as he grew older, is not in question, but it is doubtful whether he saw society or people with quite the same optimism or indeed from their point of view. But it is precisely this empathy, hopeful but never sentimental, which makes Dickens the great exemplar of a popular tradition, properly so called, of literature:

A popular tradition in literature implies, then, a literature which looks at life from the point of view of the People seen not passively but actively. Such a literature will not, of course, except at its peril, gloss over the weaknesses, the corruptions, the unpleasantness or degradation of the People . . . The essential characteristic of a popular tradition is not that it should be optimistic but that it should be true: and because it is true it will in fact be optimistic.[16]

And what finally and decisively distinguishes this view of the people from that in the social-problem novels of the nineteenth century, or from Zola or Maupassant, is its capacity to see the life of the lower depths as human in its own distinctive way: 'One of the sources of [Dickens's] artistic greatness is his capacity to look degradation in the face and see humanity there. This was possible because he looked not from above but from the level.'[17] And there the design ends.

   The achievement of the essays reprinted here is the achievement of a critic of unusually wide artistic cultivation, who can reach easily for a film of Paolo Pasolini to enforce a point about Defoe; a critic with social sympathies and a practical involvement in political activity which few literary critics think to be relevant to their professional competence, but which lies behind the force of his observation on E. M. Forster, that 'It is simply not true that one touch of

genuine regret would have made the British Empire a different institution'; or the illuminating comment that it is easier to grasp *Lord
Jim* if one translates 'Tuan Jim' into the more accessible 'Jim
Sahib';[18] a critic for whom the problems of being a good man and
being a good critic are, though distinct, in the end intimately
related; a critic with artistic, personal and political sympathies as
generous and deep as they are unsentimental. To suppose that the
elaboration of a Marxist theory of criticism, or acquaintance with
this or that European Marxist critic, would have produced better critical practice than his or improved his own criticism is, in both
senses of the word, an impertinence.

It is a unique achievement both because it was the first of its kind
and because it was, for all practical purposes, achieved single-
handed. For the fact is that Communist literary critics of Arnold
Kettle's generation had little to parallel the collective *élan* of the
Historians' Group of those years. (Roy Pascal and Alick West were
his closest, perhaps only, critical colleagues, with the great and
little-acknowledged Douglas Garman as an invaluable antidote
against the rival dogmatics of both Leavis and Lukács.) That is
what makes Kettle's work in effectively transforming the heritage of
his predecessors so singular. David Margolies has ably summarised
the main features of that inheritance as we find it, for example, in
the pages of *The Left Review* of 1934–38: 'The most general assumption was the premise that all art . . . is class art . . . The second
assumption was that social value is the proper criterion of art. . . .
The third assumption was . . . the premise that art is active (i.e.
that it *does* something rather than being merely a passive reflection).'[19] It is as safe to say that criticism based on those largely
barren propositions stood no chance of being taken seriously as it is
to say that, after Arnold Kettle, there was no chance of Marxist criticism *not* being taken seriously.

Much as that achievement owes to the influence of the Cambridge
English School, its roots spread equally deeply into the distinctive
soil of English Communism of the 1940s. A proper history of the
special *milieu* of that Communist Party, to which Arnold Kettle remained unswervingly (and unfashionably) loyal, has yet to be written
– an account which notes its generous idealism of spirit, its authentic internationalism, its intense concern for anchoring theory in
practice, for making sense to and being understood by ordinary
working people, as well as its amply recorded dogmatism, political

naivety and partisan blindness. This was what Raymond Williams found notable and admirable about his Communist contemporaries: 'What I really learned from . . . that English Marxist argument was what I would now call, still with respect, a radical populism. It was an active, committed, popular tendency . . . concerned above all to relate active literature to the lives of the majority of our own people.'[20] And Edward Thompson's authoritative refutation of Orwell's *Inside the Whale* is all the more compelling because it was written after his stormy departure from the Communist Party when no taint of special pleading or concealed partisanship could conceivably attach to his recollection of that milieu:

Who would suppose, from Orwell's indiscriminate rejection, that there were many Communists from Tom Wintringham to Ralph Fox who shared his criticisms of orthodoxy? . . . That, within the rigid organisation and orthodoxy, the Communist movement of the thirties (and forties) retained (in differing degrees in different contexts) a profoundly democratic content, in the innumerable voluntary initiatives and the deep sense of political responsibility of the rank and file?[21]

Even a partial listing of names – J. B. S. Haldane, Joseph Needham and J. D. Bernal in science, Maurice Dobb, Paul Sweezy and Paul Baran in economics, Eric Hobsbawm, Christopher Hill and Edward Thompson in history, Brian Simon in education – reminds one of the extraordinary intellectual distinction of those generations, which combined a passion for scholarship with a clear, publicly acknowledged political and moral commitment, scholars distinguishable as well by their capacity to write in simple lucid English.

That is the milieu from which Arnold Kettle emerged, and it takes a considerable effort to penetrate beyond the casually received demonology of that period to recreate a sense of the intimate link that these great scholars felt between their professional work and their political commitment. No one has conjured up that sense more convincingly than Professor Hobsbawm when he writes:

Where would we, as intellectuals, have been, what would have become of us, but for the experiences of war, revolution and depression, fascism and anti-fascism, which surrounded us in our youth? Our work as historians was therefore embedded in our work as Marxists, which we believed to imply membership of the Communist Party. It was inseparable from our political commitment and activity.[22]

That, I believe, is as true of Arnold Kettle the literary critic as it is of Eric Hobsbawm the historian, and it is indispensable to our

understanding of what I have claimed to be a signal achievement.
For if we are to seek for the sources of the lucidity and economy of
his style, or of the absence, so notable and so easily unnoticed, of any
irritable reaching after theory in his work, it is in that milieu that
we shall find them. The eschewing of theoretical pretensions is a
positive force which is too easily unacknowledged. In contrast to
a definitive critical 'explanation' grounded in some as yet undis-
covered critical theory, Arnold Kettle's critical practice holds out
the prospect of an alternative role for the critic – the role of a parti-
cipant, better informed and trained perhaps but no more infallible
than the rest of us, in a process which, far from being conclusive,
demands instead to be performed afresh for each new generation of
readers. It is a profoundly egalitarian, democratic conception of the
critic.

Nor is it only a matter of style and approach; it is a question of
substance as well. If one is to look anywhere for the sources or the
astonishing depth of perception of the hidden history of women
which, two decades before the rise of modern feminism, illuminates
the reading of *Clarissa* and *Emma*, one is likely to find it in the
influence of people like the late Dona Torr, who no doubt it was who
forced her distinguished male comrades to concede that 'we were
particularly weak on the role of women in economic life.'[23] It will be
in the particular ambience of that Communist Party that the author
of the *Introduction*, who insists so lightly but firmly on the interplay
of 'life' and 'pattern' in the making of a novel, will have learnt that
life is more important than any theory about it, including Marxism.

III

The Communist Party did not produce another critic of Arnold
Kettle's stature; the achievement of the late Alick West is of a
wholly different kind. The purpose of this essay is not, however, to
explain, but to register the claim of a great Marxist literary critic, a
Communist whose influence as a good man and a memorable teacher
is treasured by his former pupils in places as far flung as Argentina,
Brazil, the United States, France, Yugoslavia, Nigeria, Tanzania
and India; and to say that none of these achievements existed in
isolation from the others.

What did they learn from him? It would be presumptious to pretend to offer a comprehensive answer, but perhaps a few propositions

may command general assent. They learnt that literature is not to be approached by shedding one's preconceptions of what matters in life, but, on the contrary, by exposing them to the insights of the great writers. They would have sensed a certain suspicion of scholastic agility when confronted by manifestly great works of fiction; acquired a respect for the complexity of life as lived and experienced which defies, and will always defy, complete theoretical capture, and thus a respect for simplicity in one's own account of the experience of literature, a readiness to be content to 'lay down the thing as it was', in Bunyan's words.[24] They will have acquired a sense of the openness of human existence or, to put it another way, of history as a process in the making rather than as something given,[25] with real men and women as its agents, with the corollary that critics are denied access to conclusive, incorrigible verdicts immune to revision in the light of experience. They will have sensed too a profound belief in human agency, not indeed in defiance of the inheritance and constraints of history, but working in and through those constraints to create new possibilities of living: the critic and the reader thus become, rather than teacher and pupil, joint venturers in an evolving enterprise in which there can be no finality until time itself has come to a stop. They will certainly have learnt that these great works of art are not to be regarded as 'monuments of unageing intellect', but as constructions, more or less perfect, more or less complete, by 'men alive', sometimes 'whole men alive', attempting, in a real and determinable context of society and history, to order and make sense of their experience. So that the task of puzzling out their meaning and significance is no academic five-finger exercise but, rightly approached, an enrichment of our present experience, a positive instrument for coming to terms with and, who knows, occasionally even resolving the tensions and contradictions of our own situation in history. Expecting an account of how life shapes literature, they will have acquired a sense of the manifold ways in which great literature is an ever-present force in enabling us to cope with and shape our own lives.

Notes

1   This work is subsequently entitled *Introduction*; references are to volume and page number. Of the quoted sentences, Professor Richard Hoggart has acutely observed (private communication): 'Arnold often uses

these opening sentences as a gauntlet thrown down to the reader to think afresh.'

2   Kettle, 'Dickens and the popular tradition', below, p. 146.

3   Just how supple and penetrating may be seen in Professor C. B. Macpherson's pioneering study of seventeenth-century political thought, *The Political Theory of Possessive Individualism* (1960), which starts from the identical premise.

4   F. R. Leavis, *The Great Tradition* (1948), p. 2.

5   Kettle, 'In defence of *Moll Flanders*', below, p. 132.

6   Alick West, 'Daniel Defoe', in *Mountain in the Sunlight* (1958), p. 90.

7   Kettle, 'In defence of *Moll Flanders*', below, p. 134.

8   Below, p. 137.

9   Henry James, *'Our Mutual Friend'* (1865), in Morris Shapira (ed.), *Henry James: Selected Literary Criticism* (1963), p. 6.

10   Kettle, *'Our Mutual Friend'*, below, pp. 175–6.

11   *Ibid.*, pp. 171, 173.

12   *Ibid.*, pp. 173–4. That the theme of 'rising', with its accompanying moral predicaments, is no artefact of the critic might have become clearer had Kettle referred to the debate, on this very topic, at the Trades Union Congress in 1880 (TUC *Annual Report*, 1880, pp. 26–7); or indeed to the continuous debate from then to the 1960s on the 'embourgeoisement' of the British working class: see especially John Goldthorpe, David Lockwood, Frank Bechhofer and Jennifer Platt, *The Affluent Worker in the Class Structure* (1967–69). What this body of work undoubtedly shows is the historical solidity of Kettle's account of the moral structure of Dicken's novel.

13   Kettle, 'Dickens and the popular tradition', below, p. 142.

14   *Ibid.*, p. 152.

15   John Stuart Mill, 'The contest in America', *Fraser's Magazine*, February 1862; reprinted in *Dissertations and Discourses*, 4 vols. (1859–75), Vol. III (1867), p. 196.

16   Kettle, *op. cit.*, pp. 153–4.

17   *Ibid.*, p. 166.

18   Kettle, 'In defence of *Moll Flanders*', below, pp. 137–8; *Introduction*, II.161; 'Consensus on Conrad?', in *The Literary Review* (1981), p. 130.

19   David Margolies, *'Left Review* and Left literary theory', in Jon Clark, Margot Heinemann, David margolies and Carole Snee (eds.), *Culture and Crisis in Britain in the '30s* (1979), pp. 68–9.

20   Raymond Williams, *Marxism and Literature* (1977), p. 2.

21   E. P. Thompson, 'Outside the whale', in *Out of Apathy* (1960); reprinted in *The Poverty of Theory* (1978), p. 16.

22   E. J. Hobsbawm, 'The Historians' Group of the Communist Party', in Maurice Cornforth (ed.), *Rebels and their Causes* (1978), p. 26.

23   *Ibid.*, p. 37.

24   Bunyan, Preface to *Grace Abounding* (1666), in Roger Sharrock

(ed.), *Grace Abounding* and *The Pilgrim's Progress* (Oxford Standard Authors, 1966), p. 5.

25 The title of Paul Sweezy's collected essays, *The Present as History* (1953), captures this sense succinctly.

Part I

The progressive tradition in bourgeois culture

I want to take as my texts two very pregnant sentences: (i) that famous statement of Lenin's: 'There is no Chinese Wall between the bourgeois-democratic revolution and the socialist revolution',[1] and (ii) a remark of Gorky's in his speech to the First Congress of the All-Union Association of Soviet Writers: 'There is every reason to hope that when Marxists will have written a history of culture, we shall see that the part played by the bourgeoisie in the creation of culture has been greatly overestimated, especially in the sphere of literature.'[2]

It is about literature, primarily, that I want to speak. What does Gorky mean in the remark I have just quoted? Does he imply that the culture of the last four hundred years – the period of bourgeois ascendancy in the history of human society – will turn out to have been greatly overestimated? No, I do not think so. Nor does he mean that Shakespeare and Milton, Goethe and Heine, Balzac and Tolstoy and the other great writers of the bourgeois period, are not, after all, such great writers as has been assumed.

What Gorky is calling into question is the view that what gives the great art of the bourgeois period its long-term value is some specifically *bourgeois* quality, a specifically *bourgeois* contribution: the view, for instance, that Milton is a great writer because he is 'a representative of the bourgeoisie'.

I think this question is important, for a number of reasons. It raises, in the first place, some interesting *theoretical* problems. It raises the question of exactly what we mean when we speak, as Marxists, of culture or art as a 'reflection' of reality. Isn't 'reflection' too passive a word to indicate satisfactorily the nature and function of art?

Again, it raises the question of the relevance of the historical theory of 'progressive classes' to problems of art. Generally speaking, in our view of history, we speak of a class as being 'progressive' if it carries through a revolutionary change necessary for the further development of human society. Thus, in England in the seventeenth century, the capitalist class was 'progressive' because it carried through the necessary task of destroying feudal relationships which had become fetters on the development of the productive forces. Can the epithet 'progressive' usefully be transferred to an analysis of the art of the period?

Gorky's statement, the more one thinks about it, raises also *practical* questions which affect our day-to-day political work. On our interpretation of it depends our whole attitude to what we often to glibly refer to as 'our cultural heritage'. In precisely what sense is the culture of the past *our* culture? Upon the answer we give will depend our attitude to the defence of that heritage. Clearly we shall not defend with any great enthusiasm a culture we conceive to have little to do with our own values and aspirations. If bourgeois society can be considered progressive only in a historical sense and bourgeois culture is but a reflection of that society in a passive sense, then the defence of the culture of the past is unlikely to arouse in us any deep enthusiasm. This whole question links up with the vital political problem of the defence of our national independence – a concept of which most of us have, in my opinion, as yet a very inadequate understanding.

Perhaps the first consideration which will help us towards a greater clarity on this subject is to recall the nature of the bourgeois revolution itself.

It was not, in the commonplace sense, a sudden revolution. England was not a feudal country one year and a bourgeois one in the following year. If we take certain dates as decisive – 1649, 1688, 1832 – it is to indicate that at these revolutionary points the bourgeois class (or sections of that class) became established as the dominant force within British society. But that does not mean that there were no other forces. The feudal landowners, for instance, remained a very important power *after* their defeat in the Civil War and their ideology remained a power too. In bourgeois society the bourgeoisie is the ruling class; but it is not the whole of society.

It is necessary to see society, to see Britain, the whole time as something changing. Struggles are always going on, even if under the surface. In class society there is *always* a social ferment, even though the casual observer (who generally turns out, incidentally, to be more closely associated with the ruling class than with the exploited) may not be aware of it. Even in periods like the Middle Ages or eighteenth-century England, which historians often refer to as static and secure, the ferment goes on. We must not forget that eighteenth-century England is the era of Swift and Hogarth, artists whose work expresses in the most violent and extreme terms an intense and bitter social ferment.

If we realise that 'society' (i.e., for our purposes at the moment, Britain) cannot adequately be described in terms of its ruling class, and that the English bourgeois revolution was itself not a sudden, simple, decisive event, we shall not expect the cultural manifestations of that revolution to be simple and static.

The first great cultural expressions of the bourgeois revolution in Europe were the painting and architecture of the Italian renaissance and the literature of Elizabethan England.

Elizabethan literature reaches its height *before* the English commercial bourgeois achieves political power. The Elizabethan period is one of tension, of a gathering and intense struggle between the old, feudal, landowning class and the new traders, the men who were opening up the trade routes of the world and making the towns the centre of English economic life. Elizabeth herself and the Tudor monarchs in general attempted to hold a precarious balance between these two opposing classes.

Marlowe's plays are the first great artistic expression of the class struggle of the Elizabethan period. The most obvious and striking thing about these plays is the emergence of the individualist hero. Tamburlane, who seeks limitless power, Barabas who seeks limitless wealth, Faustus who seeks limitless knowledge: they are the new men of the sixteenth century, the men who reject and despise the limits, the morals, the science, the sanctities of the medieval feudal world, and yet who break themselves against the still dominant forces – material and spiritual – of that passing society. They embody in themselves the inmost aspirations of bourgeois man.

Marlowe's plays are an interesting example of the way cultural change comes about. Marlowe takes an old *form* – the medieval morality play, crude, old-fashioned, yet in the real sense popular –

and injects into it a new *content* – the clash of ideas involved in the struggle between feudal and bourgeois man. Through this injection the old form is changed, a new form is achieved. What is new in *Faustus* is the poetry, the 'mighty line', and the poetry isn't something laid on like icing, a decoration. The poetry is the expression of Marlowe's passion, the passion of the new bourgeois ideology. The poetry *is* the passion.

> Is it not passing brave to be a king
> And ride in triumph through Persepolis?[3]

Within Tamburlane's words is an assertion of the splendour of the new nation state. The king is not merely the barbaric Asiatic khan but Shakespeare's Henry V and Gloriana herself. The national tradition is somehow taken up and enriched.

Just as Faustus' vision of Helen of Troy transforms every medieval figure of the Virgin and shatters the medieval conventions of courtly love, so does his vision of the limitless horizons of science and knowledge express the new possibilities opening up for mankind with the bourgeois revolution.

> O what a world of profit and delight
> Of power and honour and omniptotence ...[4]

The passion behind the words bursts the bounds of the old medieval verse-forms.

Marlowe's colossal individualists are all defeated. There is a limit to his confidence in them. Yet the motive-force of passion behind the plays dominates and negates the defeat. Marlowe is a real bourgeois poet, and significantly the artistic limitations of his plays are bound up with this very fact. Their weakness lies in a certain lack of humanity. It is ideas rather than people which set alight his language.

With Shakespeare it is different. With him the inadequacy of describing the poet as 'a representative of the rising bourgeoisie' becomes clear.

For Shakespeare is not a bourgeois. Witness his attitude to Shylock. Witness those remarkable lines which Marx analysed to such effect, when Timon describes the effects of gold:

> This yellow slave
> Will knit and break religions; bless the accurs'd;
> Make the hoar leprosy ador'd; place thieves

And give them title, knee, and approbation
With senators on the bench ...[5]

No bourgeois could utter such words and remain a bourgeois.

Nor is Shakespeare a 'representative of the decaying feudal ruling class'. It is true that he sometimes reflects a nostalgic looking back to the days of feudal relationships (e.g., in *As You Like It*) and that he often emphasizes the virtues of stability, order, and degree (Ulysses in *Troilus*, the gardeners in *Richard II*); but such emphases do not mean that the positive driving-force of his plays can be described as 'feudal'. Indeed, to turn Shakespeare into an amiable reactionary is to drain the very life-blood from his plays. A 'feudal' dramatist could never let his characters talk like Hamlet with a supreme insolence of 'a king going a pilgrimage through the guts of a beggar'. Shakespeare's central subject is the killing of the king. The very core of *King Lear* is an exposure of the inadequacy of feudal concepts of kingship.

The positives in Shakespeare's work are neither the feudal values nor the bourgeois ones. Nor can they be the values of the masses – not yet a conscious class – though his attitude to the common people is more ambiguous than has sometimes been suggested. How, then, can we describe Shakespeare's positive values? I can only say that they are the values of *humanity*. Again and again at the supreme moments of emotion in the plays it is as a man or a woman – divested of ruling-class attitudes – that the chief characters have to stand or fall.

He was a man, take him for all in all.
I shall not look upon his like again ...[6]

says Hamlet of his father. Cleopatra, after the death of Antony, is approached by her women with the titles of majesty and rejects them:

No more but e'en a woman and commanded
By such poor passion as the maid that milks
And does the meanest chores.[7]

King Lear, a Tragedy, is yet a Triumph: Lear's progress from kingship to manhood, foolish and fond yet noble and serene.

There is, I know, a danger in thus formulating humanity as the positive value behind the plays. Humanity, abstracted from actual situations, becomes an idealist conception of no validity. Humanity does not exist in the abstract; Man is always a particular man. What I mean then by humanity in this context is *man in his fullest aspirations realisable in the concrete situation of England of the sixteenth and seventeenth centuries*, remembering always that England of the sixteenth and seventeenth centuries is the England not only of the feudal landowners and the Puritan businessmen but of Sir Thomas More and Francis Bacon and the New Model Army.

This means that Shakespeare's conception of man, no less than ours, is bounded by the limitations of a historical period. This is not, of course, to debase Shakespeare, but merely to insist that he was human. Nor is it to debase him to note in his plays elements (absolutely inevitable) of defeatism or utopianism.

It does not lessen the status of *Hamlet* to point out that Hamlet cannot solve his problems. For what are Hamlet's problems? Nothing less, I would suggest, than history itself. The court of Denmark in the play is the very epitome of a Renaissance court, governed by the typical feudal/bourgeois power values. Politics are corrupt; the counters played with are the lives of men; war is a ruling-class adventure; the morals of the court are those of a refined brothel; murder is a weapon of state; the people is a 'mob' somewhere outside the palace, thought of only in terms of political expediency. All this the young man Hamlet sees. Through the profound experience of his father's murder and his mother's infidelity, a veil has been torn from the life around him. To others life merely 'seems'; to him it 'is'. He has seen the reality of the world he lives in. And because he lives about the year 1600 there is almost nothing he can do about it, except (and it is an enormous except) *express* his vision. He cannot find actions commensurate with his experience because action which would transform class society and its values was in 1600 impossible. And so there is in *Hamlet* a certain inevitable defeatism. On one level, at least, Fortinbras gets Hamlet's voice. But the defeatism is countered all the time by honesty, by a total lack of sentimentality, a moving, humane confidence which the defeat of the hero cannot destroy.

> In my heart there was a kind of fighting
> That would not let me sleep.[8]

Hamlet is a hero and it is the hero's function to express the inner possibilities of a situation, to express men's aspirations even when history will not, at that moment, permit their successful achievement.

What I have just said about Shakespeare applies, I believe, to bourgeois realism in general. The great artists of the bourgeois period are all highly critical, in some way or other, of bourgeois society and its values. This criticism is not always consciously formulated and seldom has an explicitly *political* slant. What the realist artists of the bourgeois period were doing was, above all, telling the truth; telling the truth about − among other things − aspects of bourgeois life which from the class interests of the bourgeoisie are highly inconvenient, not to say seditious.

The novel − that great popular art form of recent centuries − arose precisely for the purpose of telling the truth critically about the life of the time. Cervantes was no more a bourgeois than Shakespeare; but *Don Quixote* had as its explicit purpose the destruction of certain central attitudes and ideas used by the feudal ruling class to maintain its ascendancy. Hence the welcome given by the bourgeoisie to *Don Quixote* and its immense influence. Hence, on a very different plane − both socially and ideologically − the tremendous popularity of Bunyan. It is worth remembering that the outstanding representative of the bourgeoisie in Bunyan, Mr Badman, is a villain, not a hero. Bunyan, who could not have written as he did but for the bourgeois revolution, speaks with the voice of the small, independent journeyman, the artisan (the 'Left' of the Revolution) *against* the capitalist. Once again we have expressed the paradox of art, that it can resolve imaginatively issues which cannot yet be resolved fully in action. And we have also here the core of the paradox which Gorky was discussing: that the greatest art of the bourgeois period is the *least* bourgeois, thrown up by the bourgeois revolution but transcending it.

The word 'transcend' is dangerous, too, because it very easily acquires an idealist slant. There are few less helpful approaches to this whole question than the attitude expressed in such phrases as 'not of one time but of eternity', or 'the great artist rises above his time and expresses eternal truths'.

The artists of the bourgeois period can only transcend the view of life of the bourgeoisie in so far as they can find a standpoint − realistic and coherent − which does in fact transcend bourgeois ideology, i.e., can solve the human problems the bourgeoisie cannot solve. This standpoint we know to be that of the class-conscious working class. Until such a time as the development of the productive relations makes the formulation of the standpoint possible there are bound to be limitations to the ability of even the finest artists to produce a fully realistic art.

These limitations we can see, as we look back on history, to be isolable in particular works of art as the expression of some residue of idealism remaining in the artist's outlook. It is an idealism which takes many forms. There is, for example, the utopian tendency expressed – in their several ways – in Shakespeare's last plays, in Botticelli's painting, in Fielding's paternalism, in Rousseau's elevation of the primitive, in Shelley's anarchism. There is the idealism of religion which substitutes a mystical resolution for a materialist one; we think of Donne's poetry, of Milton's acceptance of Christian mythology, of Gerard Manley Hopkins's Catholicism. And besides these forms of idealism there are a hundred others: the pantheistic nature cult of Wordsworth, the aestheticism of Henry James, D. H. Lawrence's obsession with sex – all in their ways alternatives to a complete and balanced realism.

I should like to take one fairly detailed example of the strength of the finest bourgeois realism and also of the nature of its limitations. Fielding's *Jonathan Wild*, written in the middle of the eighteenth century, is one of the most devastating exposures imaginable of the nature of bourgeois society. It is the story of a criminal (based on an actual case), an eighteenth-century super-spiv, the organiser of thieves and receiver of stolen property, Jonathan Wild, who lives on and – in the most precise sense – exploits the lesser fry of humdrum criminals. But Fielding's novel is in no sense an 'exposure' of criminality of the Sunday newspaper or 'crime doesn't pay' type. Fielding is interested in Wild not as a social exception, an outcast, but as a social type, a type indeed whom he does not hesitate to identify with the greatest in the land, Walpole the Prime Minister in particular. The whole point about *Jonathan Wild* is that it is a satire striking at the very heart of British eighteenth-century society. Fielding pulls no punches and his attack is often staggeringly profound:

Mankind are first properly to be considered under two grand divisions – those that use their own hands, and those who employ the hands of others. The former are the base and rabble; the latter, the genteel part of the creation. The mercantile part of the world, therefore, wisely use the term *employing hands*, and justly prefer each other as they employ more or fewer; for thus one merchant says he is greater than another, because he employs more hands.[9]

Jonathan Wild expresses his philosophy very fully when the high-wayman Bagshot expects a half share in the booty he has obtained from a robbery (Wild's part in the affair has been to tip off Bagshot of the movements of the traveller who has just won money by dishonest gambling). Bagshot, who has had all the sweat of the little enterprise, feels that he might justly be entitled to at least half-share in the profits and asks, 'Is not the labourer worthy of his hire?'

'Doubtless' says Jonathan 'he is so, and your hire I shall not refuse you, which is all that the labourer is entitled to, or ever enjoys . . . It is well said of us, the higher order of mortals, that we are born only to devour the fruits of the earth; and it may well be said of the lower class that they are born only to produce them for us. Is not the battle gained by the sweat and danger of the common soldier? Are not the honour and fruits of the victory the general's who laid the scheme? Is not the house built by the labour of the carpenter and bricklayer? Is it not built for the profit only of the architect, and for the use of the inhabitant, who could not easily have placed one brick upon another? Is not the cloth, or the silk, wrought in its form, and variegated with all the beauty of colours, by those who are forced to content themselves with the coarsest and vilest part of their work, while the profit and enjoyment of their labours fall to the share of others? . . . Why should you, who are the labourer only, the executor of my scheme, expect a share in the profit? Be advised therefore: deliver the whole booty to me, and trust to my bounty for your reward.'[10]

When Wild, at one stage of his career, lands in Newgate jail, Fielding uses the opportunity for a brilliant satire on the party system in bourgeois politics. Wild himself becomes leader of one set of prigs (thieves), another rogue, Johnson, is the present leader of the party in power. Both sets of skalliwags play on the interests and hopes of the unfortunate debtors, who are not criminals at all, who form the majority of the population of the jail. The convicts organize an election:

Newgate was divided into parties on this occasion; the prigs on each side representing their chief or great man to be the only person by whom the affairs of Newgate could be managed with safety and advantage. The prigs had indeed very incompatible interests; for whereas the supporters of Johnson, who was in possession of the plunder of Newgate, were admitted to some share under their leader, so the abettors of Wild had, on his promotion, the same views of dividing some part of the spoil among themselves. It is no wonder, therefore, they were both so warm on each side. What may seem more remarkable is that the debtors, who were entirely unconcerned with the dispute, and who were the destined plunder of both parties, should interest themselves with the utmost violence, some on behalf of Wild, and others in favour of Johnson. So that all Newgate re-

sounded with WILD *for ever*! JOHNSON *for ever*! And the poor debtors re-
echoed the *liberties of Newgate*! which, in the cant language, signifies
plunder, as loudly as the thieves themselves. In short, such quarrels and
animosities happened between them that they seemed rather the people of
two countries long at war with each other than the inhabitants of the same
castle.

Wild's party at length prevailed, and he succeeded to the place and
power of Johnson, whom he presently stripped of all his finery; but when it
was proposed that he should sell it, and divide the money for the good of
the whole, he waived that motion, saying, it was not yet time, that he
should find a better opportunity, that the clothes wanted cleaning, with
many other pretences; and, within two days, to the surprise of many, he
appeared in them himself; for which he vouchsafed no other apology than
that they fitted him much better than they did Johnson, and that they became him in a much more elegant manner.[11]

It seems to me absurd to describe such a writer, who pierces so
deep and with such devastating wit into the lies and pretences of
bourgeois society, simply as a bourgeois writer. What Fielding was
saying two hundred years ago about British society has still today an
urgency and a power which make *Jonathan Wild* anything but a
museum-piece, a relic of the days when the bourgeoisie was a rising
class. To treat it *merely* historically is therefore to do it less than
justice. Like *The Communist Manifesto*, *Jonathan Wild* emerged out of
history; that does not mean that it is dead.

On the other hand, of course, we must not pass over Fielding's
limitations, the qualities in *Jonathan Wild* which prevent its
achieving that complete realism and insight which it so nobly
attempts. There are two main weaknesses in Fielding's book. The
first is that while the negative, 'bad' characters — Wild and his
friends — are magnificently alive and convincing, the positive, 'good'
people are rather dim. Heartfree, the 'hero' of *Jonathan Wild*, the
honest jeweller, is a poor sort of hero who is quite incapable of putting up an effective fight and who accepts his tribulations as god-
given. This wouldn't matter if it were part of Fielding's plan to
show the honest man as indeed hopelessly corrupted by the
gangsters. Then, though *Jonathan Wild* would be a depressing work
it would at least be consistent. But Fielding (and it is part of his
genius that he should reject a pessimistic, despairing view of life)
cannot bring himself to let Jonathan win outright. Therefore, the
weakness of Heartfree is artistically a fault in the book. And it is
bound up with another weakness, which significantly tells us just
why Fielding, for all his honesty and genius, could not — living as

an enlightened eighteenth-century gentleman in the England of his time – create an absolutely realistic masterpiece. Since Heartfree, the hero, is too weak to defeat Jonathan Wild, and yet Jonathan has to be defeated, a new force is introduced into the book, a *deus ex machina*, 'the good magistrate', enlightened and wise, *above the State which the novel has so ruthlessly exposed*, who manages to put things right, save Heartfree and send Wild to the gallows.

Fielding was himself an enlightened magistrate who had a good record in fighting corruption. And it is not hard to see how the *artistic* weakness of *Jonathan Wild* is bound up with the limitations of Fielding's own social position. It is pointless to say 'What a pity Fielding couldn't have gone further . . . , etc.' Fielding, like the rest of us, lived in a historical situation. He also, through his writing, helped to change that situation, which is all any man can do. This is what ultimately gives his writing its vitality and makes *Jonathan Wild* not a historical curiosity but a part of the heritage of the British people, today fighting in a very different historical situation.

One final example of what we mean by our cultural heritage: a famous poem of William Blake from the *Songs of Experience*, the poem entitled *London*:

> I wander thro' each charter'd street,
> Near where the charter'd Thames does flow,
> And mark in every face I meet
> Marks of weakness, marks of woe.
>
> In every cry of every Man,
> In every Infant's cry of fear,
> In every voice, in every ban,
> The mind-forg'd manacles I hear.
>
> How the Chimney-sweeper's cry
> Every black'ning Church appalls;
> And the hapless Soldier's sigh
> Runs in blood down Palace walls
>
> But most thro' midnight streets I hear
> How the youthful Harlot's curse
> Blasts the new-born Infant's tear
> And blights with plagues the Marriage hearse.

I find it difficult to talk about this wonderful poem, so immensely powerful that to read and think about it is, literally, almost unendurable. It is a poem written a hundred and fifty years ago but still capable today of burning its way into our consciousness.

Indeed, like much of Blake's poetry, history *adds* to its power. (I believe that only after many years of socialism and communism will the full richness of this great poet come to be understood.)

The immediate, down-to-earth impact of the poem is established in the first two lines. 'Charter'd' means, of course, sold, let out by charter as a monopoly. And the whole poem is a hideous picture of what bourgeois society involves. No one has ever produced a more magnificent phrase for the power and significance of ideas than that image of the 'mind-forg'd manacles'. We talk of the battle of ideas, of the power of the ideology of a class to be a weapon – even a deadly weapon – in its hands: but it is the power of this poem that it can give a content and intensity to phrases that are often a little abstract and theoretic.

Again, the images of the chimney-sweeper and the soldier are effective not because in a general, theoretical way they link exploitation and suffering with the ruling class and its ideologists but because the images they create are concrete, many-sided ones, as full and rich as life itself. The 'black'ning Church' – linked at once with corruption, the soot of an industrial society (the soot the chimney-sweeper is condemned to seek), the spire and the factory chimney are brought together unforgettably. Blake does not say, abstractly, 'the rulers are responsible for the suffering of war': in a superb image he smears the palace walls with blood. As for the final stanza, the power here is quite overwhelming. For Blake is not saying, what anyone can easily agree with, that prostitution is bad; he is making us know that prostitution is an integral part of London – bourgeois London – and that its horror is not simply what it does to the harlot, but what it does to us. The marriage hearse: the symbol of love turned into death.

Is it a limitation of this poem that it does not 'point the way forward'? I do not think so. In a sense, of course, it does point a way out, for in making us understand more profoundly the nature of capitalism and arousing our deepest, most human indignation it organises us spiritually, making us better able to play our part in the destruction of capitalism. To respond fully to Blake's *London* is to respond to the nature of reality and hence to come nearer to its mastery.

It is right and necessary that we should understand the limitations of the work of the great artists of the bourgeois epoch, should recognise the virtual impossibility within the framework of class society and ruling-class thinking of the achievement of a total realism. History before the achievement of socialism is, as Engels said, pre-history, with the limitations that implies.

But the men and women of pre-history cannot be brushed aside as sub-men. We must never fall into the easy, abstract temptation of adopting a patronising attitude to the masters of bourgeois realism, any more than to the other great progressive fighters of the past. There is something insulting and essentially inhumane about treating great artists is mere pegs to hang our judgements on. The assumption that we know the truth and they, poor creatures, were merely groping, is not one which does us or them any kind of credit. Before we glibly say 'Yes of course *we* know John Donne really meant Necessity when he says God . . .' or talk too easily about 'elements of utopianism in Botticelli' let us remember with humility that no working-class poet has yet expressed with a quarter of Donne's intensity the paradox of social giving and taking, the relation of the individual to the whole, the dialectical sense of advance through conflict; nor has any modern painter expressed with the insight of Botticelli the potentialities of what Blake called the Human Form Divine.

Let us not forget that for us it is comparatively *easy* to see the limitations of, say, Marlowe's view of life or Milton's theology. But for Shakespeare to have created *King Lear*, for Fielding to have written *Jonathan Wild*, Swift *Gulliver's Travels*, Blake the *Songs of Experience*, Emily Brontë *Wuthering Heights*, a spiritual struggle was involved, a grappling with life of almost unconceivable intensity and magnitude. Before we criticise *Hamlet* for leaving problems unsolved we must be sure that we have solved our own. What gives art its value is not the abstract correctness of its message or its conscious ideology but the concrete richness of its expression of life in its full complexity.

I stress this point not, heaven knows, to play down the work of our own artists or to belittle the possibilities of socialist realism, which like socialism itself opens out potentialities hitherto unknown to man. I stress the point because we shall not be proud of our British heritage unless we are also humble about it. And unless we are proud of it we shall not defend something which, I have tried to show, is a part of our very bones and brains and a treasure which we alone can discover and pass on to future humanity.

Notes

1 'On the fourth anniversary of the October Revolution', *Pravda*, 1 October 1921.

2 *Problems of Soviet Literature* (Moscow, 1935), p. 32.

3 *Tamburlaine the Great*, 11. 758–9.

4 *The Tragicall History of Dr Faustus*, 11. 81–2.

5 *Timon of Athens*, Act IV, Sc. iii, 11. 33–7.

6 *Hamlet*, Act I, Sc. ii, 11. 187–8.

7 *Antony and Cleopatra*, Act IV, Sc. xv, 11. 72–5.

8 *Hamlet*, Act V, Sc. ii, 11. 4–5.

9 *Jonathan Wild*, Book I, Ch. 14.

10 *Ibid.*, Book I, Ch. 8.

11 *Ibid.*, Book IV, Ch. 3.

The artist and politics

The question of art or culture and its relation to politics is a very real and immediate political question. It has recently cropped up in a particularly dramatic and inescapable form with the question of Pasternak, and *Doctor Zhivago*.* It was the major theoretical pre-occupation of the two most distinguished modern German literary intellectuals, Thomas Mann and Bertolt Brecht. It has been the subject of intense discussion in France, especially since the war and occupation, as illustrated for instance in Simone de Beauvoir's novel *The Mandarins*. And it has recently, again, in Britain been the subject of a notable book by John Berger, the novel *A Painter of our Time*.

Art and society

I think it is particularly important not to treat the question of the relation of the artist to society in an abstract way. Society is not itself an abstraction and if we generalise about society as such we do so at our peril. Because man is a social being and cannot live and develop without other men he is bound, always, to enter into relationships with other men, to live in a society. But the relationships that bind men together have been, and are, of many kinds. What all societies have in common is not more important than what differentiates one society from another. The question of the relation of the artist to society has got to be seen as part of a larger question: the way men's social relationships, in all their complexity, change and develop.

The word artist changes its meaning and significance like every-

* i.e. in the late 1950s (eds)

thing else. The position of the artist in modern British bourgeois society is very different fróm that of the artist 400 or even 2,000 years ago. Yet bourgeois artists and critics, and some who would be insulted to have the adjective bourgeois applied to them, nearly always talk as though their own highly individualist, historically-speaking very exceptional, view of the artist were hallowed by centuries of experience and general agreement. This is partly due to an instinct for self-protection. Probably no society has ever been quite so inimical to humane culture as modern industrial capitalism which turns everything into a commodity and whose typical representatives have for the most part not even bothered to conceal their contempt for and impatience with art. Mr Podsnap's view, which Dickens so brilliantly expressed in *Our Mutual Friend*, really is what at bottom the bourgeoisie feels about art.

Mr. Podsnap's world was not a very large world, morally; no, nor even geographically . . . the world got up at eight, shaved close at a quarter-past, breakfasted at nine, went to the City at ten, came home at half-past five, and dined at seven. Mr. Podsnap's notions of the Arts in their integrity might have been stated thus. Literature: large print, respectively descriptive of getting up at eight, shaving close at quarter-past, break-fasting at nine, going to the City at ten, coming home at half-past five, and dining at seven. Painting and Sculpture: models and portraits representing professors of getting up at eight, shaving close at quarter-past, break-fasting at nine, going to the City at ten, coming home at half-past five, and dining at seven. Music: a respectable performance (without variations) on stringed and wind instruments, sedately expressive of getting up at eight [etc.] . . . Nothing else to be permitted to those same vagrants the Arts, on pain of excommunication.[1]

It is not hard to see why so many sensitive nineteenth-century artists, loathing Podsnappery and rejected by it, became rebels, passionately dissociating themselves from the values and morality of Victorian capitalism, becoming, in the eyes of the rulers of that society, 'anti-social'. Nor is it hard to see why their rebellion should, typically, have taken a largely individualist and anarchistic character. It was not easy for the nineteenth-century artist, himself almost inevitably of bourgeois or petty bourgeois background, to associate himself in his rebellion with the still relatively weak working-class movement. Some of the deepest spirits did, of course, in different ways and with varying degrees of success, manage to make this transition: one has only to mention Dickens, Ruskin, William Morris, Bernard Shaw. But the far more common pilgrimage was towards either an ivory tower — what Tennyson so aptly called the Palace of Art – or a more sordid Bohemia from which one thumbed one's nose at all 'respectability'. And it is probably true to say that these two tendencies were even stronger among painters and musicians than among writers. It is interesting that when the typical late nineteenth-century artist (Flaubert is a good example) attacks 'bourgeois' ideas what he principally has in mind is not capitalism as an economic and social system but the smug and narrow complacency of the petty bourgeoisie. Respectability rather than exploitation is what most angers him.

The artist in bourgeois society

One can only mention a few of the by-products of this situation. One, of course, has been the very widespread tendency of the artist, in the last hundred and fifty years or so, to see himself as a lone figure, supported no doubt by other like- and high-minded individuals, fighting a desperate battle to preserve his integrity against the alien and corrupting forces around him – forces which he easily comes to identify with 'society' as such. In such a situation to be 'anti-social' quickly comes to be seen as a positive virtue. The permanent alienation of the artist from society comes to be seen as a feature, not of capitalism, but of life. So that a *Manchester Guardian* reviewer can let fall without fear of contradiction the sentence:

The artist or the intellectual is in a relationship with the rest of society which can only be expressed in terms of 'I' and 'they'. (*Manchester Guardian*, 7.10.58.)

Socially acceptable art becomes, in such a context, associated with those who have sold their souls, compromised with the philistines, entered the Royal Academy. And the working class comes to be seen less as an *alternative* to the bourgeoisie, a hope for the future, than as a more or less inarticulate slab of humanity itself largely corrupted by the set-up – call it industrialism, capitalism, what you will. For though the typical petty-bourgeois artist in capitalist society feels far more sympathy for the workers than for the bourgeoisie and will tell you – especially after a few pints – how much humanity and decency and fellow-feeling he has found among working class people, yet he also feels, *vis-à-vis* the working class, extremely *unappreciated*. He knows from experience that the average worker doesn't like his painting or his sonata any more than the philistine millionaire. And so, unless he is rather exceptional, he turns more and more to the company and to the values of other people like himself, other artists and literary[2] intellectuals, people who care about art and things of the mind, people who understand him. The 'classless' world of the intelligentsia absorbs him, not completely, since by its nature it is not a complete world, but with a powerful and often a seductive force.

Equally important is the particular connection that the word Art has acquired in this situation. It is, in the sense it is now commonly used, a comparatively new word,[3] and it makes remarkable claims for itself. The artist is seen not primarily in terms of contributing to the life and knowledge of the community but in terms of some almost mystical act of 'self-expression' or in direct relation to some absolute abstraction like Truth or Beauty. It is necessary to try not to oversimplify these tendencies. Marxists sometimes talk as though most contemporary bourgeois artists and critics consciously sub-scribe to the late nineteenth-century theory of 'art for art's sake'. In fact nowadays very few artists *consciously* sympathise with this posi-tion and become very indignant if you suggest to them that they do. Nevertheless, even though they may not realise it, most contem-porary artists do in practice take up a position which is in essence not very far from 'art for art's sake', for by insisting that art has little or no *direct* social effects (they will generally admit it has indirect or 'long-term' ones) they do in actuality remove it out of the sphere of social activity and judgment.

The word Art has, in the last 200 years or so, acquired a remark-able aura of something like divinity. For a great many intellectuals it has in fact replaced religion as the idea to which is given the highest of all sanctions. The artist is seen, if not precisely as a god, as the nearest approach to god that twentieth-century intellectual scepticism will permit. The artist is the man who, above all others, perceives and expresses the truth about the world we live in. He teaches us to see what had previously escaped our observation, he defines what had previously escaped full comprehension. He is at once 'committed' (for life in all its ramification is his province) and disinterested, above partisan considerations because uncorrupted by political power.

It is necessary for us especially if we do not normally mix in circles in which these things are much discussed – to appreciate the force with which these convictions about the supremacy of art are held. Otherwise we shall not understand what is behind many of the reactions which take place among people interested in the arts. I think it is not easy, for instance, for most workers to understand how passionately intellectuals can feel about such an issue as the publication of Pasternak's *Zhivago* or whether or not such-and-such a film should be censored. No doubt there is very often a great deal in such reactions which is in fact unbalanced, hypocritical and indefensible; but we shall only tackle such problems effectively if we recognise – to put it crudely – what we are up against.

Commitment and liberalism

The very people who talk most about 'commitment' and the duties of the artist to humanity are very often among those most deeply imbued with a liberal individualist view of the position of the artist. In *Declaration*, that rather dim symposium of the more or less Angry, one comes for instance upon a passage by Doris Lessing in an essay which is in many ways sympathetic and progressive in tone and intention:

I think that a writer who has for many years been emotionally involved in the basic ethical conflict of communism – what is due to the collective and what to the individual conscience – is peculiarly equipped to write of the dangers inherent in being 'committed'. The writer who can be bludgeoned into silence by fear or economic pressure is not worth considering; these problems are simple and the dangers easily recognisable. What is dangerous is the inner loyalty to something felt as something much greater than one's self. I remember, in Moscow, when this question was discussed, a writer replied to an accusation of being bludgeoned by the Party into false writing by saying: 'No one bludgeons us. Our conscience is at the service of the people. We develop an inner censor.' It is the inner censor which is the enemy.[4]

It is worth examining some of the implications here. In the first place Doris Lessing is right when she says that commitment has its danger. Of course it has. Everything has – especially what is important. The danger of the writer becoming a yes-man is a real one. But the way Doris Lessing poses the question seems to me wrong, especially when she poses the individual conscience *against* the collective. For one thing we have to recognise that 'conscience' is itself a weighted word. If we use the word 'judgement' the whole problem immediately looks a little different – and, I think, clearer. I remember a colleague coming to me in great distress at the time of the Hungarian crisis and saying that his conscience would no longer allow him to be a member of the Communist Party. I was distressed, too, and said with equal emotion that my conscience would not allow me to leave the Communist Party. After that it was surprising how much better we both felt for we both realised that what was at stake was not conscience versus lack of conscience but one man's conscience versus another's – in other words a difference of *judgement*. And having established this we were able to discuss the real problems about Hungary, whether certain decisions taken were – all things considered – the right ones or not. And I think the same sort of process needs applying to Doris Lessing's remark.

It is the inner censor which is the enemy [my italics].

Is it really? Should the writer, alone among human beings, really render himself immune to that inner censor which prevents us at certain times saying or doing things which we feel – all things considered – will be unhelpful – and this in the sacred name of conscience! Should the writer really be committed to the view that he should *always* say what first comes into his head or that he should always say what he has a particularly strong impulse to say, *regardless of the consequences*? I think this is an untenable position and that to pretend that it is the answer to the difficult problem of whether or not an individual should submit his personal judgement to the collective judgement is quite unsatisfactory. So is the use by Doris Lessing a little later of the word expediency. Another weighted word. Of course if you organise a battle between conscience and expediency everyone knows from the start which ought to win. Yet expediency, minus its pejorative associations, means doing what seems, all things considered, to be right, making what seems to be the best, most helpful decisions. I cannot see any other basis for making decisions – moral, political, artistic, public, private, long-term, short-term or what have you. And I think it is nonsense for artists to claim that they can have any other tenable basis for taking their decisions.

Not that one would suggest for a moment that there are not enormous difficulties involved, innumerable possibilities of error. What has to be insisted is that the only valid basis of judgement is whether any particular book or film or action will or will not serve humanity, not humanity in the abstract but human beings in the actual situation in which they find themselves. It is no good for artists to claim exemption from this general criterion, to claim, for instance, the right to say at all times exactly what they feel like (which isn't the same, incidentally, as suggesting they ought to say what they don't feel). There are times when it is better not to say certain things even when they are true. I am quite sure a novelist living in Notting Hill could write a perfectly truthful novel – in the sense that chapter and verse could be given for all the facts mentioned – in which most of the West Indian and African characters turned out to be knife-carriers, drug-pedlars and ponces. And if someone complained that this was not the whole truth he would reply quite justly that he never said it was the whole truth and anyway no novel can ever tell the whole truth. Yet I believe that an author who tried to publish such a novel would be not merely irresponsible, but guilty within his particular sphere of crimes against humanity.

Art is important

There is, however, a real danger that we may seriously underestimate the whole importance and supreme value of art. Art *is* one of the essential ways of discovering what men and their world are really like and, not least, what their potentialities are. Art is tremendously important and valuable precisely because it is not what culture-snobs think it is, a pleasant and elegant trimming to our lives, the icing on the cake. It increases not simply our enjoyment of life (though it does that) but our knowledge and understanding releases new energy in us, helps us to change the world. As George Thomson has put it: 'The artist leads his fellow men into the world of fantasy, where they find release, thus asserting the refusal of the human consciousness to acquiesce in its environment, and by this means there is collected a hidden store of energy which flows back into the real world and transforms fantasy into fact.'[5]

It is right to emphasise that the relation of the artist to *any* society is likely not to be an altogether simple one. This is due to a number of complexities in the situation, but I would mention only two of them.

Fantasy and reality

(i) There is no doubt that the history of class society in general and of capitalism in particular has led us to over-emphasise the singularity, oddity, individualism of the artist. In particular it has stressed the quality of intensity and individual creative struggle involved in the production of good art. In a society based on human co-operation I feel sure that attitudes to art will be more relaxed and rational, less centred on titanic personal grapplings. Yet, even so, there is a certain paradox involved in artistic creation which even in the most rational society will, I think, still have to be recognised. I mean the fact that the artist does, in an important sense, withdraw from life in order to master and participate in it. The painter alone with his canvas, the writer wrestling with the words that are his medium, the film director shooting time and time again a particular scene to get it 'right': each of them is involved in a process which has its own logic and its own contradictions – not of course separate from or in contradiction to the processes and needs of life but nevertheless, because it involves absorption in fantasy, raising its own peculiar and complex problems. It is true, of course, that this applies to some extent to any skill or craft. The precision engineer working on a new apparatus withdraws, in a sense, into a field of activity, a world which has its own laws and, in the old-fashioned, craft sense, 'mysteries'. And, like the composer, he musn't be disturbed, as his wife has long ago discovered. Yet there is a difference between the contradiction involved in precision engineering and the concentration involved in composing a symphony and the difference is that the artist is involved in what is best called fantasy. He creates a world which he and everyone else knows is not the real world. No one supposes that Paul Robeson is *really* Othello. And this is a problem with which the engineer is not concerned; there is no element of fantasy in what he is doing, though there is, let us not forget, the quality we commonly call 'imagination', which I take to be the creative element involved in scientific research, and is the expression of man's power to project the experiences of the past into the future, the power of the architect to envisage a building which has not yet come into existence but will.

I do not think the creation of fantasy is quite so different from scientific activity as is generally assumed. For the fantasy world of art is, of course, in some sense or other, however complex, a reflection of the real world, just as the architect's plans are. But the complexities involved are very considerable and they arise largely because the artist, as opposed to the architect or the engineer, has as his raw materials human beings and their relationships. And the complexities are so great that they create what is in effect a new problem.

In practice the new problem can be seen in the difficulties which arise when a society tries to help its artists develop their art. In bourgeois society this question by and large simply does not arise. Since, through the very nature of class society, you cannot have social planning in the people's interests, the only kind of culture that gets official encouragement is the kind that bolsters up class privilege and class thinking. For the rest, the artists either have to come to terms with the moneybags or else work out their own salvation as best they can. The honest culture is the culture produced *against* the grain of the Establishment, with the help, acknowledged or not, of the progressive movements of the people against the bourgeois state. But when, as in the Soviet Union or other socialist countries, a society arises which takes a responsible attitude towards culture (i.e. sees it as its job to encourage the good and discourage the bad) and attempts to help its artists to develop in a way which will serve and enrich the people as a whole, then certain new problems crop up, especially at first.

Problems of Soviet culture

Soviet culture today is an infinitely healthier, infinitely richer — because more popular — culture than the culture of the capitalist world. Yet the difficulties the Soviet leadership have had in persuading Soviet artists to produce new works really commensurate with the all-round human advances of socialist society are no secret. No doubt the abuses of the Stalin period and their considerable and often disastrous effects on many areas of Soviet intellectual life made the difficulties far greater. Yet I think we would be wrong to see the problem as primarily one created by these abuses. Even without the bad things of the Stalin period the business of transforming bourgeois attitudes towards culture into socialist ones would have been difficult enough and one of the dangers of blaming all the weaknesses of Soviet culture on to the Stalin period is that — as our revisionists demonstrate — this can so easily lead to a sheer crude liberalism which is utterly inadequate to meet the issues concerned.

The principal difficulties, in my opinion, which have been met in the Soviet Union on this front are (*a*) that old individualist attitudes to art among intellectuals die hard and are not easily buried, and (*b*) that it is not easy to evolve ways of giving necessary help and guidance to artists without at the same time inhibiting initiative.

(*a*) The problem of getting rid of bourgeois ideas among Soviet intellectuals has undoubtedly been hampered by the necessary but dangerous policy of giving intellectuals and cultural workers rather exceptional privileges. This was inevitable. The Soviet people, emerging from oppression and illiteracy, demanded books and films, music and ballet on a scale hitherto undreamed of, and the writers and ballerinas undoubtedly became privileged members of Soviet society, often living lives which cut them off to some extent from Soviet reality. But whereas the whole activity of ballet-dancing requires corporate effort and 'team spirit', which no doubt counteract to a considerable extent other tendencies, the activity of writing a novel or painting a picture tends to have the opposite effect. It is easy enough to elevate the inevitable isolation of the writer in the throes of creation into some kind of mystic 'apartness'.

In addition to this, intellectuals, through their whole way of life, tend to be most subject to cosmopolitan attitudes and influences, to cling most nostalgically to a past in which a cultural élite of every country felt more in common with its prototypes in other lands than with the workers of its own country. This attitude, for instance, wends its way through Pasternak's *Zhivago* as unmistakably as it does through Dostoievsky's *Possessed*, even though both writers, obviously with sincerity, make much of their 'Russianness'.

(*b*) It doesn't do very much good simply to tell writers what they ought to write. Art, of all activities, needs the most complete absorption, the most utter conviction. Even if you manage to persuade an abstract painter intellectually that he ought to paint representational pictures the chances are that for a long while his representational pictures won't be much good. Art is a great revealer, it will reveal more surely than anything else the weaknesses of a man's philosophy, the hollowness of his pretensions and the limitations of his good intentions. So that the business of giving guidance to artists isn't simple, quite apart from the fact that most of them will resent it like the plague.

Does this mean that guidance shouldn't be given, that the Party should leave such matters to chance or history? Obviously it doesn't. As Comrade Gomulka points out in the last number of *Marxism Today*, 'The cultural revolution is an indispensable element of a socialist revolution.'[6] A Communist Party cannot possibly remain indifferent or neutral in ideological or cultural matters. Every parent discovers that some of the forms of pressure or influence he exerts on his children are ineffective if not worse; but it is a very foolish parent who then jumps to the conclusion that he should therefore exert no pressure or influence at all. It doesn't do much good simply to tell writers what they ought to write; but that doesn't mean that the pressures of a society should not be consciously exerted to try to convince artists that they should be responsible rather than irresponsible, that they are subject to the same obligations and duties as everyone else – and indeed more so, because their very articulateness imposes an extra obligation.

Why *Zhivago* was not published

The liberal principle of cultural *laisser-faire* has no place in a Marxist outlook. I think this is not always sufficiently realised. There is a tendency among Left intellectuals who are not at all to be classed as anti-Soviet to imagine, for instance, that the Soviet decision not to publish *Zhivago* is a sort of temporary aberration from liberal principles due almost entirely to the immediate exigencies of the Cold War. I think this is self-deception and that the editors of *Novy Mir* meant what they said when they wrote to Pasternak:

It seems to us that your novel is profoundly unjust and historically prejudiced in its description of the revolution, the civil war and the years after the revolution, that it is profoundly anti-democratic and that any conception of the interests of the people is alien to it. All this, taken as a whole, stems from your standpoint as a man who tries in his novel to prove that, far from having had any positive significance in the history of our people and mankind the October Socialist Revolution brought nothing but evil and hardships. As people whose standpoint is diametrically opposed to yours, we naturally believe that it is out of the question to publish your novel in the columns of the magazine *Novy Mir*.[7]

Now whether or not the editors of *Novy Mir* were right in their estimate of the novel is a quite separate question. What I think is clear is that the decision not to publish *Zhivago* was due neither to an unsuccessful attempt to prevent the capitalist world making use of the book nor to a groundless fear that it would corrupt large numbers of Soviet readers, but rather to the general principle that a socialist society feels no obligation to publish work that is fundamentally opposed to and has the effect of misrepresenting the human advances and ideals of the socialist revolution. Obviously such a principle is not one that will be found sympathetic by those

who do not see the ending of exploitation as a basic human advance
or a socialist society as a higher form of society than its predecessors:
but to the millions who have actually emerged from class oppression
into socialism it seems merely common sense. To them it is the idea
that the stronger and more secure a socialist society becomes the
more ready it should be to publish anti-socialist literature that is
hard to comprehend.

Creating a popular culture

(ii) A second real problem which has to be recognised in the creation
of a satisfactory popular art is that such things take a good deal of
time. As John Berger's painter hero says in *A Painter of Our Time*:

> The artist's justification lies in creating new relevances; but it takes a long
> time. To create a heavy industry in five or ten years is an heroic but possible
> aim. To create a heavyweight art in the same time is impossible.[8]

Just because the production of art is the kind of process it is, we
should not be surprised that the establishment of a new tradition in
art takes a long time. The business of absorbing experiences and
ideas at the level necessary to turn them into mature and worthy art-
products is immensely hard. That is the reason why there has been,
for instance, so little adequate literature about the two world wars.
It is not that artists have not felt strongly or held very definite
opinions about these wars; the problem is to find ways of organising
and expressing these feelings and opinions in art. The creation of a
new tradition in which the artist can work easily and confidently is
something very tricky. It is not by chance that writers have nearly
always written about the past, even if it is the fairly immediate past.
Scarcely one of Shakespeare's plays is set in Elizabethan England.
Even Dickens (an unusually topical writer) set his early novels
twenty or thirty years back in history, like *Pickwick*, presumably
because he felt that this was what he had most fully absorbed. Many
artists continue to write about the world of their childhood and early
manhood all their lives – and this isn't necessarily escapism, though
of course it can be. Some critics have expressed astonishment that
Pasternak could have lived through forty years of the Soviet revolution and yet remain so intractably bourgeois in his outlook. But
Pasternak was twenty-seven in 1917 and the surprising thing, to
anyone familiar with the development of artists, would have been if
he had much changed. I am not suggesting, of course, that artists,

alone of living creatures, are not subject to the laws of change. But I
think it should be recognised that the kind of absorption and comprehension of material involved in the production of art is not something that can well be rushed. To write a novel or paint a picture
unless you feel the experiences involved upon your pulses and are
absolutely in control of your material is to court superficiality and
triviality.

But of course this kind of argument applies to other people as well
as artists. It is all very well for a painter to write, 'To create a heavy
industry in five or ten years is an heroic but possible aim' but does he
quite realise all the implications here of the word heroic? It involves
– if one thinks of, say, Soviet industrialisation in the thirties or the
Chinese efforts of the last two years or for that matter of the British
war effort – not merely tremendously hard work and sacrifice in the
more obvious senses, it also means to the individual craftsman a certain sacrifice of his perfectionist standards and to the research scientist a deliberate concentration on immediate and perhaps rather
humdrum needs when he would no doubt sooner be working among
the broader vistas of longer-term investigation. It is notable that
every great heroic industrial advance of our time has been made
against the views of the relevant 'experts', whose conceptions of the
possible are significantly limited by their very expertness. It takes
the mass of the people, politically mobilised, to produce new standards in possibility, new heroes of our time. Is there any real reason
why the artist should not be asked to make similar sacrifices, to
become a similar sort of hero? Is not the tendency of the artist to
claim the sort of special privilege that he does chiefly a reflection of
his tendency – historically explicable but no longer justifiable – to
see himself as in some way above the struggle, above humanity and
its actual needs?

It seems to me that centuries of individualist thinking and
practice have led us all (including no doubt myself) to exaggerate the
purely personal nature of artistic creation. The art of primitive, pre-
class societies is communal and anonymous; I have no doubt that
future art will tend to be so again, though obviously on a far higher
level of consciousness and complexity.

How different is the artist?

I think that we ought to destroy the whole thing that the artist is different
from anyone else.

A recent remark of Christopher Logue's seems to me true and healthy and apt. Of course, in one sense, an artist is different: he is an artist. But there are two kinds of different artists. One sees himself as having a special *sort* of sensibility, some special *sort* of direct contact with truth and reality, which makes him superior to and in that sense different from other people. This is the basis of snob art, *élite* culture, intellectual arrogance. The second artist sees himself as different from other people only in the sense of being better able to express what all feel. This is the basis of a responsible and democratic attitude to art.

Notes

1   Book I, Ch. II.
2   I use the word 'literary' to distinguish them from the scientists. There is relatively little contact in our society between the scientific and literary intelligentsia: even in a university, where Arts and Sciences are studied within the same institution, this is true.
3   Raymond Williams, in his *Culture and Society 1780–1950*, a non-Marxist work of great interest, has some relevant material on the subject.
4   Tom Maschler (ed.), *Declaration* (1957), p. 20.
5   George Thomson, *Marxism and Poetry* (1947), p. 61.
6   *Marxism Today* (February 1959), Vol. 3, No. 4.
7   Edward Crankshaw, *Khruschev's Russia* (Harmondsworth, 1959), appendix, p. 171.
8   *A Painter of our Time* (1958), pp. 65–6.

Part II

The Mental Traveller

I

This extraordinary and difficult poem has been generally recognised as one of Blake's most remarkable achievements but very few critics seem to have risked speculating as to what it means. Those who have done so have either lost themselves in the maze of the Prophetic Books or brought forth interpretations of a highly mystical, not to say metaphysical, complexion. The immediate objection to such interpretations is that they bear so little relation to the kind of impact the poem makes. It is in no sense a misty poem, the imagery is extremely concrete, the language entirely direct. Above all it is a terrible poem, almost unbearable in the physical impact of its unshrouded images. Any 'explanation' which reduces or muffles that impact or turns it into something different in quality must be suspect. I believe that the difficulty of the poem, like that of most of Blake's lyrics, is of a different sort from that generally assumed. It is a difficulty that springs less from idiosyncrasy than from unexpectedness. The Prophetic Books are highly idiosyncratic: the mythology is private, the thought obscure and sometimes perverse. But the lyrics are public poetry, complete in themselves, demanding of the reader only that he shall open his consciousness to their fullest impact. The difficulty lies in the nature of that impact. What Blake has to say is odd in the sense that it is seldom said at all and never said precisely as he says it. But it is not odd in the sense of being off-centre, psychopathic, queer. And the difficulty of 'receiving' his poetry lies in ourselves rather than in the poetry. What he says is so unexpected – and to many so unpalatable – that the reader can scarcely believe his senses.

   In any attempt to interpret a poem like *The Mental Traveller* – that

is to say, any attempt to say not just what it 'means' but what it is —
the reader's greatest temptation is to read into the poem what he expects or would like to find there. It is a temptation which must be
frankly recognised, but it is also important, that having recognised
it, we should not topple over into a temptation even more insidious,
the view that denies to a poem any objective existence at all and
says, in effect, one man's guess is as good as another's. This view —
surprisingly common among literary critics (surprisingly because in
fact it makes literary criticism an impossibility) — is as dangerous as
it is defeatist. We might as well recognise at the outset that no one
ever reads any poem with a blank mind, i.e. a mind free of previous
experience. The important thing when we read poetry is not that we
should try to cast aside all our previous experiences and attitudes but
that we should be conscious of them and be prepared to have them
changed. My interpretation of *The Mental Traveller* is that of a
Marxist, i.e. of a reader whose previous total experience has led him
to a certain standpoint which is indicated by the word Marxist. If
I were not a Marxist I should probably not see in Blake's poem what
I do see. But that is no proof that what I see may not be there.
The only test must be in a comparison between my interpretation
and the words Blake wrote. Other poems of Blake, including the
Prophetic Books, may provide useful corroborative evidence and
may, in particular, prepare one's mind for the sort of impact this
particular poem has. But if I have forced Blake's poem into a pre-
conceived mould of my own then my interpretation is of no use. The
point I want to make is that every reader *does* begin with a precon-
ceived mould, conscious or not. The operative word is 'forced'.

Another problem of method is likely to be raised. Cannot the
poem have more than one meaning? It seems to me very probable
that it can. Images have a significance and validity on more than one
level of experience. But in any case it must always be remembered
that the best, the truest interpretation does not take the place of the
poem. In an important sense you can never do anything with a poem
except respond to it. You cannot put it into other words. The purpose of literary criticism is not to paraphrase literature but to help
the reader to come to it prepared.

II

The Mental Traveller is the description (a word which does not adequately convey what poetry does) of a cyclical process, but the cycle

it describes is not symbolic of the whole of life itself. We are taken immediately in the first verse into an imaginary world (mental = imaginary in Blake's language) which *is* a symbol of and closely relevant to our world, and it is *within* this imaginary world that the cycle takes place. This is very important because the temptation is to equate the cycle in the poem with life and the Babe with man. But in fact the imaginary world of the poem has an existence of its own quite outside the cycle of the Babe. The imaginary world of men and women goes on even when the cycle is not operative, i.e. before the birth of the Babe and when (verses 22–3) the people in the cycle have become impotent. The *ordinary* people of the imaginary world – lovers, shepherds, those who build cities – are terrified of the Babe and of the whole process of the cycle. Indeed it is only in these verses (2, 22, 23) that describe life outside the cycle that a calm and almost pastoral imagery prevails. Fruitfulness and hope are here dominant whereas in the rest of the poem any images of healthy normality are quickly given a twist which hideously inverts them.

This, then is basic to any satisfactory reading of the poem: the cycle (which forms the essential subject of the poem) is a cycle which takes place within (and is therefore not to be identified with) the life of the imaginary world.

What is the relation of the imaginary world to the real world? It *is* the real world, i.e. it is a vision of the real world in which the life and values of men and women are relevant. And yet (by the paradox of Art) it is more real than the real world. By comparison the people of the real world are 'cold' and even not quite natural. The imaginary world is, in fact, Blake's poetic vision of human life, not *different* from our life but more intensely seen, its potentialities more profoundly realised. Through the fantasy evoked by the poet's imagination a firmer grasp on reality is to be achieved. Within the world of the poem the cycle of the Babe, the Old Woman, the grown Man and the Female Babe is imposed and enacted. It is a cycle which begins in joy and is thenceforward hideous and destructive, withering all healthy life of humanity and nature. Three episodes of the cycle are presented to us.

The first and most immediately powerful episode (verses 3–7) is the relationship of the Babe and the Old Woman (the mother). It is a relationship in the revelation of which the most potent insights of Freud are made to seem cold and abstract. To speak of it as a revelation of the full horror of the Oedipus complex is to debase Blake's poetry, for what is presented here is not to be adequately described

as 'psychological'. With the woman preying on the child are associated images of the most profound significance: the crucifixion, the
Promethean legend, the golden cup of the holy grail (itself a sexual
symbol going back to primitive fertility ritual), the gold of the
miser, the virgin mother, the chains binding mankind, the fertility
of the husbandman. Almost the entire cultural, religious and economic foundations of our society are being evoked. And they are
evoked to deepen and to colour an image utterly hideous: the woman
living upon the shrieks of the child until the situation is reversed
and he lives upon her.

In the second episode (verses 8–11) the sum of the achievement of
the cyclical man's life is presented; the cottage filled with gems and
gold (note the insistence on gold throughout the poem). And we are
left in no doubt as to what the wealth represents in terms of human
suffering and frustration. It is perhaps worth recalling here the final
verse of *The Human Image* (first draft for *The Human Abstract*):

There souls of men are bought and sold
And milk-fed infancy for gold;
And youth to slaughter houses led,
And beauty for a bit of bread.

It is against this revelation of the basis of the man's wealth that we
note his charity and again a stanza from the poem just quoted is not
irrelevant:

Pity would be no more,
If we did not make somebody poor;
And mercy no more could be,
If all were as happy as we.[1]

The wealth, which is his meat and drink, is also his grief. These
verses have all the paradox of Blake's dialectic, all the moral profundity of his social vision.

The third episode deals with the relationship of the man and
woman within the cycle. The Female Babe is all compact of the elements associated with the poem's horrors. Like the Male Babe she
withers all she touches and her substance is of gems and gold, the
significance of which we have already learned. At this point it is
emphasised that the people of the cycle are not simply lone individuals – there is more than one of them. The Maiden whom the Man
wins is not, apparently, the same Female Babe who has sprung from
the fire, but she is similar, involved in the cycle, and will become a

Woman Old, playing her allotted part. The relationships of the three cyclical men and women to whom we are referred are both cruel and dreadful in their implications. The first relationship, introduced in the deceptive language of romantic love –

> But she comes to the man she loves,
> If young or old, or rich or poor,[2]

– involves immediately the driving out and reduction to beggardom of the old man. The second relationship – that of the old man and the maiden – is even more destructive. Again we are at first given the impression of a romantic fulfilment (verses 15–18). The two lovers become involved entirely in each other, oblivious of the outside world, which shrinks away (cf. 'This bed thy centre is, these walls thy sphere'). In verse 18 it seems – especially if we have given the words 'fear', 'shrink' and 'desart' in the preceding stanzas less than their full value – as though Blake is building up an image of the bliss of the isolated "soul-mates". The first two lines of verse 19 continue the process; but then comes the shock:

> And on the desart wild they both
> Wander in terror and dismay.[3]

And once more we see that the images of living on one another are in fact associated not with the fulfilment but with frustration. The lovers – she beguiling him with all her arts, he living on her beguilement – are not happy but wildly unhappy. A labyrinth of fear and hatred is all that they are creating and finally, like the other characters in the cycle, they are reduced to impotence. Then and only then does life – the positive life of men and nature – assert itself, only to be again forced out as the Babe is once more found and the cycle recommences.

III

The cycle represented in the poem is acquisitive society. The appalling horrors of the poem have all the same source, possessiveness. And the poem is not an allegory. It is not the representation in symbolic terms of an abstract idea. The Babe does not 'stand for' acquisitive society (in the way that most interpretations of the poem I have read make him 'stand for' one of Blake's hobby-horses) any more than the Tiger in his most famous poem stands for God or the

Devil, as some critics have tried to make out. The Tiger is a tiger, the Babe is a babe. That is the first thing to insist. That they have significance and relevance beyond that of an isolated, non-symbolic image is true; but it is not an *abstract* significance. The Babe does not stand for acquisitive society; he is a babe within acquisitive society, his potentialities warped and distorted by the possessiveness first of his mother and then of himself.

In the three episodes of the cycle the source of horror is the same. The mother lives upon the child; the man lives upon the mother and then upon the gems and gold, finally upon the maiden. In each case the images are those of eating and drinking: the mother 'catches his shrieks in cups of gold'; to the man the gems and gold are meat and drink; it is honey and bread and wine of the maiden which he eats and drinks. And in each case the horror is associated directly with these images. It it also associated in each case with images of wealth. 'The countless gold of the akeing heart' is one of the central, unforgettable images of the poem, and it is linked with the mother numbering the nerves of the child like a miser counting his gold and with the very essence of the maiden who is the product of fire and gems and gold. It is from these two central, recurring sets of images that we shall get the core and meaning of the poem. They are images of possessiveness and exploitation.

They hold together the three episodes of the poem, which at first appear to have little organic connection. For what Blake is saying is that the psychological and emotional problems of personal relationships are inextricably linked up with the social and economic basis of human activity. This is indeed the principal 'discovery', the very essence of the poem. The dreadful mother–child relationship and the no less desperate frustration of the two lovers are presented to us not merely as ghastly, isolated phenomena but as part and parcel of a situation in which human beings spend their lives preying upon each other. Each of the characters in the cycle seeks his satisfactions at the expense of others and what Blake is saying is that personal exploitation is the other side of and inseparable from economic exploitation.

In this vision of bourgeois society Blake goes so deep that to most bourgeois readers the poem is incomprehensible. Since possessive relationships and economic exploitation seem to such readers either natural or inevitable, they find it almost impossible to realise what Blake is driving at; consequently they are disturbed by the poem but cannot understand it. That the cherished symbols of Christianity and the scarcely less sacred concepts of individualist romantic love should be associated with a way of life represented as hideous and frustrating is more than they bargain for in a work of art.

For Blake is not stating in this poem the perfectly respectable view that the Oedipus relationship is common and interesting but that it is typical and horrible. He is not saying that economic success carries with it the obligation to be charitable, but that the good of charity is a poor and inadequate thing beside the evil of exploitation and no generosity can compensate for the situation of either exploiter or exploited. Above all Blake is saying that possessive individualism makes a happy relationship between men and women impossible. The image of the bourgeois man and woman wandering in terror and dismay in the desert which they have created for themselves is one of the most extraordinary insights in our literature. The man and woman, in their desperate attempt to achieve a complete fulfilment in one another, turn away from the social world. Ecstatically they try to live upon each other, the woman using her every art to beguile the man, he desperately desiring to be beguiled. And actually within the relationship there is not security but fear. Love and hate become inseparable. Instead of fulfilment there is a labyrinth of frustration. In Blakean language the emanation is for ever defeated; the spectres triumph.

Inevitably they triumph, for the men and women of the cycle have sacrificed humanity to possessiveness. It is only when humanity triumphs that the emanation – the potentialities of the individual – can be realised and the spectre – the frustrating elements – defeated.

> Each man is in his Spectre's power
> Until the arrival of that hour,
> When his Humanity awake
> And cast his own Spectre into the Lake.[4]

The meaning of *The Mental Traveller* is that as long as the cycle of acquisitive society continues man is his spectre's power. It is not a propagandist poem. It does not tell how the cycle can be broken. But with a passionate and dreadful clarity it illuminates the human situation which it reveals.

Notes

1 *The Poems of William Blake* (ed. W. H. Stevenson), Longman, 1971, pp. 157–8.

2   *Op. cit.*, p. 579.
3   *Op. cit.*, p. 580.
4   *William Blake's Writings* (ed. G. E. Bentley), Oxford, 1978, Vol. II,
p. 932.

From *Hamlet* to *Lear*

I will first put, as a hypothesis, a description of *Hamlet* which, though obviously oversimplified, I think gets somewhere near the heart of the play, what it is about.

Hamlet is a sixteenth-century prince who, because of certain extremely disturbing personal experiences, the death of his father and his mother's marriage to his uncle, comes to see his world in a different way. This new vision affects everything: his attitude to his friends and family, his feelings about sex, his view of the court and its politics, his image of himself. The experience is so all-embracing and so shattering that he is not at first sure that his new vision can be true or, if it is, whether he can endure it. But as the situation clarifies he becomes convinced of its validity and comes to understand its implications better. In this he is helped by two things: his education, which has predisposed him towards a humane and rational approach to life, and his friendship with Horatio, another young man who, though much less brilliant than Hamlet, is also a humanist scholar and who stands firm in loyalty and affection when the rest of the world treats him as a pitiable or dangerous neurotic.

At first Hamlet, though of an active disposition, is almost overwhelmed by the difficulty of solving his problems – especially with regard to his uncle – in terms of his new way of looking at things. He more or less deliberately prolongs the business of testing-out his well-founded suspicions and allows his uncle to get back the initiative and ship him out of the country. At this point, however, he comes to the conclusion that he cannot avoid acting, even if the actions he takes cannot satisfactorily meet all the problems he has unearthed. He acts very decisively therefore on the voyage to England, returns to Denmark and, moved beyond measure by the suicide of Ophelia and the reactions of her stupid but not ineffectual brother, puts on once more the bearing and responsibilities of a prince and solves the situation in action in the only way he can, by killing the king, leaving Prince Fortinbras to reign in his place, and begging Horatio to live on to tell the tale.

The degree to which Hamlet, in the last act, capitulates to the values he has previously rejected – the extent to which he gives up the battle to act as a man rather than as a prince – corresponds, I suggest, to the actual possibilities in the year 1600 of putting into practice the ideas of the new humanism or, perhaps more accurately, holds the mirror up to nature in the sense that certain limitations in sixteenth-century humanism and discrepancies between humanist theory and practice are revealed.

Hamlet's new view of the world he lives in is, essentially, the view of the world of the most advanced humanists of his time. It rejects as intolerable the ways of behaviour which formed the accepted standards of the contemporary ruling class. The basic view of man of the feudal ruling class had been, in theory, a metaphysical one which saw man as a fallen creature seeking to win redemption through submission to and service of God, in practice a highly conservative one which saw each man as having a specific, appointed place within existing society, and wisdom as acceptance of this fact. Within this view abuses of responsibility – tyranny, cruelty, murder – were theoretically condemned but in practice sanctioned by political custom. There was no lack of all three in Elizabethan England. The revolutionary nature of Hamlet's view of the world is that he sees tyranny and murder and inhumanity not as unfortunate abuses but as the norm and essence of the court of Denmark, not as blots on a society he can accept but as integral parts of a way of life he now finds intolerable.

In other words, Hamlet can no longer base his values and actions on the accepted assumptions of the conventional sixteenth-century prince. He ceases to behave as a prince ought to behave and begins behaving as a man, a sixteenth-century man, imbued with the values and caught up in the developing and exciting potentialities of the new humanism. The words which Hamlet comes back to in his deepest moments of need and trouble are the words man and friend.

He was a man, take him for all in all   (I. 2. 187)

is the best he can say of the best of men, his father. And when, dying, he stretches out his hand to Horatio it is with the words 'As

thou art a man, Give me the cup.' He scarcely speaks, even in the
two great soliloquies most relevant to his public position and behaviour ('O, what a rogue and peasant slave am I!' and 'How all
occasions do inform against me') of his duties and obligations as a
prince, except in so far as he happens to be the son of a murdered
father who was also a king; always the question is, what should a
man do? He scarcely refers to what, in any of the Histories, would
have been uppermost in the thoughts of a prince whose father has
been murdered: his own claims to the throne.

Throughout the play he is obsessed by the contradiction between
his own desperate unease and his vital sense of the potentialities of
man, so noble in reason, infinite in faculty, 'the beauty of the world,
the paragon of animals' (II. 2. 292ff.). It is this contradiction that
provides the underlying dramatic and verbal tensions of the soliloquies and makes them so much more than exercises in melancholic
introspection. It is Hamlet's optimism and vitality that give his
pessimism and misery their únique power to move us. He is so un-
bearably horrified by a man like Claudius because he has recognised
the possibility of being a different kind of man. What most disgusts
him about Rosencrantz and Guildenstern is their betrayal of friendship, but when Horatio uses the conventional 'your poor servant
ever' he at once replies

> Sir, my good friend. I'll change that name with you.   (I. 2. 163)

When Polonius is asked to see the players well bestowed, he says,
thinking to please the Prince who has been expatiating on their
virtues,

> My lord, I will use them according to their desert

and Hamlet cuts back with

God's bodkin, man, much better. Use every man after his desert, and who
shall scape whipping?   (II. 2. 523–5)

Obviously Hamlet is not a twentieth-century democrat; his thinking remains deeply sixteenth-century in its flavour. But within the
context in which he is operating his humanism has very definite
democratic implications – as any able actor doing the part before a
modern audience quickly discovers – especially when it is contrasted
with the social and political attitudes of Claudius, Laertes, Polonius
and Fortinbras.

At the centre of any discussion of *Hamlet* must always be what he

himself calls his 'mystery'. I think it is important to recognise that
this mystery, though it includes a psychological 'state', cannot be
adequately described in purely psychological terms. It involves not
only Hamlet but the world he lives in. If his view of that world had
no real basis, if it were at bottom a delusion, then one would be
justified in seeing Hamlet, as his interpreters on the stage often
seem to see him, as a 'case', a neurotic. But Shakespeare is at pains to
show that Hamlet's view of his world in the opening scenes of the
play is not a delusion. It is the worldly-wise of the play, in particular
the Queen and Polonius, who are time and time again shown to
be deluded. In his very first speech, after his three sardonic puns,
Hamlet states the problem. The King and Queen are trying to persuade him to be sensible about his father's death. Everyone dies. To
die is common.

> If it be,
> Why seems it so particular with thee?

asks his mother, immediately treating Hamlet as the queer one. But
he, whose experience has made him aware of the double edges of
words as well as deeds, immediately seizes on her least-considered
assumption and throws it back:

Seems, madam? Nay, it is. I know not seems.

It is not his superficial behaviour, the forms, moods and shows of
grief, that can denote him truly.

> These indeed seem;
> For they are actions that a man might play;
> But I have that within which passes show,
> These but the trappings and the suits of woe.   (I. 2. 74–86)

The contrast between 'seems' and 'is' is a key question in the play.
And it is not treated metaphysically. The contrast between appearance and reality which Hamlet at once emphasises is not at all an
abstract philosophical problem: it is a problem of behaviour and
human values. When he cries out agonisingly

That one may smile, and smile, and be a villain;

he adds at once

At least I am sure it may be so in Denmark.   (I. 5. 108–9)

The phrase 'I have that within that passes show' means not only 'I cannot express what I feel' but 'What I have experienced makes further pretence at conformity impossible'. Hamlet is putting the issue quite bluntly: which way of feeling and behaving corresponds most fully to the situation? The Queen's and the court's, or his? Who is putting on a show? Is it the conventional, 'normal' behaviour of the court that 'is', so that he 'seems' the odd man out, or is it *their* behaviour that involves dissimulation and self-deception, the rejection of reality?

Hamlet, at the beginning of the play, is on the verge of suicide, seeing life as entirely weary, stale, flat and unprofitable. The delineation of this state of mind is so convincing and indeed so clinically precise that it immediately entitles Shakespeare to an honoured place in the history of psychology. But the limitation of Freudian interpretations of the play[1] is that, though they can throw light on the nature of Hamlet's experience and reactions – the effects on him of his father's murder (which he already half-suspects) and his mother's marriage – they tend to draw attention away from the real dramatic significance of that experience, that it makes him see the world differently in ways which have little to do with the experience itself. The personal crisis Hamlet has been through is the *occasion* of his new vision but does not explain it or help us to judge its ultimate validity. We are so used to separating 'personal' from 'public' issues in our thinking that is not easy for us to recognise that Hamlet's discontent is not merely private: on the contrary, it is deepened and validated by his perception that the values and attitudes which corrupt personal relationships are essentially the same values and attitudes which reside at the corrupt core of the public world.

Shakespeare goes out of his way to emphasise that what Hamlet is up against is not a problem of personal relationships simply but a whole society. 'Something is rotten in the state of Denmark.' The rottenness is not psychological (though it has its psychological manifestations all right) but social. This is stressed right through the play. The King and the state are reflections of one another.[2] It is the *time* that is out of joint, not Hamlet. The difficulty of his dilemma is that he sees all too clearly for his comfort that it is only by setting the time right that he can set himself right. This and not some metaphysical mole is the 'cursed spite' behind his mystery.

That is why it is unforgiveable to act Hamlet as though he were a neurotic instead of a hero and why one must reject as hopelessly on

the wrong track any interpretations of the play which offer us a
'negative' Hamlet skulking in the wings of a sanity represented by
the Court of Denmark.

What Hamlet has come to see, as a result of the goings-on in his
family, is, I would suggest, nothing less than what, from the point
of view of an advanced sixteenth-century humanist, the Renaissance
court of Denmark is actually like. The King, whom a generous-
minded modern critic like Professor Wilson Knight can describe as
'a good and gentle king'³ he sees as a drunken, lecherous murderer.
The Queen is 'stew'd in corruption'. The politicians are time-servers
and machiavels, without a decent principle between them, to whom
the lives of the common people mean nothing except as a factor in
personal struggles for power. The women are mere pawns in the intrigues of the court, generally willing pawns reducing themselves to
the status of whores. Friends cannot be trusted. The values of love
are those of the stud or the stock-market.

And all this does not 'seem' but 'is'. Shakespeare makes sure that
we are in a position to check up on Hamlet's judgements, to see
whether he is deluded or not. It is not only the authenticity of the
Ghost and the conscience of the King that are tested out in the play
scene but also the moral values of the Danish court. Shakespeare
leaves much to the imagination but nothing to chance, permitting
no escape into metaphysical generalities about 'the human condition'. We are spared no detail of Polonius's attitude to his son's taste
of *la dolce vita* in Paris or of Claudius's complex political manoeuvres
at home and abroad. The predatory Norwegian army crosses Denmark on its way to Poland before our eyes and we are left to choose
between two comments, the cynical acceptance of the Norwegian
captain who sees this as the way of the world (Claudius has already
expressed his attitude succinctly with 'It likes us well') and Hamlet's immediate linking of the project with the rottenness in the
state of Denmark:

> This is th' imposthume of much wealth and peace,
> That inward breaks, and shows no cause without
> Why the man dies.   (IV. 4. 27–9)

The pitiless humiliation of Ophelia is revealed in pitiful detail. In
one of the most painful scenes in all literature the words of human
dignity and rationality enter like daggers into the ears of the
wretched Queen and cleave in twain her corrupt but human heart.

The state of Denmark that unfolds before our eyes is presented with extraordinary realism and at the same time against an almost continuous undercurrent of thoroughgoing criticism. The criticism comes, of course, largely from Hamlet himself, especially in the soliloquies and the graveyard scene, but in some form or other it impregnates every scene in which he appears. It is this deep, insistent strain of irreverent, daring and radical criticism that represents the essential change wrought by Shakespeare upon his sources – the Danish chronicle from which, via an earlier 'revenge' play, he took his plot.[4] In the earlier play Hamlet's problems had been purely physical – how, when and where to get a revenge, the implications of which were never questioned. Shakespeare's rejection of the old feudal concepts of revenge (based on the feudal lord's refusal to accept any justice other than his own) first in *Romeo and Juliet* and then in *Hamlet* shows how far he had come from the more primitive morality which Kyd, only a few years earlier, had accepted as the moral and dramatic driving-force of his plays.[5]

Not that there is anything abstract or schematic about the insistent note of social criticism that gives *Hamlet* its particular flavour. On the contrary, the solid and detailed realism of the presentation of the Danish court is such that it is not surprising that readers and audiences who take the ways and values of class-divided society for granted should have tended to take Claudius's Denmark at its face value as the human norm.[6] Yet if one examines, say, Polonius's speech of advice to the departing Laertes – a speech which generations of schoolboys have had to get by heart as one of the ultimates in human wisdom – it turns out to be (quite appropriately in the context) a compound of stuffy platitudes and unconscious ironies culminating in the words (which I remember a worthy uncle inscribing in my autograph book as a child)

> This above all: to thine own self be true,
> And it must follow as the night the day,
> Thou canst not then be false to any man.   (I. 3. 78–80)

The glib simile should be warning enough. If it followed as inevitably as that there would be no problem, and it is not the only time in the play that Polonius uses this particular image to reinforce his quarter-truths.[7] The 'moral' of his speech simply enshrines the cheerful self-deception of the individualist who cannot face the fact that his individualism brings him to an insoluble impasse.

Hamlet has seen through Polonius. His contempt for him is so complete that he cannot even spare him a moment's pity when he has run his sword through him by accident.[8] For Hamlet, who knows that a tear is an intellectual thing, has come to see the horror, in terms of human misery and betrayal, of what Polonius stands for. That is why it is wrong for an actor to play the Lord Chamberlain simply as a clown: he is a responsible figure who, in the context within which he works, knows perfectly well what he is doing and boasts of how skilfully he can 'By indirections find directions out'.[9] Politically he is a machiavel: morally, as Hamlet tells him to his face, a fishmonger. Before he has 'loosed' his daughter to Hamlet (a good stock-breeder's term) he has expatiated at length to her on her value on the marriage-market, fearing she has taken Hamlet's 'tenders for true pay Which are not sterling' (I. 3. 105–6) and describing his vows as 'brokers, Not of that dye which their investments show' (I. 3. 127–8).

It is not, of course, only Polonius that Hamlet has seen through but the morality of a whole society which sees nothing wrong with Polonius except his garrulousness. Hamlet has loved Ophelia, but now, in the light of his new vision of the Danish world, he sees her as, though personally innocent, a pawn in the corrupt intrigues of the court. This is what lies behind his contradictory and paradoxical shifts in his scene with her – 'I did love you once' and then, immediately, 'I loved you not' (III. 1. 115, 119). He loved her, but now he sees her – and women in general – differently, and what he sees he cannot love. She were better in a nunnery. That is before he realises that Ophelia has been 'loosed' to him. After that he is pitiless and in the play scene treats her with the utmost brutality as a prostitute, humiliating both himself and her.

Hamlet's problem is the appallingly difficult one of finding actions commensurate with his new vision of what 'is', what the world he lives in is actually like. He is not afraid of action as such. He has been, we are told more than once, a capable and popular prince. All through the play he acts boldly and decisively whenever he needs to – in following the ghost, in organizing the play, in facing his mother with the brutal facts, in killing the old man behind the arras, in coping effectively with the situation on the ship bound for England: and about none of these actions does his conscience bother him particularly, though his enigmatic display immediately after the death of Polonius shows his awareness of the moral complexities of that act. But it is really only over the killing of the King that he hesitates and that is certainly not because he dare not do it or looks on the killing as in some absolute way 'wrong'. The 'Now might I do it pat' speech (III. 3. 73) expresses as clearly as any of his utterances his sense of the inadequacy of *merely* killing the King, of achieving nothing but the minimal formalities of revenge.

It is not good enough to describe Hamlet as a man who cannot make up his mind. More adequately one might say that he is faced with a situation which it is almost impossible for him to resolve satisfactorily in action. For, to put it crudely, what adequate actions could a young man take who, in the year 1600, could no longer look at society from the point of view of the ruling class? He might kill the king (as was, within fifty years, to happen in Britain) recognising him as the source not only of his personal ills but of the corrupt state, the prison that is Denmark. But what then? Especially if young Fortinbras, just back from a successful mopping-up operation in Poland, is to reign in his stead.

It seems to me essential to see Hamlet's problem historically. To do so helps resolve one of the issues that has always worried actors who tackle the part: how can Hamlet be at the same time – what almost everyone feels instinctively he must be – a hero, yet also ineffective? It is this problem that has led to the tendency to sympathise with Hamlet *because* he is ineffective. I think this tendency, though wrong, is a tribute to the significance of the situation Shakespeare has put his finger on, a situation of great general interest in the modern world and the one which makes everyone recognise the typicality as well as the uniqueness of Hamlet. Hamlet is not merely a Renaissance prince. Along with Marlowe's Faustus he is the first modern intellectual in our literature and he is, of course, far more modern as well as much more intelligent than Faustus. And his dilemma is essentially the dilemma of the modern European intellectual: his ideas and values are in a deep way at odds with his actions. Thinking and doing have got separated, basically because power is in the hands of a class whose values humane people feel they must repudiate. Power and effectiveness tend therefore to be suspected by the intelligentsia who retreat physically into a world removed from vital power-decisions and mentally into a realm of ideas and art which they value above the world of action and try to defend from the corrupting inroads of cynical expediency.

In Hamlet all these tendencies and temptations are to be found, though, being a sixteenth-century prince, the practical possibilities of an escape from the world of action are not, for him, very great. But the lost young man of the opening acts, acutely conscious of 'not belonging', contemptuous, sardonic, even a bit exhibitionist, talking a language different from those around him,[10] speaks directly to the experience of the modern intellectual who proceeds to idealise this unhappy young man into the supreme expression of the eternal human condition epitomised in being an intellectual.

Shakespeare does not permit this idealisation. Hamlet, having stood on the brink of despair, comes back to the court of Denmark, refusing to continue to contemplate the possibility of a separation of thought from action. From the moment at which, recalled to actuality in the graveyard by the death of Ophelia, he leaps into the grave with a cry 'This is I, Hamlet the Dane!' (V. 1. 250–1), he puts behind him the most desperate of his haunting doubts.[11] The atmosphere of the fifth act, with its tense, controlled, unemphatic prose statements, is one of sad, almost (but not quite) passive acceptance of the need to act. The readiness is all. Hamlet is not taken in, nor has he become cynical: in his heart there remains a kind of fighting that will not let him sleep. Although all's ill about his heart he will meet the challenges that come bravely, without cynicism and without humbug.

The fifth act does not involve, it seems to me, a dramatic resolution of Hamlet's dilemmas in any full sense of the word, but rather some kind of salvaging of human decency and a rejection of philosophic idealism. Hamlet, the prince who has tried to become a man, becomes a prince again and does what a sixteenth-century prince ought to do – killing the murderer of his father, forgiving the stupid, clean-limbed Laertes, expressing (for the first time) direct concern about his own claims to the throne but giving his dying voice to young Fortinbras, the kind of delicate and tender prince that Hamlet himself could never again have been. Horatio, it is true, lives on, pledged to tell the truth and bearing the aspirations of the humanist cause; but Horatio without Hamlet will not be, we feel, a decisive force. The end then, is, in one sense, almost total defeat for everything Hamlet has stood for. But it is an acceptance of the need to act in the real world, and that is a great human triumph.

A twentieth-century spectator may well recall, at this point, another humanist hero, born in the same year as Shakespeare, confronted with problems more like those of Hamlet than at first seems

obvious, and interpreted to our own time by the only twentieth-
century dramatist whose name can be mentioned in the same breath
as Shakespeare's. Galileo would have known what Hamlet was talking about when he says

> Thus conscience does make cowards of us all,
> And thus the native hue of resolution
> Is sicklied o'er with the pale cast of thought,
> And enterprises of great pith and moment,
> With this regard their currents turn awry,
> And lose the name of action.   (III. 1. 83–8)

Neither Hamlet nor Shakespeare, in the year 1600, could resolve
in action, even tragically, the dilemma of a young man from whose
eyes the veils which shrouded so many truths about class-divided
society had been torn. Shakespeare could do nothing about Hamlet's
dilemma except express it with profound realism. But the 'except' is
a tremendous one, pointing to the way art works and helps.

We begin to see the link between *Lear* and *Hamlet* when we
recognise that Lear, unlike Hamlet in so much, is, like him, a hero.

A hero is a figure to whom, irrespective of faults and weaknesses,
we feel a deeply sympathetic commitment. We do not, in the day-
dream sense of the word, identify ourselves with him; but we do in a
decisive way identify our hopes and fears with his career. It is not his
more purely individual characteristics – his personality or his charm
– that make a man a hero, nor his actions as such – he can (like
Coriolanus) be strong or even brave without being heroic. What
makes the hero, or heroine, heroic, is that he bears on his shoulders,
sometimes without realising it, something of the actual aspirations
of humanity in its struggles to advance its condition. Prometheus is
the greatest of heroes in that he embodies human aspiration itself.
Most of his successors have a more limited burden and, because
human aspiration is not something absolute and abstract but real
and changing, the hero cannot as a rule be fruitfully taken out of
his actual historical situation. The heroes of Renaissance drama are
the men and women whose lives and struggles express the actual
attempts of people at that time to extend the frontiers of human
possibility. We commit ourselves to the career of Romeo and Juliet,
though we know their love is in the pejorative as well as the sympathetic sense 'romantic', because we recognise the need of advanc-
ing men and women to choose their own lovers rather than subscribe

to marriages arranged by their parents for dynastic or family purposes. In our attitude to a hero we are always *partisan*; to be indifferent to his fate would be to be indifferent to the outcome of our
own lives. But our partisanship, even when it seems intuitive, is
based on an assessment of the forces and values involved in his situation which has to bear the scrutiny of *objective* analysis. This, I think,
is what Brecht was getting at in his insistence that a revolutionary
drama must at the same time be 'committed' (i.e. committed to the
solving of actual problems, to the changing of the world) and, in his
sense of the word, 'epic' (i.e. involving the conscious realisation by
the spectator that he is watching actions that are outside himself, so
that in one sense he must remain cool and uninvolved). Scientific
humanism is the basis on which we can come both to *feel* our
commitment (our identity as human beings with other human
beings and our impulse to take the right side in human choices) and
understand it (submit it to the tests of argument and experience).

Lear's story begins where most stories end. The old man seems to
be at the finish of his reign and time. But in fact his journey has not
yet begun. The opening scene is a statement – the statement of
where we and Lear start from – and Shakespeare has neither the time
nor the concern to make it naturalistically convincing in its every
detail. Lear is there, every inch a king, disposing of his kingdom.
Essentially one has to see him as a feudal king, but in saying this
I refer less to the social and economic relations of feudalism than to
its characteristic ideology. The point, and also its significance, becomes clear, when we remember that within Lear's kingdom there
are, inside the ruling class, two tendencies or camps, which are not
simply or primarily a matter of conflicting generations or social
status. On the one hand are those who accept the old order (Lear,
Gloucester, Kent, Albany) which has to be seen as, broadly speaking, the feudal order; on the other hand are the new people, the individualists (Goneril, Regan, Edmund, Cornwall) who have the
characteristic outlook of the bourgeoisie.

These correspondences are underlined – as Professor Danby has
very suggestively pointed out[12] by the differing ways in which the
people of the two camps use the word Nature, a key-word which
crops up nearly fifty times in the course of the play. To Lear and
those associated with him Nature is essentially a benignant traditional order, like the 'Natural Law' of the Middle Ages, in which
human and divine society are at one. In Lear's language the 'offices of
nature' are always linked with such concepts as

> bond of childhood,
> Effects of courtesy, dues of gratitude. (II. 4. 177–8)

Goneril and Regan become, to him, 'unnatural hags', and Gloucester, from his side, talks of 'the King falling from the bias of Nature, there's father against child'.

Such uses of the word are in direct contrast to Edmund's forthright

> Thou, Nature, art my Goddess; to thy law
> My services are bound. Wherefore should I
> Stand in the plague of custom . . .? (I. 2. 1–3)

Here Nature is seen as the opposite of custom, tradition, hierarchy, established order. And Professor Danby shrewdly points out that Edmund's use of Nature is precisely the use which, within half a century, the most remarkable and most consistently materialist of the early bourgeois philosophers, Thomas Hobbes, was to give the word. Hobbes, as is well known, saw the state of Nature as a state of war. Man was to him not *naturally* a social animal but had to be made one. The author of the *Leviathan* would not, of course, have approved of Edmund's worship of the Natural man; but he would have understood it and, in a wry way, appreciated its 'realism'.

In *King Lear* Shakespeare reveals, from the very start, a society in turmoil in which (in contrast to *Hamlet*) it is the representatives of the old order who feel that everything is out of joint:

> . . . love cools, friendship falls off, brothers divide; in cities, mutinies; in countries discord; in palaces, treason; and the bond crack'd 'twixt son and father. . . . We have seen the best of our time: machinations, hollowness, treachery, and all ruinous disorders, follow us disquietly to our graves.
> (I. 2. 110–20)

It is Gloucester speaking and the particular speech is not a deep one (Gloucester himself being a conventional and – as he comes appallingly to realise – blind old man); but it is, from his point of view and, indeed, objectively, a quite true description of the state of affairs in Lear's kingdom. And it cannot but remind us of such a poem as Donne's *First Anniversarie*, written in 1611, in which the state of the contemporary world is strikingly expressed.

> 'Tis all in peeces, all cohaerence gone;
> All just supply, and all Relation:
> Prince, Subject, Father, Sonne, are things forgot,
> For every man alone thinkes he hath got
> To be a Phoenix. . . . [13]

Gloucester, in the speech I have just quoted, superstitiously links the social crack-up with the eclipse of the sun and moon. It is all, he insists, thoroughly unnatural. And he wanders off, scratching his head, leaving his bastard son Edmund to pour scorn in a brilliant soliloquy on his superstitious unscientific outlook: 'An admirable evasion of whoremaster man, to lay his goatish disposition on the charge of a star.' Edmund has none of his father's amiable, conservative illusions. He is intelligent, active and ruthless. His immediate personal motive is simple — 'Legitimate Edgar, I must have your land.' No beating about the bush. Edmund is emancipated. The ancient sanctities of law (he is in every sense illegitimate) and order (kingship, the property rights of fathers, primogeniture, the identity of the man-made hierarchy with a God-made one), these mean nothing to him. He is the new man of the incipient bourgeois revolution, the private enterprise man, the man who thinks he has got to be a phoenix, the individualist go-getter, the machiavel, Marlowe's aspiring hero taken to his extreme conclusion: man with the lid off.

Edgar of course is Edmund's opposite. The brothers are contrasted at every point, and it is not the crude static moral contrast of the good and the bad, even though something of this — the structure of the old Morality plays — remains in *Lear*. Edgar is the loyal son of the feudal father, pious, resourceful, kind, and above all legitimate, and when in the last act he steps forward at the third trump to defend the right, he carries on his shoulders all the glamour and the chivalry of a formalised feudal past.

Edgar defeats Edmund. Gloucester, though hideously punished for his moral laxity and political blindness, is avenged, even redeemed, gaining in his suffering, through his contact with Poor Tom, an insight which, seeing, he had lacked. His profoundest moment is when he gives Tom his purse:

> Here, take this purse, thou whom the heavens' plagues
> Have humbled to all strokes: that I am wretched
> Makes thee the happier: Heavens, deal so still!
> Let the superfluous and lust-dieted man,
> That slaves your ordinance, that will not see
> Because he does not feel, feel your power quickly;
> So distribution should undo excess,
> And each man have enough.   (IV. 1. 64–70)

It is a wonderful moment, the full significance of which lies in its echoing of some of Lear's own words which I will refer to in a moment. The power Gloucester has not seen because he has not felt it can only, in the context, be that of common humanity, embodied in Poor Tom. Yet in the Gloucester story, even though Tom does save Gloucester and help him onwards, this outburst, moving as it is, is not really developed. It is not developed because the relation between Tom and Edgar remains ill-defined or, rather, too well-defined. Edgar simply pretends to be Tom and then becomes Edgar again. Tom is a richer character than Edgar because he includes Edgar, whereas Edgar doesn't include Tom. Edgar is not really changed by being Tom, though the play is, through the experiences of Lear and Gloucester. But the Edgar of the last act is essentially St George, the feudal hero, and he has to be, for he will become king. Only in the four final lines of the play does a doubt creep in and we are allowed to wonder whether Edgar perhaps remembers Tom.

The Lear story is deeper, more complex and more variously moving than the Gloucester story, for Lear, unlike Gloucester, is a hero.

At the beginning of the play he is not a hero at all, but a king to whom the forms of kingship and hierarchy are the basis and reality of the world. It is Cordelia who, at this stage of the story, is the heroic one, for it is she who speaks the words of aspiring humanity. When she has to define her feelings about her father she can only say

> I love your Majesty
> According to my bond; no more nor less. (I. 1. 92–3)

The words bear close scrutiny. Obviously they are not the words of a twentieth-century daughter, royal or common. Their form is essentially feudal, as the word 'bond' emphasises. Yet it becomes clear that by 'according to my bond' Cordelia is not thinking in formal feudal terms but defining as realistically and truthfully as she can a human relationship between two people, of whom one happens to be her father and a king and therefore has special claims on her. I think Cordelia's view of love is very much akin to that expressed two hundred years later in another poem about an innocent child faced with angry authority. In Blake's 'A Little Boy Lost' the child says to the inquisitor Priest:

> 'And Father, how can I love you
> Or any of my brothers more?
> I love you like the little bird
> That picks up crumbs around the door.'

Such heresy, the expression of a relationship honourable and *natural*
in senses which neither party in the *Lear* world can accept, leads the
child to the stake as it leads Cordelia to the gallows. And it is interesting that, near the end of the play, in a beautiful scene which
shows us a Lear and a Cordelia who have come through to 'a better
way', the old man uses the very Blakean image

> We two alone will sing like birds i' th' cage.
>
> (V. 3. 9)

It is also interesting that Cordelia's phrase 'no more nor less' is
echoed by Lear when, the great rage dead, he comes to describe himself in the terms of his new understanding:

> I am a very foolish fond old man,
> Fourscore and upward, not an hour more or less;
> And, to deal plainly,
> I fear I am not in my perfect mind.   (IV. 7. 60–4)

He is now, like Cordelia, dealing plainly, describing the situation
realistically. He has reached the view of Nature implicit in her first
statement. I can find no better way of describing it than as the
humanist view of nature. And in the course of discovering it Lear has
become a hero. His story, put in its simplest terms, is the story of
his progress from being a king to being a man, neither more nor
less. It is a story so fearful and yet so wonderful that all human
society is shaken by the terrible beauty of it and at its supreme
moments man and the universe are seen in relationships which it is
scarcely possible for words other than Shakespeare's own to describe.

When I say that *Lear* is the story of how a king becomes a man I
do not mean at all that it is an allegory or that we should use a word
like 'symbolic' to describe it. For Shakespeare does not work in
abstractions. He is a supremely realistic writer who presents us all
the time with actual situations, actual relationships, and what general conclusions he offers are always based on particular observations
and insights. He is not, of course, a *naturalistic* dramatist, attempting a 'slice of life' kind of realism, and he uses every resource of his
teeming imagination to create means of penetrating, through words
and fantasy, to the inner processes of the situations and people he
presents. The storm in *Lear* 'works' artistically on a number of
levels: the elemental storm, the social storm which shakes the
divided kingdom, the inner storm that drives Lear mad, all are
interconnected and reinforce one another to achieve what is, I
suppose, the most extraordinary and harrowing representation of

crisis in the whole of art. But every device of art is used to produce, not some effect above or beyond reality, but the deepest, most complex exploration of the actual nature of reality, its texture and its implications, its movement and its interconnectedness.

In the first three acts of *Lear* we have almost unrelieved horror and pessimism, broken only by isolated gleams of human decency and hope. It is one of Shakespeare's triumphs that, without compromising for a moment on their hideousness, he does not make the opponents of Lear crude villains. Edmund, with his gusto and energy, is in many respects a more vital creature than the rather colourless Edgar. Goneril and Regan have a terrible common-sense effectiveness, almost a normality, about them. Their very baiting of their father by the reduction of the numbers of his retainers is not mere insolence: they have a strong case and argue at least partly in the terms of a modern-sounding contempt for the hierarchical principle.[14] They are at once shrewd, able, shallow and morally impervious, and they are rivals because they are alike.

It is the new people with their heartless rationalisation – 'the younger rises, when the old doth fall' – who bring down Lear. And his friends, the ineffectual unseeing Gloucester and the loyal but too simple Kent, are unable to save him from the new ruthlessness. Kent's role in the play is interesting because he is of all the 'feudal' characters the most courageous and least corrupt. And he is able to shield Lear to some extent. But his ultimate failure to cope with the situation – he is unable to hold Lear within the bounds of sanity and is in fact of far less use to him than either the Fool or Poor Tom – is echoed by his own prognostications of his death in the final scene. The ultimate inadequacy of Kent despite his decent, old world virtues, is one of the expressions in the play of the impossibility of a return of the feudal past.

What we have, then, in the first three acts of *Lear* is a world in which the old order is decadent and the new people unprincipled and both, as the treatment of Cordelia shows, inhuman. Horror dominates. The terrible curse on Goneril – made by Lear in the name of Nature –

Into her womb convey sterility!
Dry up in her the organs of increase,
And from her derogate body never spring
A babe to honour her! If she must teem,
Create her child of spleen, that it may live
And be a thwart disnatur'd torment to her.   (I. 4. 287–92)

— this curse, whose imagery overflows into the verse of scene after scene, is a measure of the depth of the horror; but not its ultimate expression. For the equal horror is Lear's own impotence. When Goneril rejects him he still can threaten vainly to 'resume the shape' of the past — to be king again. When Regan's cruelty is added to her sister's, and personal ingratitude is, so to speak, turned into a system, he is literally unable to express his emotion, though he still mutters of revenge.

> No, you unnatural hags,
> I will have such revenges on you both
> That all the world shall — I will do such things
> What they are, yet I know not, but they shall be
> The terrors of the earth.   (II. 4. 280—4)

Lear has, literally, no resources of action, language or even emotion to be able to cope, within the bounds of the consciousness he has so far achieved, with the situation which faces him. From here to madness is but a short step. And the very word madness needs our thought. It can no more be taken for granted in *Lear* than in *Hamlet*. The more one examines the play the more one comes to feel that Lear's madness is not so much a breakdown as a breakthrough. It is necessary.

In the storm scene comes the first hint of resolution, the first turning-point of the play, the first breakthrough of humanity, coincident with the words 'My wits begin to turn'. For the phrase is followed by some words to the Fool:

> Come on, my boy. How dost, my boy? Art cold?
> I am cold myself. Where is this straw, my fellow?
> The art of our necessities is strange,
> That can make vile things precious. Come, your hovel.
> Poor fool and knave, I have one part in my heart
> That's sorry yet for thee.   (III. 2. 68—73)

The words represent a change in direction: away from self-pity, pride, revenge and kingliness, towards fellow-feeling and co-operation, the minimum qualities of humanity. I do not want to present Shakespeare as some kind of 'unconscious' precursor of Engels; but I think it is very interesting that at this crisis of the play, when Lear is first beginning to feel his way towards a new freedom, Shakespeare should use the word 'necessities' and use it in a context which forbids any but a materialist significance.

It is through his madness – his incapacity to deal with reality any longer within the framework of his accepted standards of sanity – that Lear comes to a new outlook on life. The moving prayer just before his meeting with Tom is now fairly generally recognised as a crux of the whole play.

> Poor naked wretches, wheresoe'er you are,
> That bide the pelting of this pitiless storm,
> How shall your houseless heads and unfed sides,
> Your loop'd and window'd raggedness, defend you
> From seasons such as these? O! I have ta'en
> Too little care of this. Take physic, Pomp;
> Expose thyself to feel what wretches feel,
> That thou mayst shake the superflux to them,
> And show the Heavens more just.   (III. 4. 28–36)

This speech, echoed so soon by Gloucester's words to Tom, in which precisely the same ideas are expressed and the word 'superflux' returned to, is absolutely central to the structure and meaning of the play. Lear's incapacity to deal with the inhumanity of the new people is what drives him into a solidarity, and, later, an identification, with the poor. For in his powerlessness he is forced to recognise the pervasive helplessness of the poor in the face of the power of the rich, whose who have property. Thus his direct personal contact with ruling-class inhumanity leads him to question the validity of property itself and the authority and exemption from elementary human moral values it confers. In this, Lear's development is not at all unlike that of later seventeenth-century radicals like Winstanley.

There is method, Polonius discovers, in Hamlet's madness; and Edgar, listening to Lear's mad wanderings, remarks to the audience 'Reason in madness!' The speech he is referring to contains some of the deepest and acutest social criticism in all Shakespeare, or indeed anywhere.

> . . . A man may see how this world goes with no eyes. Look with thine ears: see how yond justice rails upon yond simple thief. Hark, in thine ear: change places and, handy-dandy, which is the justice, which is the thief? Thou hast seen a farmer's dog bark at a beggar?
> *Gloucester.* Ay, sir.
> *Lear.* And the creature run from the cur? There thou mightst behold the great image of authority: a dog's obey'd in office.
> Thou rascal beadle, hold thy bloody hand!
> Why dost thou lash that whore? Strip thy own back;
> Thou hotly lusts to use her in that kind

For which thou whip'st her. The usurer hangs the cozener.
Through tatter'd clothes small vices do appear;
Robes and furr'd gowns hide all. Plate sin with gold,
And the strong lance of justice hurtless breaks;
Arm it in rags, a pigmy's straw does pierce it.
None does offend, none, I say none; I'll able 'em:
Take that of me, my friend, who have the power
To seal th' accuser's lips. Get thee glass eyes,
And, like a scurvy politician, seem
To see the things thou dost not. Now, now, now, now!
Pull off my boots; harder, harder; so.   (IV. 6. 151–75)

When that speech has the currency of Polonius's advice to Laertes it
will be seem less strange to British readers to refer to the democratic
content of the bourgeois–democratic revolution and to link Shakespeare's greatness with his humanism.

   If we describe Lear's, or Gloucester's, experiences as 'spiritual',
that is to say, involving a change not just in fortune and circumstance but in values and quality of being, it is essential to recognise
that Shakespeare links this change at every step with actual actions
and social attitudes. The social emphases are not more or less casual
sidethoughts but are absolutely basic to the whole conception of the
play. You cannot understand it without them. The new humanity
which Lear achieves is not simply a self-knowledge acquired by introspection or any kind of mystical or religious experience; it is an
outlook gained through experience and action, through the necessity
that has been forced upon him of exposing himself to feel that
wretches feel, of facing reality in all its horror and splendour, of
judging men and women by their simplest, most essential actions,
and of learning who his friends are. The experience results in a
turning upside-down, handy-dandy, of accepted social assumptions.
The pulling off of the boots at the end of the speech I have just
quoted is, everyone realises, significant. Already in the hovel in the
storm Lear has insistently taken off his clothes, feeling them an
impediment, a mark of rank, preventing complete identification
with Poor Tom. 'Off, off you lendings' he cries. The phrase is almost
a summary of the play. Lear, the king, reduced by the new people of
the bourgeois world to the depth of human humiliation, falls only to
rise, and becomes a man. And the people who help him to achieve
humanity are by no means the wise or great or powerful, but a Fool
and a beggar who has gone mad.

The turning point of the play is Lear's losing of his wits to find them; and it is followed by a decisive moment of action – the first instant in the play when the evil characters are checked in their deeds. Up to the moment of the blinding of Gloucester the decent people have seemed impotent. And then of a sudden a blow is struck – and again it is not by the great or the wise, but by the servant who, his humanity outraged by the torturing of Gloucester, kills the Duke of Cornwall. Regan's horrified comment is more eloquent than a long speech:

A peasant stand up thus? (III. 7. 79)

And from now on a fight is put up.

I have said nothing so far of the role of the Fool. We should not sentimentalise him or exaggerate his importance. He is less significance to Lear's progress than Poor Tom. But his comments – the shrewd and cynical paradoxes, the irreverent thrusts at Lear's dignity – form a kind of choric counterpoint of the main themes of the play which not only adds a depth and complexity but helps define the essential 'popular' element within this play of kings and nobles. It is not easy to get a consistent pattern from the Fool's remarks. His Blakean prophecy (at the end of Act III, Sc. 2) is puzzling and apparently inconsistent, yet it expresses with an exciting vividness the historical tensions and contradictions which lie behind the whole play. Perhaps it is the cynical realism of his comments which is most striking. He has been ground down too long to have much hope of salvation, so that his resilience is spasmodic, his pessimism deeprooted. He reminds one a little of the old soldier whose hatred and contempt of the army has been fed on a lifetime of chastening experience and who cannot – for all his irreverence – shake off the habits of servitude he despises. One might describe him as the opposite of the eternal butler, an eternal batman, a sort of Elizabethan Schweik.[15]

When Lear awakes from his madness the Fool is no longer with him, but Cordelia. The realm of Albion has indeed come to great confusion and Lear has come through to a new state of mind. He has not merely been purged of pride and learned a proper humility, as Christian critics point out, he has changed his whole attitude to people and society and there is, most significantly, no desire in him to get his throne back. On the contrary, the court is mentioned only

with contempt, not at all unlike the contempt of Hamlet: Lear and
Cordelia will

> hear poor rogues
> Talk of court news; and we'll talk with them too,
> Who loses and who wins; who's in, who's out,
> And take upon's the mystery of things
> As if we were God's spies: and we'll wear out,
> In a wall'd prison, packs and sects of great ones
> That ebb and flow by th' moon.   (V. 3. 13–19)

The whole emergent world of bourgeois politics is somehow evoked
and placed in that single sentence and a modern reader can scarcely
fail to hear in *Lear* constant pre-echoes of Swift and Blake.

Towards the end of the play Cordelia, with whom Lear now un-
equivocally associates himself, is seen explicitly as the alternative to
the old order (which by her honesty she has exposed) and to the new
people who hate and fear her.

> Patience and sorrow strove
> Who should express her goodliest. You have seen
> Sunshine and rain at once: her smiles and tears
> Were like, a better way.   (IV. 3. 17–20)

'Sunshine and rain at once', the image of the rainbow, the pledge of
future harmony arising out of contradiction, is associated with
Cordelia. She seems to express in her very person the 'better way' to
which Lear has come through. If there is a kind of utopian promise
here – the sort of thing Shakespeare comes back to in his final plays –
the suggestion is achieved without a removal of the play into the
realms of abstraction or metaphysics. For it is because of what she
does and thinks, not what in some safe way she 'is', that the new
people cannot let Cordelia live. And Lear, too, in this ineffably
beautiful yet most terrible play, must die. He cannot be set back –
an even older but a wiser man – upon his throne. Shakespeare has
revealed a struggle more desperate than such a resolution could
encompass.

It is worth comparing the end of *Lear* with that of *Hamlet*. In both
plays the protagonist has been defeated, not by his enemies or by his
weaknesses but by history. Both plays end with the implied acces-
sion of a new king, a promise of continuity as opposed to death; but
in neither case does the new king in any serious sense fill the bill.
The point about Fortinbras, as we have seen, is that he is incapable

of understanding what Hamlet has understood; so that there is, despite the survival of Horatio, a distinctly hollow sound in the closing commonplaces of the play. The most that can be said for Edgar is that he is something to be going on with. But he is, nevertheless, a considerable advance on Fortinbras. The final words of *King Lear* are moving and curiously profound.

> The weight of this sad time we must obey;
> Speak what we feel, not what we ought to say.
> The oldest hath borne most; we that are young
> Shall never see so much nor live so long.   (V. 3. 323–6)

That the experience and meaning of the play cannot be confined within the limits of seventeenth-century social thinking is implicit in these lines. Conventional assessment (what we *ought* to say) is quite inadequate. What raises Edgar so far above Fortinbras is that he recognises his own inferiority; he has not seen what Lear has seen, but he has seen and felt enough to recognise the quality of Lear's experience, to know that he does not know. Perhaps, after all, he has not quite forgotten Poor Tom.

Notes

1   As, for instance, Ernest Jones, *Hamlet and Oedipus* (1949).

2   This is brought out particularly in Act I. Sc. 4.

3   *The Wheel of Fire* (1930). Professor Knight recognises, of course, that this is only one side of Claudius; but he argues that Claudius is presented as being 'human', Hamlet 'inhuman'. Hamlet is no doubt in the right but his philosophy is the negation of life. I think Professor Knight grants Claudius far too much and underemphasises Hamlet's realism.

4   The chronicle was the *Historica Danica* of Saxo Grammaticus, a twelfth-century Dane whose work was translated in the sixteenth century into French, German and possibly English. The old *Hamlet* revenge-play, which may have been by Kyd, has never come to light but we know it to have existed from contemporary references and a German play *Der Bestrafte Brudermord* based on it. Some critics, like J. M. Robertson, have tried to explain the difficulties of Shakespeare's *Hamlet* primarily in terms of the unsuitable plot Shakespeare was saddled with. There is, of course, something in this, but it does not touch the principal point – why Shakespeare made the changes he did in his original source material.

5   While there is still no central national state strong enough to enforce its law and order, revenge is the individual's only means of getting justice. The decline of the 'revenge-tragedy' and changes in the feudal concept of 'honour' run parallel to the strengthening of a centralised state apparatus in the later years of Elizabeth's reign.

6   Alternatively, like Laurence Olivier in the film, they abstract the significance of the play by offering an Elsinore in the clouds, a *Hamlet* with plenty of Prince but no Denmark.

7   See Polonius's sycophantic speech in Act II. Sc. 2 after the exit of the Ambassadors from Norway.

8   He does say, a little later, 'For this same lord I do repent', but adds immediately 'but heaven hath pleased it so' (III. 4. 175). For the death of Rosencrantz and Guildenstern he feels even less remorse:

Why, man, they did make love to this employment;
They are not near my conscience; ... (V. 2.57–8)

9   Act II. Sc. 1.66. Professor Harry Levin in his *The Question of Hamlet* (1959) is good on Polonius and the court's political morality.

10   Literally as well as metaphorically, as his baiting of Osric (V.2) shows.

11   It is worth noticing that Shakespeare delays Hamlet's description of his adventures on the voyage to England (V. 2) until *after* this moment, though the events occurred before and could quite plausibly have been related to Horatio in the graveyard (V. 1). This is surely because Shakespeare wants Hamlet to emerge as a man of action only after the funeral of Ophelia, thus linking the two.

12   John F. Danby, *Shakespeare's Doctrine of Nature* (1949).

13   Ll. 213–17. I have drawn attention elsewhere (*Zeitschrift für Anglistik und Amerikanistik*, Vol. X, Berlin, 1962) to the number of phrases in this poem which are directly reminiscent of some of the key phrases of *Hamlet*, e.g.:

Then, as mankinde so is the worlds whole frame
Quite out of joynt, almost created lame

and Donne's vision of

Corruptions in our braines, or in our hearts,
Poysoning the fountaines, whence our actions spring ...

14   When Goneril and Lear argue about the question of Lear's retainers they use the word 'need' in different senses. Goneril uses the word to mean something like 'efficiency'; Lear's use of the word is very different.

15   The most effective Fool I have seen on the stage was that of a German actor, Edwin Marian, in a production at the Deutsches Theater in East Berlin in 1957. This Fool was a plain, down-to-earth, somewhat Brechtian peasant, neither fey nor eccentric, like must British interpretations.

Bernard Shaw and the new spirit

It has seemed to me for some time that much Marxist or left-wing assessment of the work of Bernard Shaw has been less than satisfactory. It is true that Shaw was in many respects a vulnerable figure. Both in his life and his art he offered a great many hostages to fortune, and fortune – in the form of the deepening crisis of capitalist society through which he lived so long – wasn't slow to take advantage of the situation. Yet when one has totted up the errors and the sillinesses, the false hunches and the jokes that fell flat or rebounded against him, what remains is greatly impressive and, like so much good writing, not easily predictable. It is not hard to see in a general way how he emerges out of the stresses and contradictions of his time; yet it is no easier to 'explain' him than it would have been to foresee those others he so much admired: Mozart and Wagner, Dickens and Ibsen. And perhaps what one most wants to say of him is that it is in the end to that company that he belongs.

What follows cannot of course be in the nature of a reassessment of Shaw's work. That would need far more than a short essay. All I can hope to do is to suggest certain approaches and perspectives that might make possible a more full and satisfactory estimate.

Caudwell in his essay on Shaw in *Studies in a Dying Culture* strikes a note I would want to query.

Faced with proletarianisation, he clung to the bourgeois class. In the same way, faced with the problem of ideological proletarianisation in his reading of Marx, he resisted it, and adhered to Fabianism, with its bourgeois traditions and its social respectability.[1]

Well, yes, one sees what he means all right. And it isn't untrue. But is it really what most matters, what most needs to be said? Isn't there perhaps even something rather dangerously Platonic in the

approach, a setting up of ideal standards, embodied in the word proletarianisation, and an insistence on judging not only a man's life
but also his work against that ideal standard. One hesitates to use
that argument with Caudwell who did himself make precisely that
effort – and at the cost of his life – which he accuses Shaw of
shirking. Yet the suspicion remains that, in concentrating so single-
mindedly on what Shaw *wasn't* or on what he might have been,
Caudwell runs the risk of missing what he was, what he brought to
the movement he always tried, with whatever foibles and failures, to
serve. To stress too much the role of Shaw as misleader is unsatisfactory not because the charges that can be made against him may
not have truth in them, but because it becomes so easy, in the process, to miss what is truly original, the contribution no one else did
or could make.

It is interesting to recall that Caudwell's criticism, which rather
too readily equates Shaw's weaknesses with his Fabianism, is not in
some ways so very different from that of Shaw's own Fabian friend
and colleague Beatrice Webb. She too was shocked by what seemed
to her Shaw's frivolity or irresponsibility, feeling that he sold the
pass for the sake of effect or applause or some sort of bourgeois approval. In 1905, the day after taking the (Tory) Prime Minister to
see *Major Barbara* at the Royal Court, she wrote in her diary:

I doubt the popular success of the play: it is hell tossed on the stage – with
no hope of heaven. G. B. S. is gambling with ideas and emotions in a way
that distresses slow-minded prigs like Sidney and me . . . But the stupid
public will stand a good deal from one who is acclaimed as an unrivalled
wit by the great ones of the world . . . [2]

I think that what both Caudwell and Beatrice Webb underestimated
is the liberating effect of good art and, in particular, the complexity
of the way that effect can work. It is true that the 'moral' of *Major
Barbara seems* to be that the capitalist realist Undershaft holds all the
cards. But the deeper burden of the play is that power can never be
effectively challenged by idealism and Shaw's ability to open up *that*
question for his audience is in the long run worth a score of easier
moral victories to comfort the converted.

A more recent assessment of Shaw from the left – by Raymond
Williams – seems to me representative of what a great many people
nowadays think about Shaw:

Shaw's dynamic as a dramatist is surely weakening, and it seems impossible
that it can, as a major force, survive the period of which he was a victim.

Respect for his ability to laugh at a great deal of persistent nonsense will certainly endure; and respect for his great wit and for his skilful forensic and burlesque . . . but the emotional inadequacy of his plays denies him major status. He withered the tangible life of experience in the pursuit of a fantasy of pure intelligence and pure force.[3]

It is a formidable dismissal and all the more so because it stresses Shaw's role as 'victim', isolated and frustrated by the socio-historical situation of his time and especially by the weaknesses of the British Labour movement and the strength of British bourgeois philistinism. But, again, it seems to me to go somehow wrong and to grant Shaw too little. And in this respect it is in striking contrast with the views of Shaw's most persistent defender among twentieth-century dramatists: Bertolt Brecht.

Brecht did not idealise Shaw. But he recognised him generously as one of the writers with whom he had special affinities. When he was working on his *Life of Galileo* his mind would go back to Shaw's *Saint Joan*, another twentieth-century chronicle-play set in the past and one he had watched from behind the scenes in the course of production in the twenties, when Max Reinhardt directed it in Berlin and Elisabeth Bergner was Joan. Brecht saw Shaw's Epilogue, in which Joan reappears, so to speak, both in and outside history, as his attempt to achieve the sort of 'distancing' or 'objectivising' effect that Brecht called *Verfremdung* and regarded as so important to his own drama. He was not satisfied with Shaw's solution and when, in East Berlin after the war, he himself worked on a Joan play for the Berliner Ensemble (an adaptation of a radio play by Anna Seghers entitled *The Trial of Joan of Arc at Rouen* 1431) he produced his own solution by writing a final scene for the play, placed squarely in France in 1436, by which he avoided the mystical element in Shaw's Epilogue. I mention the point merely to establish that Brecht's relationship to Shaw isn't just of the 'literary-history' sort, or my own hunch.

I think it can be fruitful to look at Shaw in the light of Brecht's subsequent achievement because the tendency has been to see Shaw's work too much as a failure to establish a socialist drama and insufficiently as a creative move in that direction. This tendency, I'd suggest, is what leads to Raymond Williams's dismissal which I have quoted, and it seems to me to inform also much of what is by far the most serious and rewarding Marxist study of Shaw – Alick West's *A Good Man Fallen among Fabians*.

To achieve the perspective I am proposing – a perspective more revelatory of what is truly valuable (and progressive) in his drama – it is necessary to see Shaw historically, not only in relation to the socialist movement of his time but also in relation to the development of modern European drama.

My hypothesis is that there are two very great modern European dramatists, dominant in the sense we can now see Shakespeare to have dominated the drama of his time and after. These are Ibsen and Brecht. They are great not simply in themselves, measured in terms of the quality of their individual output, but in terms of their centrality to their times and, consequently, the depth of their influence, which will outlast superficial movements of taste and fashion.

Ibsen, starting from an unlikely base in Scandinavia and a slightly more promising German tradition, wrought a fully serious drama out of the most basic human dilemmas and developments of mid-nineteenth-century bourgeois Europe. If one calls it a bourgeois drama, that is not because most of the characters belong to the middle-class nor because Ibsen is uncritical of bourgeois society and its values; but rather because it is a drama that operates and makes its effect within a structure of feeling and – to a large extent – ideological assumption that is at bottom bourgeois. Ibsen's people are stripped – before us and each other and themselves – of layer after layer of ideological comfort and illusion and falsity; but scarcely a hint of an alternative way of living emerges: as with Wagner, the redemptive vision of the love of a good woman is sometimes offered, but it in no serious way resolves the contradictions that have been revealed with that remorseless technique for the uncovering of ghosts that Ibsen perfected. As with Shakespeare and Brecht, Ibsen brings a world out into the open. Yet 'open' is not really quite the word one wants, for his art – even in *Peer Gynt*, the most 'open' of his plays – is much less open than theirs, much more caught up in the obsessions and neuroses it portrays, with a certain ingrowing overintensity against which Brecht himself was consciously in reaction in *his* sustained attempt to open up the world for twentieth-century men and women.

Between Ibsen and Brecht the best of the dramatists – Chekhov, Strindberg, Synge, O'Casey, even Pirandello – all contributed to the opening up of Ibsenite drama. Of all these the most original, the most brilliant and the hardest to characterise, is Bernard Shaw. His plays are remarkably unlike anyone else's, so that in seeing him historically, as one must, one is in no danger of undermining his idiosyncrasy. And since he saw himself historically, never for an instant considering his art timeless or spaceless, there is no excuse for our not doing so.

Unlike Brecht, who frequently used Ibsen's middle-period plays as examples of the sort of drama he mistrusted and sought to avoid, Shaw looked on Ibsen as a liberator and presented him as such to the public, especially in *The Quintessence of Ibsenism*, first published in 1891, but later revised in 1913 after Ibsen's death. *The Quintessence*, everyone agrees, tells us more about Shaw than about Ibsen. It makes Ibsen's plays seem more didactic and self-consciously 'progressive' than they are and exaggerates those elements which it suited Shaw's own purposes to stress in his determination to *épater le bourgeois*. Shaw seized on Ibsen because his plays, unlike almost all contemporary drama, struck him as truly serious. He represented, Shaw said, that 'new spirit' which alone could grapple with the needs of the time.

The 'new spirit' is not altogether easy to define. Shaw associated it explicitly with Mozart and Wagner, Chekhov and Tolstoy, Samuel Butler and the later Dickens: figures whose highest common factor of novelty doesn't spring spontaneously to mind. Put negatively, the new spirit was what George Eliot and Matthew Arnold hadn't got. Its absence struck him particularly in the work of Henry James, one of whose plays he described in the nineties in the following terms:

Mr Henry James' intellectual fastidiousness remains untouched by the resurgent energy and wilfulness of the new spirit. It takes us back to the exhausted atmosphere of George Eliot, Huxley and Tyndall, instead of thrusting us forward into the invigorating strife raised by Wagner and Ibsen.[4]

This gives us an important clue if we link the mention of George Eliot, Huxley and Tyndall with another statement of Shaw's, made in connection with his discovery of the supreme importance of the 'economic base'. This time he is describing (to his biographer Archibald Henderson) his experience of listening in 1882 to a speech of Henry George and suddenly seeing his own intellectual development in a new light.

It flashed on me for the first time that 'the conflict between religion and science', . . . the overthrow of the Bible, the higher education of women, Mill on Liberty, and all the storm that raged round Darwin, Tyndall, Huxley, Spencer and the rest, on which I had brought myself up intel-

lectually, was a mere middle-class business. Suppose it could have produced a nation of Matthew Arnolds and George Eliots — you may well
shudder . . .[5]

This explicit linking of the intellectual forces he had come to reject
with 'a mere middle-class business' seems to me very important.
Shaw never committed himself to a Marxist position and kept up a
running battle against Marxian economics; but reading *Capital* was a
decisive event in his intellectual development and, even before that,
he had clearly been influenced by the sort of approach we have come
to call Marxist. That description of so much serious Victorian thinking as a 'mere middle-class business' indicates what it was that
attracted him about the creative artists in whom he recognised a
'new spirit'. Wagner, Tolstoy, the later Dickens, Ibsen had all
broken through to forms of art which couldn't justly be subsumed
within the category 'a mere middle-class business'. Their work expressed and stimulated an 'invigorating strife' which their more
class-bound *confrères* sought to muffle or cover up. The art imbued
with the 'new spirit' had the effect of opening up the nature and
problems of bourgeois society in a manner which those whose work
could be described as a mere middle-class business were without the
resources to achieve.

What linked the purveyors of the 'new spirit' was not a shared
philosophy in the more formal sense of the word. Nor was it something easily covered by even a loose use of the word 'ideology'. It
was, rather, the ability to 'open up' through their art the world into
which they had been born. What *The Magic Flute, Little Dorrit, The
Ring of the Nibelung, Peer Gynt, Anna Karenina, The Cherry Orchard*
and *Heartbreak House* have in common isn't at all easy to define.
Marxists have tended to use the word 'realism' — indicating that
good art uncovers reality — and perhaps there is no better word: yet
one can't help feeling that it's a word with as many snags as advan-
tages, implying either too much or too little and tending to play
down the importance of artistic form. If I stress the phrase 'opening
up' it is to try to suggest that an important part of the achievement
of those in whom Bernard Shaw recognised the new spirit was their
reaching out for *forms* that liberated themselves and their audience or
readers from a certain kind of emotional relationship towards art
which generates its reduction into a mere middle-class business.

Shaw picked out two aspects of Ibsen's plays which particularly
appealed to him. One he called 'realism', which he associated with

an extension of subject-matter – the serious treatment of people (servants, workers, 'common people') and situations which remained on the fringes of ruling-class art; the other he called 'discussion' – and he claimed that the introduction of this analytical element into his plays was Ibsen's most significant technical innovation. Shaw probably exaggerated the 'discussion' element in Ibsen (the sort of thing that occurs in the last act of *A Doll's House* when Nora insists on *analysing* her marriage); but if he did so it was, from his point of view, in a good cause; for what he was urging was the need for a drama that made the audience think as well as feel and forced them to re-examine cherished emotional attitudes and assumptions. His remark that 'the question which makes the (Ibsen) play interesting ... is which is the villain and which the hero?'[6] indicates what attracted him to Ibsen and also the extent to which he was himself rejecting the Aristotelian view of drama with its emphasis on some kind of 'identification' of the audience with the progress of the hero.

Yet, for all his propaganda on behalf of Ibsen, Shaw always recognised that his own plays were quite different in kind from the Norwegian's: 'My own drama' he wrote (in 1904) 'is utterly unlike Ibsen in its stage methods and socialist view of human misery.' It is an important statement, not only because it should warn us against thinking of Shaw as a sort of Ibsen *manqué*, but also because of its linking of form with ideas. It was Shaw's *socialism* that made him want a new *form* of drama, not simply a drama which might have a propagandist usefulness, though he didn't despise that.

Shaw played up Ibsen and played down Shakespeare. Brecht did the opposite. Shaw, despite the important distinction between himself and Ibsen I have just emphasised, saw Ibsen primarily as a liberating force. Brecht, operating nearly half a century later (though he died only six years after Shaw) and in a very different socio-historical situation, had to reject Ibsenite drama. This was not, of course, because he didn't *appreciate* Ibsen or recognise his greatness, but because – a committed Marxist in a sense Shaw never was – he felt himself able to develop a dramatic theory far more thoroughgoing and radical than Shaw – caught up in the British situation – was able to contemplate. Through his rejection of the whole Aristotelian theory of drama, with its emphasis on ritual, catharsis and the special role of the hero, Brecht was able to evolve a new basis for the opening up of the drama as an integral part of the opening up of the social world. He saw Ibsenite drama as, for all its power and honesty, trapped in the categories of bourgeois ideology and dragging its audiences into a sort of complicity with the bourgeois attitudes it so relentlessly exposed. Shaw, as we've seen, to some extent took a similar line, emphasising his differences from as well as his debt to Ibsen: yet he was unable to develop for his own practice a theory as basically helpful as Brecht's 'epic theatre'.

It is not difficult for us, with our easier hindsight, to recognise that Shaw was tentatively but insistently feeling his way towards the kind of dramatic theory that was to serve Brecht. And it is not yet possible, in any case, to make a long-term assessment of the value of Brecht's theories (nor would he, with his insistence that the proof of the pudding is in the eating, want us to rush into one). Yet it seems to me useful to look at Shaw's practice in the light of Brecht's theory and I suspect that some of the current underestimation of Shaw's writing comes from a failure to see the two outstanding socialist dramatists of the twentieth century sufficiently in relation to one another.

When Raymond Williams writes (in the passage quoted above) of the 'emotional inadequacy' of Shaw's plays he seems to me to be expecting a Shaw play to be essentially *like* an Ibsen play in structure and mode of operation. That is to say, he seems to assume that the shape and structure of the play is governed by the shape and structure of the emotional situation which the dramatist is concerned to convey, so that the experience of the audience involves a high measure of 'identification' with the movement of the situation which is evoked on the stage. Now, I would not wish to argue that Shaw never works in this way: the endings of *Candida* and *Saint Joan* are instances and they are examples of Shaw at his most vulnerable. But I see them as somewhat exceptional: not in the sense that there are necessarily more good bits than bad ones in a Shaw play, but in the sense that they lead us away from his most basic originality.

That originality, I would suggest, lies most centrally in his concern about ideology and in his discovery of a dramatic structure — based on wit — which frames that concern in a creative way. The concern with ideology I have already touched on, his determination to create a drama that was more than a mere middle-class business. Shaw's plays are about power: it is his obsession, and an obsession which marks him out from the bulk of nineteenth-century British writers who run away from questions of power as from the plague

and accept a bourgeois view of politics as a sort of professional tech-
nology. That is why it is misleading to describe his plays as 'drama
of ideas'. What he is interested in, above all, is the power of *ideology*
– that is to say, collections of ideas, attitudes, feelings and prejudices linked together by their relationship to certain general needs
and aims, the needs and aims of certain people at a certain time. The
coherence of an ideology lies, in practice, in the part it plays in
serving the needs of a class. The very conception of an ideology rests
on the recognition that ideas are themselves not 'pure' but gain their
hold over men's minds through the importance they acquire as *forces*
serving or preventing the realisation of felt and discovered needs.
This Shaw came to understand, as a sort of revelation, in the eigh-
teen-eighties. It took him a decade to discover how to incorporate
his knowledge in a style. But a style is precisely what differentiates a
play like *Mrs Warren's Profession* (in the nineties) from the bourgeois
drama of the day. Because its subject is prostitution it took thirty
years for the curtain to rise on a public performance of *Mrs Warren's
Profession*, but when it goes up, the curtain (an ordinary west-end
curtain in a west-end theatre, as middle-class as you like) goes up on
an ordinary west-end theatrical scene and the people on the stage
seem to be just like the people Pinero or Henry Arthur Jones or Tom
Robertson or Wilde (at least before *The Importance of Being Earnest*)
put there. But when they begin to talk you discover they are not the
same people at all: or, rather, the same sort of people revealed in
quite a new way and therefore different people. It is Shaw's style that
has transformed them and that style is by no means a matter of tricks
or technique or 'literary' qualities. The style is the ability to convey
the power of ideology in the shaping of a human situation.

When Raymond Williams writes that despite our respect for his
great wit we have to recognise the emotional inadequacy of Shaw's
plays I think he is underestimating the part wit plays in Shaw's dramatic art. Wit, in a play like *Major Barbara*, is not an embellish-
ment which improves the play, it is the motive-force which informs
its very structure and movement. There is a moment in the second
act of that play, set in the Salvation Army shelter in the East End,
when Barbara introduces her father, the capitalist arms-manufac-
turer Undershaft, to the poor man Peter Shirley who has been
forced, to his humiliation, to accept help from the Army. The following exchange takes place.

BARBARA   . . . By the way, papa, what is your religion? in case I have
to introduce you again.

UNDERSHAFT   My religion? Well, my dear, I am a Millionaire. That is
my religion.

BARBARA   Then Im afraid you and Mr Shirley wont be able to comfort
one another after all. Youre not a Millionaire, are you, Peter?

SHIRLEY   No; and proud of it.

UNDERSHAFT (*gravely*)   Poverty, my friend, is not a thing to be proud
of.

SHIRLEY (*angrily*)   Who made your millions for you? Me and my like.
Whats kep us poor? Keepin you rich. I wouldnt have your conscience,
not for all your income.

UNDERSHAFT   I wouldnt have your income, not for all your conscience,
Mr Shirley.[7]

What is involved here is not a dramatic situation embellished by a
prettily-turned exchange *of dialogue*. The wit is basic to the whole
enterprise and informs its very nature including the conception and
presentation of character. The perception that a society in which one
has to choose between conscience and income is intolerable is precisely what Shaw's play is about: not about the love-affair (if that's
the word for it) between Barbara and Cusins or the family problem
of who is to inherit the Undershaft millions. What I am driving at is
that the dialectical wit which everyone recognises as a feature of
Shaw's plays is the very basis of his dramatic method and the struc-
tural principle on which the plays are built. This is why people who
expect Ibsen-type plays often complain that Shaw's 'fizzle-out', fail
to achieve the sort of emotional climax the audience, imbued with
Ibsen/Aristotelian anticipations of how a play should work, expects.
If the endings of Shaw's plays are often arbitrary and almost incidental it is because the resolution of the situations – the interplay of
forces – he has evoked remains for the future to work out: the air-
raid in *Heartbreak House*, for example, brings the play to an end but
is in no sense emotionally 'inevitable': it has no cathartic effect on
the audience and the producer who tries to impose such an effect is
wasting his time.

Running through a good deal of criticism of Shaw as a dramatist
lies the complaint that, for all his talent, he is not truly serious: he
spoils his good mind. There is, of course, plenty of justification for
such criticism in the sense that the plays are very uneven with far too
many bad jokes and irritating idiosyncrasies which time has not
been kind to. But basically, I believe, the complaint is a disastrous

one, sweeping aside Shaw's triumphs along with his failures. Again, Brecht can help put the perspective right. Writing in 1926 when he was in his twenties and Shaw was seventy, he said:

Shaw has applied a great part of his talent to intimidating people to a point when it would be an impertinence for them to prostrate themselves before him.
It will have been observed that Shaw is a terrorist. Shaw's brand of terror is an extraordinary one, and he uses an extraordinary weapon, that of humour . . .
Shaw's terrorism consists in this: that he claims a right for every man to act in all circumstances with decency, logic and humour, and sees it as his duty to do so even when it creates opposition. He knows just how much courage is needed to laugh at what is amusing, and how much seriousness to pick it out. And like all people who have a definite purpose he knows that there is nothing more time-wasting and distracting than a particular kind of seriousness which is popular in literature and nowhere else.[8]

Brecht was not, of course, so naive as to use the word terrorist blindly. He knew very well that terrorism in the revolutionary movement implies attitudes characteristic of the petty bourgeoisie rather than the working class and he wouldn't have disagreed with Caudwell's (or Lenin's) analysis of Shaw's political position. The word terrorist does indeed indicate one of Shaw's artistic weaknesses: just as the political terrorist easily becomes bomb-happy, the intellectual one tends to be idea-happy and Shaw could seldom resist a bright idea, even when it disrupted his own deeper purposes. But Brecht's remarks do much more than put a finger on one of Shaw's weaknesses: they also indicate his strength.

Behind what Brecht has to say about Shaw lie his own experiences of and reaction against a 'particular kind of seriousness', the German kind which found its expression not just in the heaviness of so much Romantic art but in a technique of obfuscation to which Marx in particular brought his special attention. Brecht's description of Shaw as a 'terrorist' is extraordinarily apt, especially when the word is linked with an emphasis on his humour or (as I would prefer to call it) wit. That image of Shaw the terrorist upsetting an applecart containing bourgeois concepts of what is and what isn't serious seems to me very much to the point, not only because it characterises Shaw's role in a plausible way but because it forces us to think about the whole concept of seriousness.

One of the most helpful ways of looking at much 'Modernist' literature of the early twentieth century is, I think, to recognise its role as puncturing or undermining the *sort* of seriousness, the sort of consciousness and therefore the sort of art which nineteenth-century capitalist society all the time tended to generate and encourage. Shaw and the modernist writers of his time had little sympathy for one another (T. S. Eliot said that Shaw as a poet was stillborn) but I think it may be fruitful to stress what Shaw and Brecht and the modernists had in common: an assault on the *forms* of bourgeois realism.

Notes

1   Christopher Caudwell, *Studies and Further Studies in Dying Culture* (Monthly Review Press, 1971), p. 14.
2   *The Diary of Beatrice Webb* (eds. Norman and Jeanne MacKenzie), 1987, Vol. 2.
3   *Drama from Ibsen to Brecht* (1968), p. 256.
4   *Our Theatre in the Nineties* (Standard Edition, 1932), pp. 194—5.
5   Archibald Henderson, *George Bernard Shaw, a Man of the Century* (1956), p. 261.
6   'The quintessence of Ibsenism', *Major Critical Essays* (Standard Edition, 1932), p. 139.
7   *Collected Plays* (Bodley Head, 1971), Vol. III, p. 111.
8   John Willett (ed.), *Brecht on Theatre* (New York, 1964), pp. 10—11.

W. H. Auden: poetry and politics in the thirties

Since this is by no means an exhaustive or 'authoritative' essay, I had better start by mentioning the limits of what I want to say in this piece, which is chiefly about Auden and the young middle-class poets who were involved in left politics and the anti-fascist movement of the thirties. I am not interested in claiming that they were or ought to have been more or less 'political' than they actually were. I am not much interested in assessing precisely how 'Marxist' Auden or his poems were. Nor am I concerned to propose some impregnable general 'theory' about the relation of poetry and politics. I *am* interested in considering what can be learned from the experiences of the thirties (for better and worse) about the ways in which writers can become more involved in the needs and struggles and issues of their time, the time of the transformation of a basically bourgeois society into a basically socialist one, and how the socialist movement can profit from the insights and experiences of writers who use language in a creative way because their perceptions penetrate to truly important aspects of reality.

The case *against* the young middle-class poets of the thirties, made with varying emphases but considerable regularity over the subsequent decades, is, essentially, a political case emerging from the Cold War and the brainwashing which was one of its aspects. This is not to say that none of the hostile criticism has anything in it. But the Cold War element is so powerful that unless the literary critic is conscious of it from the start he stands little chance of coming up with a reasonably objective assessment of the literature of the period.

It is now quite the thing, for instance, to quote Auden's description of the thirties (from the poem 'September 1, 1939')[1] as

'a low dishonest decade', as though it referred indiscriminately to
left and right and to see his withdrawal from political commitment
in simple terms of 'disillusionment'. It is not nearly so simple as
that. 'September 1, 1939', which begins:

> I sit in one of the dives
> On Fifty-Second Street
> Uncertain and afraid
> As the clever hopes expire
> Of a low dishonest decade . . .

is indeed a kind of farewell, not just to the thirties but to the
English Auden. And no doubt among the clever hopes and dis-
honesties evoked are errors and sillinesses and deceptions of the left
in general and of Auden and his friends in particular.* The poem
does indeed mirror the poet's own movement from a more generous
commitment to popular causes to the flickering affirmation of one
who sees himself as an ironic point of light in a doomed world. But
the general tone and burden is not anti-left or indeed anti-political
at all. The 'love' which is a keyword is not clearly or primarily a
socio-political concept, but neither is it alternative to politics. To
read the poem as though it chronicled the escape of Auden from the
spider's web of left-wing politics, with Stalin as the spider, is,
simply, to misread it.

When Auden wrote (of New York):

> Into this neutral air
> Where blind skyscrapers use
> Their full height to proclaim
> The strength of Collective Man,
> Each language pours its vain
> Competitive excuse . . .

he had certainly not entirely forgotten or rejected what he had
learned from Marxism. And the final lines of the same stanza:

> Out of the mirror they stare,
> Imperialism's face
> And the international wrong.

may not be the last word either in poetry or political analysis; but

---

* Including the kind of thing referred to in the lines beginning 'Our hopes were
still set on the spies' career' which Auden himself expressed in 'August for the
people . . .', a poem of 1935 dedicated to Christopher Isherwood.

they are not the words of a writer overcome by revulsion against the horror of Left-Book-Club politics.

Of course the situation is complicated by the fact that the later Auden himself not merely connived at but went out of his way to encourage such misreading of his earlier poems, this one in particular. By pretending that the words 'we must love one another or die' were rubbish (because we will die anyway) and revising the poem in ways that shatter its coherence, he paid his own peculiar grotesque tribute to the potency of cold-war attitudes. But fortunately the poems had already appeared and are irrevocably a part of the thirties, as the editor of *The English Auden* very sensibly and properly recognises.

I have started with 'September 1, 1939' not because it is one of his best poems but because, while full of moving resonances for the reader steeped in Auden's poetry, it is also a good point for the new reader to come in at, with its simple relaxed diction, its relatively straightforward allusions (you have to connect Hitler with Linz), and its clear historical context. Written a few months after Auden and Isherwood had decided to settle in America it is rightly included by Edward Mendelson in his *English Auden* volume, for it is indeed a kind of 'Envoi' and Auden's own later mutilations of his poems can only underline the nature of the crisis he and his generation faced.

The mutilations also raise the complex yet necessary question as to how far any of Auden's poems (some would say the poems of anyone) can be treated as directly autobiographical anyway. I have referred to 'September 1, 1939' as though the 'speaker' of the poem were, necessarily and simply, the poet himself. But obviously it isn't quite like that. Many of Auden's poems are more like dramatic monologues, spoken by a 'persona' who isn't necessarily to be identified with the poet himself, any more than you can identify Macbeth with Shakespeare. Some of them have strong elements of parody in them. 'Brothers, who when the sirens roar,' sometimes entitled 'A Communist to Others', is one such; and indeed it is always naïve, not to say dangerous, to assume that any sentiment or opinion in the poems is the author's own, just like that.

Yet it is equally naïve to treat the poems, or Auden's revisions of them, as though they wrote themselves or operated on the basis of some pure, autonomous aesthetic principle. In *some* sense, even if it's often an elusive and deliberately cagey one, they 'reflect' his own journeys and choices. History and ideology get into them all.

'September 1, 1939' can be read, quite properly, as a vital step in Auden's movement away from political poetry. But, again, it is not a simple story. Auden and Isherwood went to America not just because they were disillusioned with European politics (though, of course, like everyone else they were depressed and fearful about the advances of fascism and the growing likelihood of a new world war). They also went to America for personal reasons connected with their search for satisfactory homosexual relationships. Isherwood has made this quite clear in the last pages of *Christopher and His Kind*[2] and when Auden explained to his friend, Professor E. R. Dodds, in a letter (dated 11 March 1940, and made public in the 'Young Writers of the Thirties' exhibition at the National Portrait Gallery in London in 1976) why he stayed in America, he did not mention politics but wrote: 'For the first time I have a happy personal life.'

In emphasising this point I do not want to play down the importance of political events like the defeat in Spain, the Moscow purges and the Soviet-German Non-Aggression Pact of 1939 in striking at the hopes and self-confidence of the British left of the thirties. Nor, of course, do I want to gloss over the failure of the left to build a movement strong enough to defeat fascism without a second world war and all that involved. But to see this failure and the collapse of the left – including left poetry – after 1939 primarily in terms of wickednesses of the international communist movement and 'disillusionment' with the Soviet Union (communism as the God that failed) strikes me as hopelessly superficial and inadequate and is precisely what I mean by cold-war brainwashing.

The gains of the thirties – including the appearance of a body of poetry more wide-ranging, democratically relevant and humanly progressive than the bulk of British twentieth-century poetic production – were not in some total sense negated either by weaknesses within them or by the Cold War that followed them. On the contrary, the experience of the thirties – including the Seventh World Congress, the forging of weapons of corporeal and mental fight against fascism, the poetry of W. H. Auden – was an important contribution to all the gains made since. It was presumably because he realised this that Auden, when he became positively anti-political, spent so much of his time revising the poems he thought the most politically effective. An interesting point here is how generally and poetically disastrous the revisions were. I do not see how any reasonably objective assessment of his revision of, for example,

'Now the leaves are falling fast' (not a particularly 'political' poem at all) could prefer the revision to the original. And I can only draw the conclusion that the position of the later Auden involved an all-round retreat.

Though the British left in the thirties was undoubtedly very ignorant, sometimes in a dangerously self-induced way, about what the Soviet Union was really like, it is also true that blind faith in the Soviet Union was never the principal basis on which the Communist Party — let alone the left movement as a whole — built its campaigns, its thinking and its hopes. That there was a powerful element of 'the Soviet Union right or wrong' in communist thinking it would be idle to deny; but this certainly wasn't the principal motive-force of the move to the left of millions of people, including the young writers. The Soviet Union or hopes about it entered very little into the poetry of the period. The shock and fear of fascism, contempt for the British ruling class, a sense of solidarity with people battling against poverty and exploitation, were far more basic ingredients. The Soviet Union was, it is true, seen sympathetically and hopefully by most people who became involved in the left movement. And there was good reason for this. It was the *only* part of the world not dominated by the drives and needs of the capitalist system; it was a struggling socialist country (not regarded by anybody as a 'great power') which had resisted the attempts of the surrounding powers to smash its revolution; and it had the only government consistently trying to achieve collective resistance to fascist aggression. The principal role of the Soviet Union in much left thinking in the thirties was therefore as a kind of 'opposite' — the opposite of capitalism and of fascism — whose very existence proclaimed the possibility of a different and better way. Of course such an attitude did, and was probably bound to, involve a good deal of self-deception and utopianism: but it was nothing like as unrealistic, or unhelpful, as the outlook which saw 'Communism', embodied in the Soviet Union, as the enemy and blinded people to what was going on, not in another very different and complex part of the world, but under their noses.

The left-wing poets of the thirties were primarily interested neither in the Soviet Union nor in Communism in the abstract but in the problem of making sense of their own dilemmas and of the society and the world into which they had been born. It was the First World War, its consequences and, above all, its *meaning*, that lay behind their lives and consciousness. The differences between the

Britain of 1907, when W. H. Auden was born, and that of 1931,
when he was twenty-four, were so great that no one could be
unaware that he or she was living through some sort of deep social
and political crisis: yet at the same time, because there had been no
invasion, no occupation, and 'victory' rather than 'defeat', it was
surprisingly easy to pretend that nothing much (except the slaughter, softened into the word 'sacrifice') had really happened. The
Empire remained, the City of London remained, the General Strike
failed, only the Liberal Party seemed to have taken an irrevocable
knock. The death of liberal England was something that writers, especially the middle-class writers with their traditional education and
most of their traditional privileges intact, had to discover. They discovered it in their poetry.

> Our hunting fathers told the story
>   Of the sadness of the creatures,
> Pitied the limits and the lack
>   Set in their finished features;
> Saw in the lion's intolerant look,
> Behind the quarry's dying glare,
> Love raging for the personal glory
>   That reason's gift would add,
> The liberal appetite and power,
>   The rightness of a god.
>
> Who nurtured in that fine tradition
>   Predicted the result,
> Guessed love by nature suited to
>   The intricate ways of guilt?
> That human ligaments could so
> His southern gestures modify,
> And make it his mature ambition
>   To think no thought but ours,
> To hunger, work illegally,
>   And be anonymous?

Auden's poem,[3] written in 1934, is one such exploration into the
strange death of liberal England. It opens with an evocation of im-
perialism — images of big-game hunting and the individualist ethic
— and finishes with a quotation from Lenin. It does much more than
that of course, playing on words like 'hunting', 'finished', 'intoler-
ant' and 'liberal' with a marvellous sense both of their ambiguities
and their historical and anthropological dimensions. I can think of
few short poems of the post-1945 period (Ted Hughes's 'Pike' would
be one) with so much that is stimulating and imaginative to say
about the changing condition of England.

Auden's poem doesn't merely offer us an apprehension of the contradictions involved in the exposure and overturning of the liberal
tradition; it does so with a peculiar note and energy characteristic of
the best poetry of the thirties and in marked contrast to the note
which T. S. Eliot, in *his* exploration of the death of liberal England,
had sounded in the twenties. To Auden and his friends Eliot's poetry
had indeed been a kind of revelation (C. Day Lewis in his essay *A
Hope for Poetry* saw Hopkins, Eliot and Wilfred Owen as the main
immediate poetic ancestors of the left poets). But in the later twenties and thirties Auden moved left while Eliot, reacting to the same
crisis in a different way, went steadily to the right.

Eliot shared with the left poets a sense of the inadequacies of
bourgeois-democratic society. In 1932 he was writing

The present system does not work properly, and more and more people are
inclined to believe that it never did and that it never will: it is obviously
neither scientific nor religious. It is imperfectly adapted to any purpose
except that of making money; and even for money-making it does not work
very well ....[4]

But when it came to the consideration of an alternative, not only his
general idealist mode of thinking but some pretty crude class prejudices prevented any sort of sympathy with any move in the direction of a more democratic, let alone socialist, society. Though
proclaiming himself 'interested in political ideas, but not in
politics', Eliot didn't hesitate to express himself – in the *Criterion* or
in critical work like *After Strange Gods* – on political issues. In 1930
he was regretting that 'the one most rational form of representation
in the House of Commons, the representation of the Universities, is,
if the Labour Party has its way, to be abolished'.[5] 'The *great* danger,'
he wrote in April 1937, 'seems to me to be the delusion of the
Popular Front', and in October 1938 he was still taking occasion (in
the *Criterion*) to pour scorn on 'irresponsible anti-fascists' and
specifically on 'the heirs of liberalism who find an emotional outlet
in denouncing the iniquity of something called "fascism"'.[6] Well,
no one is going to claim that all the anti-fascists of the thirties were
always wise and responsible; but one doesn't have to have very
exalted standards of political judgment to question whether, a
month after Munich, six months before Franco's victory in Spain and
a year before Hitler's invasion of Poland, anti-fascism of any sort was
among the more irresponsible political attitudes of the day.

'I should think better of Communism', Eliot had written in

1932, 'if I learned that there existed in Russia a decent leisure class.' He was saddened by the idea of being able to afford only one 'very hardworking' servant and felt it would be far more desirable 'to employ a large staff of servants, each doing much lighter work but profiting by the benefits of the cultured and devout atmosphere of the home in which they lived.'[7] The use of the word 'home' in this last context seems an odd one for a person not normally insensitive in his dealings with language.

One might dismiss much sentiments, perhaps, as mere unrealistic eccentricities, like Winston Churchill announcing in 1945 that he had not won the war in order to preside over the dismantling of the British Empire; but I don't think it is reasonable to let the right off as lightly as that. Churchill was not able to prevent the dismantling of the Empire; but he was able at Fulton to add his contribution to the Cold War, which is still with us. And in *After Strange Gods*, published in the year of Auden's 'Our hunting fathers' and *after* Hitler had come to power, Eliot could write, of the society he desired,

The population should be homogeneous . . . What is still more important is unity of religious background; and reasons of race and religion combine to make any large numbers of free-thinking Jews undesirable. There must be a proper balance between urban and rural, industrial and agricultural development. And a spirit of excessive tolerance is to be deprecated.[8]

I bring in Eliot partly to make the point in passing that those who have subsequently felt that the left-wingers of the thirties should show adequate remorse for their political gullibility in those days don't generally seem to have felt that *his* political stance required much remorse; but, more importantly, to try to get the role of the left poets in the thirties into historical perspective. For Eliot, one of their masters, had now become one of the influences they reacted against.

The first thing nowadays everyone says about Auden and Spender and MacNeice and the others is how very middle-class they all were. And of course it's true. They came from comfortable, cultivated professional middle-class families and the cultivation was of the Oxbridge kind with all that implies in elitism, intellectual snobbery and privilege. Also language. Auden's 'Our hunting fathers' is an example. It is a politically radical poem saying more in a few lines about the slogan 'Forward from Liberalism' than Stephen Spender could manage in a whole book or T. S. Eliot could bring himself to face at all. But the *mode*, the language, is pure Oxbridge. Take the adjective 'southern' in the middle of the second stanza. I think it is a brilliantly effective word, managing to combine a whole number of references and suggestions including Keats' beaker full of the warm south, Eliot's line from *The Waste Land* ('I read, much of the night, and go south in the winter'), and the whole tropical way of life of the white colonialists (from topees and tiffin to 'mopping-up operations' on the frontier, and the stiff upper-lip when Rhodes meets Living- stone). But no one could pretend that the culture behind that word 'southern' had anything 'popular' about it. This raises a problem. One of the recurring obsessions of many of the left poets was their unresolved doubt as to whether they ought really to be poets or politicians. Their books and letters are full of self-doubt. Spender writes a letter to Day Lewis (November 1938): 'You seem to assume that, given the present situation, the only thing a poet can do is to merge himself in the working-class movement, completely.'[9] Edward Upward's autobiographical novels hinge almost entirely on the *choice* he felt he must make between being a poet and being poli- tically responsible.

It is a rather strange situation. Here were poets who wanted to be radical, felt deeply that capitalist society was rotten, but could only reach a certain point in their sense of political commitment, partly at least because they couldn't quite resolve the problem of writing poetry which they could feel was really poetry, yet progressive. Be- cause taking part in the 'struggle' seemed to involve abjuring the only sort of poetry they could conceive of, they often felt themselves trapped by a false choice. It is rather as though they had taken aboard Wilfred Owen's statement: 'All a poet can do today is warn,' and added, 'but not by writing poetry.'

Some of the responsibility for the difficulties the poets found in reconciling their vocation with their politics must no doubt rest with the Marxist left, including its most serious and effective organ- isation, the Communist Party. Philistinism is a persistent and dif- ficult problem in the British labour movement. And there was also undoubtedly a tendency (not discouraged by Soviet example) to oversimplify the relation between literature and politics and to want poetry to be 'political' in a rather narrow 'tactical' or propagandist way, which was not much help to artists who needed to develop their *art* as well as (indeed as part and parcel of) their political understanding.

But it won't do to blame the whole business on sectarian attitudes within the Communist Party or the weaknesses of the Marxist literary criticism of the day. As a matter of fact most of the critical pages of *Left Review*, which it is now fashionable to dismiss as 'Stalinist', compare favourably with much of the left literary criticism of the seventies.

The problems of the Spenders and Upwards were at least partly due to their own extremely naïve view as to what 'poetry' or 'being a poet' involved, a naïveté which (one can see now as one looks back on it) fed about equally on neo-romantic and modernist views on literature, and emerged in their rather self-centred personal perspectives and their essentially purist conception of the poet's role.

The poets of the thirties whose work has stood up best seem to me to be those who plumped hard (at this stage of their careers) for an 'impure' poetry of a very open kind.

Louis MacNeice's essay on *Modern Poetry*, first published in 1938, is a case in point. It is a survey of contemporary poetry — his own and other people's — and is a plea for '*impure* poetry, that is, for poetry conditioned by the poet's life and the world around him'.[10] Starting from the point 'poets today are working back from luxury-writing and trying once more to be functional' MacNeice wrote:

I consider that the poet is a blend of the entertainer and the critic and the informer; he is not a legislator, however unacknowledged, nor yet, essentially, a prophet. . . .

The poet, he argues, is 'in a sense man at his most self-conscious, but this means consciousness of himself as man, not consciousness of himself as poet'. And he goes on to suggest that poets, for more than a hundred years, have been suffering from the wrong kind of self-consciousness;

They have felt that their expressed attitude to the world must be peculiarly the attitude of *poets*, that therefore much of the world was unfit subject for poetry because it was itself unpoetic.[11]

I am less concerned to discuss the 'correctness' of MacNeice's position than its significance as a breakthrough to a more 'open' view of poetry with democratic and progressive implications. Its implications in MacNeice's own work can best be seen in *Autumn Journal* but is also behind such a poem as 'The Sunlight on the Garden' (1938)[12], a lyrical poem which I quote because it expresses so well — and so objectively — the *political* situation in which T. S. Eliot could think of nothing better to lament than the irresponsibility of anti-fascists.

> The sunlight on the garden
> Hardens and grows cold,
> We cannot cage the minute
> Within its nets of gold,
> When all is told
> We cannot beg for pardon.
>
> Our freedom as free lances
> Advances towards its end;
> The earth compels, upon it
> Sonnets and birds descend;
> And soon, my friend,
> We shall have no time for dances.
>
> The sky was good for flying
> Defying the church bells
> And every evil iron
> Siren and what it tells:
> The earth compels,
> We are dying, Egypt, dying
>
> And not expecting pardon,
> Hardened in heart anew,
> But glad to have sat under
> Thunder and rain with you,
> And grateful too
> For sunlight on the garden.

MacNeice's sense that poetry must work its way back from luxury-writing and become more 'functional' is a sort of echo of Hugh MacDiarmid's plea, in the *Second Hymn to Lenin* (1935),[13] that

> Poetry like politics maun cut
> The cackle and pursue real ends.

What MacDiarmid is saying is not that poetry can or ought to be replaced by sloganising (he has already brought Burke and Joyce and Paul Morand into his argument). He takes his stand on behalf of 'a poetry of erudition, expertise, and ecstasy' and argues that what is involved is 'a many-sided active delight in the wholeness of things'. Auden – less directly politically committed than MacDiarmid – has his own version of the same need expressed, not inappropriately, in his 'Letter to Lord Byron'[14]:

> I want a form that's large enough to swim in,
>   And talk on any subject that I choose,

From natural scenery to men and women,
  Myself, the arts, the European news . . .

What Auden did supremely well in his early poetry was to explore
and speculate on the condition of Britain in the period between the
wars. One of the characteristics of this poetry is that it has at the
same time a very individual, idiosyncratic sometimes private flavour
(which at its least successful depends on a certain cliquishness and on
'in' jokes) and is yet preoccupied with general, public, impersonal
yet central factors and ideas. His lyrics are as intellectually subtle
and sometimes as intellectually challenging as his more obviously
argumentative poetry. It has been well pointed out that what allows
him to be 'unselfconsciously personal' is 'his awareness of being the
spokesman for, or representative of, many people'.[15] His almost
constant use of a 'persona' is a device which allows him to dramatise
situations without depersonalising them or adopting the rather
heavy, hectoring tone which poetry concerned with public issues can
easily fall into.

He had an extremely sharp instinct for significant trends and for
contemporary atmosphere and he was interested in everything. If
psychology was his major preoccupation, to emphasise this can
easily give a false impression, partly because it wasn't just Freud but
a wider selection of 'healers' (Lawrence, Blake, and Homer Lane)
whom he drew on, partly because there was so much else that interested him: many aspects of science and scientific theory, history
and anthropology, music, religion and philosophy and of course –
supremely – literature. What he had to say was not always true but
it was always intelligent and stimulating and very seldom sentimental. So that his poetry at its best had the effect of opening up the
modern world rather than leading the reader inwards into his personal obsessions and limitations. Although clearly a very unusual
and quirky man, he managed on the whole, as a poet, to see himself
objectively and humorously.

Auden's involvement in political struggle during the thirties,
though it never brought him to a theoretical position which
Marxists would be likely to consider very satisfactory, seems to me
to have been an altogether positive factor in his development as a
poet for several reasons. In the first place, it led him to explore continuously the connections between his private or purely personal experience and the public, historical developments of the time. In the

second, it encouraged him to find out what he had in common with other people and to see himself as a part of a social situation, not merely as one lonely man, uncertain and afraid. In the third place it helped him, at least for a time, towards a view of language and indeed of poetry itself which was fruitful precisely because it was outward-turning and socially orientated.

Now it is true that by the end of the thirties Auden was denying the active, social role of poetry:

> Art is not life, and cannot be
> A midwife to society (1939)[16]

and

> For poetry makes nothing happen: it survives
> In the valley of its saying where executives
> would never want to tamper;
> . . . it survives,
> A way of happening, a mouth (1940)[17]

But a few years earlier he had written

> No artist, however 'pure', is disinterested[18]

and

You cannot tell people what to do, you can only tell them parables; and that is what art really is, particular stories of particular people and experience, from which each according to his own immediate and peculiar needs may draw his own conclusions.[19]

This last statement is a rejection of poetry as propaganda; but it is an acceptance of the political role of the poet and of the fact that poetry can and does make something happen. And it was during the period in which he held this view that his strongest and most political poetry was written.

For a poet to think of himself as a 'mouth' or 'voice' is fair enough. Saying things is what he is good at. It is when the voice becomes abstracted from changing reality that the trouble starts. It is then that it is likely to begin talking, as Auden in his later years did more and more, about the poet's duty or responsibility being to 'the language', rather than to something impure like human need. This is what purism involves: the treatment of 'language' or 'poetry' or 'art' as though they had some unchanging purity of their own, some autonomy like that of the celestial voice which crops up at cri-

tical moments in Italian opera, though always in practice in a specific human context. Celestial voices are all right as long as everyone
agrees (even if they don't quite say so) that they are just another convention to help get past difficult moments. But when the poet *really*
thinks his duty is to the Language or to Poetry, what actually happens is that he capitulates to conceptions of language and poetry that
the ideologists of those with power have found suitable to their
deeper purposes.

Auden had been enormously influenced by his experiences in Ger-
many in the late twenties and early thirties. On one level what
attracted him to Berlin was no doubt the discovery of a homosexual
underworld of working-class bars, unemployed young men, experi-
mental psychiatrists and a variety of *Wandervögel* of several national-
ities. But what he also learned in the Weimar Republic was the
necessity of politics, the possibility of human solidarity, the nature
of the Nazi movement, the corruption of bourgeois democracy and
the potency of expressionist and radical art, particularly in the
cinema and the political and satirical cabarets.

> Easily, my dear, you move, easily your head
> And easily as through the leaves of a photograph album I'm led
> Through the night's delights and the day's impressions,
> Past the tall tenements and the trees in the wood;
> Though sombre the sixteen skies of Europe
>   And the Danube flood.

The poem[20] which begins this way was written towards the end of
1934. It is in one sense a highly personal, even private, one, partly
because the head is almost certainly a boy's head (although the poem
was called 'A Bride in the Thirties' when published in *The Listener*)
and seems to link with other love poems like 'Lay your sleeping
head, my love'; but also in the sense that the trees in the wood are
also symbols of 'false attitudes of love', linking, through other
poems of the same period, with the wood in which the babes are lost
in the fairy story, the dangerous forest of the Freudian unconscious,
the wood of the peat-bog soldiers in the Nazi concentration camps
and the crosses in the war cemeteries spread out beneath the skies of
Europe. Purists may object to such cross-references between different poems (they are nearly as common in Auden as in Yeats), but
I do not see why it should be felt to be essential that each poem
should stand entirely on its own – something which doesn't in practice ever happen anyway.

This poem of Auden's (and it is typical of a whole number of his poems of the period) goes on, using the resources we often associate with film techniques:

> Ten thousand of the desperate marching by
> Five feet, six feet, seven feet high;
> Hitler and Mussolini in their wooing poses
> Churchill acknowledging the voters' greeting
> Roosevelt at the microphone, Van der Lubbe laughing
>   And our first meeting.
>
> But love, except at our proposal,
> Will do no trick at his disposal;
> Without opinions of his own, performs
> The programme that we think of merit,
> And through our private stuff must work
>   His public spirit.

I don't know whether such quotations can quite convey the energy or originality of Auden's verse. What he is saying – that the private is entwined with the public life, that our conceptions of love and its possibilities are themselves determined by the sort of society we live in and our attitudes to it – is not of course in itself profoundly original; but I do not think any previous English poet had made so vigorous an attempt to write poetry that absorbed and coped with the relation of the mass media to the nature and quality of our perceptions and assumptions.

'Spain 1937'[21] was one of the poems Auden himself was to mutilate most drastically. It is also – partly for this very reason – a poem one has to return to in any attempt to define or assess the nature of Auden's political poetry. Why did he come to dislike it quite so much? It is not in any crude sense a propaganda poem exhorting the already converted to support a clearly-defined cause. It centres around the importance of choice, and Spain becomes the moment of choice for reasons which, embodied as they are in a series of disparate images, are – purposely one feels – not easy to disentangle or fix priorities to.

> On that arid square, that fragment nipped off from hot
> Africa, soldered so crudely to inventive Europe;
>   On that tableland scored by rivers,
> Our thoughts have bodies; the menacing shapes of our fever
>
> Are precise and alive. For the fears which made us respond
> To the medicine ad, and the brochure of winter cruises
>   Have become invading battalions;

And our faces, the institute-face, the chain-store, the ruin

Are projecting their greed as the firing squad and the bomb.
Madrid is the heart. Our moments of tenderness blossom
  As the ambulance and the sandbag;
Our hours of friendship into a people's army.

In an interesting and sympathetic discussion of this poem Samuel
Hynes has said

The striking thing about these lines is that they treat the Spanish war in
psychological, not political terms, as an eruption of the sickness of modern
society. In Spain, the enemy is *us* — our fears and greeds (as usual Auden
involves himself in the class he condemns), and the people's army is psychological, too, a sort of metaphor for loving feelings. It is more than a
metaphor, though; in Spain 'our thoughts have bodies', what was mental
has become physical, and therefore mortal.[22]

I am not sure that this is the right way to put it (and I quote Hynes
because the way he reads the poems seems to be a usual one). It is
true, of course, that the passage, and indeed the whole poem, keeps
associating or linking psychological attitudes with a political situation, private neuroses with public events, and that the public events
— the war — are never analysed in an overtly political way. But when
the speaker of the poem says that in Spain 'the menacing shapes of
our fever are precise and alive' is he really interpreting the Spanish
war in psychological terms, that is to say treating the mental as
more basic than the real? I would have said that the precise relationship between the private and the public in 'Spain' is left open
and that the general view of that relationship emerging from the
poem is similar to that implied by MacNeice when in *Autumn
Journal* (written in 1939) he looks back at his pre-war visit to Spain
and writes that he could not then know that

    ... Spain would soon denote
      Our grief, our aspirations;
    Not knowing that our blunt
      Ideals would find their whetstones, that our spirit
    Would find its frontier on the Spanish front,
      Its body in a rag-tag army.[23]

Auden in 'Spain 1937' seems to be saying that the political decisions or choices which have to be made about Spain today are essential because history (a keyword in the poem) is not a force outside
men and their dilemmas and neither are men and their dilemmas
outside history. I would suppose that the reason he took so violently

against the poem, particularly the final statement, later on was indeed because he recognised that in it the balance between materialism and idealism was so fine. He was to assert, intemperately, that the final lines of the poem,

> History to the defeated
> May say alas but cannot help or pardon

expressed the 'wicked doctrine' which equated goodness with success. Since this is patently *not* what the lines do express, the explanation of his treatment of them can only be, I think, that at some level he remained conscious of their authenticity and feared it. 'Spain 1937' is in a number of respects a vulnerable poem, but not in those that its author in his revisions chose to fix on.

'Spain' is certainly an unusual sort of political poem, schematic in its structure (past – 'struggle' – future), and somewhat abstract in much of its effect because the 'struggle' tends to be oddly isolated from the historical processes within which it is evoked. The images, though themselves specific and 'concrete' and sometimes rich and vivid (such as the lines describing the coming of the volunteers to the International Brigades), are related to one another mainly through their place in the structure of the argument, which is about history and necessity and choice. Yet, though it is in this sense 'about' theoretical and philosophical questions, it doesn't come up with any very satisfying or conclusive theoretical insight. There is also the problem that one may suspect, without being quite sure, that homosexual tensions get deeper into the poem than the words quite admit. It is indeed a very 'impure' poem, and Marxists of a predominantly theoretical cast of mind have always tended to find it unsatisfactory.

Its strength, as it seems to me, lies in the way, for example, Auden succeeds in giving the words 'Madrid is the heart' a remarkable sense of the way political action can become central, involving choices whose implications and consequences reverberate through every area of life and consciousness. He isn't saying, 'We must forget our personal obsessions for a bit and take part in the struggle, which is the "real" thing', or 'The Spanish War is "really" a kind of reflection of our personal problems.' Rather, he is asserting a close and complex connection between personal fears and political possibilities and leaving the precise nature of the connection open.

This is what, from the first, gave 'Spain' its particular power and no doubt explains Auden's strong subsequent revulsion against it.

I remember the first time I heard the poem read aloud (by Ian Watt) at a lunch-time meeting in Cambridge which ended with a collection for Spanish medical relief. It was certainly an example of poetry helping to make something happen: but I don't think any of us in the audience thought we were being hectored or got at.

And I remember, nearly forty years later, while Franco was still there, being taken by a young Spanish colleague who could not remember the war, to see the vast appalling monument of victory which the Nationalists had built in the hills outside Madrid, near the Escorial. After we had walked round in silence I said to my Spanish friend: 'What were you thinking about?' 'About the Republican prisoners who had to build the thing,' he said. 'What were you thinking about?' 'About my friends,' I said, and there was a line of poetry I couldn't get out of my head:

> History to the defeated
> May say alas but cannot help or pardon.

Political poetry, I would suggest, is poetry in which the question of power gets recognition and expression. Experience is presented not in a cocoon (the poem's form tending all the time to separate it from everything outside itself), not in some sort of purity and isolation as an autonomous whole, but in a way that gives a sense of the power-forces present in the situation evoked. Too strong an emphasis on the autonomy of any human experience or activity always tends to remove it from the pressures, the power-forces, which go towards making it what it is. Poetry that makes us conscious of power opens up the world rather than attempting to enclose a part of it in some sort of mystic purity. One of the virtues of the best poetry of the thirties was that it arose out of and helped define the power struggles of the time.

The impact of Auden's poetry on young intellectuals in the thirties was so great, I think, not because he was offering them the theoretical truth or the confirmation of their existing prejudices but, rather, because with great intellectual and verbal energy his poetry probed and explored many areas of consciousness – scientific, psychological, sociological, political, aesthetic – and came up with striking and stimulating connections embodied in phrases and images of vivid contemporary resonance. It is rather as though H. G. Wells had had a poet's creative way with language, or Harold Pinter had actually got something interesting to say. And the 'poetic' quality is not of course a 'technical' linguistic knack or an abstract theoretical correctness but a quality of perception in which the verbal form and the 'content' (in so far as one can abstract either of them even for descriptive purposes) are one. The lines which begin

Lay your sleeping head, my love,
Human on my faithless arm[24]

will exemplify as well as any what I mean.

Notes

1   Edward Mendelson (ed.) *The English Auden* (Faber & Faber, 1977), p. 245.
2   Christopher Isherwood, *Christopher and his Kind* (Eyre Methuen, 1977).
3   *The English Auden*, p. 151.
4   *The Criterion*, vol. XI, p. 467.
5   *Ibid.*, Vol. X, p. 482.
6   *Ibid.*, Vol. XVII, p. 59.
7   *Ibid.*, Vol. XI, p. 275.
8   T. S. Eliot, *After Strange Gods* (Faber & Faber, 1934), pp. 19–20.
9   'Young Writers of the Thirties' Exhibition, National Portrait Gallery, 1976.
10   Louis MacNeice, *Modern Poetry* (OUP, 1938), Preface.
11   *Ibid.*
12   Louis MacNeice, *Collected Poems* (Faber & Faber, 1966), p. 84.
13   Michael Grieve and Alexander Scott (eds.), *The Hugh MacDiarmid Anthology* (Routledge & Kegan Paul, 1972), pp. 191ff.
14   *The English Auden*, p. 172.
15   Monroe Spears, *The Poetry of W. H. Auden* (OUP, 1963), p. 89.
16   W. H. Auden, *The Double Man* (Random House, 1941), p. 17 (published in England as *New Year Letter* (1941)).
17   *The English Auden*, p. 242.
18   *Ibid.*, p. 334.
19   'Psychology and Art To-day', in *The Arts To-day*, ed. Geoffrey Grigson (Bodley Head, 1935), pp. 18–19 (quoted in Samuel Hynes, *The Auden Generation* (Bodley Head, 1976), p. 168, reprinted in *The English Auden*, p. 341.
20   *The English Auden*, p. 152.
21   Robin Skelton (ed.), *Poetry of the Thirties* (Penguin, 1964), p. 133–6.
22   Samuel Hynes, *op. cit.*, pp. 253–4.
23   Louis MacNeice, *Collected Poems*, p. 112.
24   *The English Auden*, p. 207.

Part III

The precursors of Defoe: Puritanism and the rise of the novel

The connections between the development of Puritanism in seventeenth-century Britain and the rise of the novel are complex but interesting and seem to throw a certain amount of light on both phenomena and also the tricky but central question of the growth of 'realism'.

For a consideration of the earlier aspects of the problem – what was happening before the seventeenth century – we can turn to Margaret Schlauch's *Antecedents of the English Novel, 1400–1600*.[1] But Professor Schlauch does not follow the story beyond the Elizabethans. Her final section, 'Fiction for the new Middle Classes', leaves us with Deloney, who died in 1600. But Defoe – Deloney's successor – was not born till 1660 and didn't begin writing what we recognise as novels until the eighteenth century; so there is a whole century to account for, the century of the Puritan Revolution, which somehow or other gave Defoe the opportunity to extend the whole scope and sweep of 'realism', to add to Deloney's down-to-earth but rather provincial sense of bourgeois reality and sharp ear for middle-class colloquial talk, a new dimension which it is perhaps safest to call 'moral' but which also involves the sheer vigorous self-confidence of a class that has come through; which is perhaps the same thing.

One can, of course, approach the gap by way of the 'picaresque' tradition, and a fairly recent book by Professor Parker[2] does this elegantly and suggestively; but as far as Britain is concerned there is very little development of the picaresque in the seventeenth century (to see Mr Badman in that tradition is surely to miss the whole point)[3] and one is left with the same problem: what is it that makes *Moll Flanders* so much *more* than a picaresque novel?

I am assuming, of course, that *Moll Flanders is* more than a picaresque story and that Defoe is one of the masters of the novel, a view I used not to hold (or held only half-heartedly), perhaps because I was cowed by Dr Leavis's patronising references in *The Great Tradition*.[4] I have not the space here to establish convincingly my conviction of Defoe's greatness, but since my argument to some extent depends on it I had better state it. *Robinson Crusoe* and *Moll Flanders* are great achievements in realism because Defoe brings to his material not merely a superb ability to conjure up 'verisimilitude' but an equal (and, I think, closely connected) awareness of the moral tensions of his time which he embodies in the essential form of his books. *Moll Flanders* is built upon and around the contradiction between Moll's resilence as a human being and the corrupting nature of the life she leads. To put it another way, the tension is between Moll's aspirations and her actual life. In more literary terms one might say that deeply embedded in Defoe's novel (and determining its *form*) is a tension between two sorts of realism. On the one hand there is the shrewd realism of *acceptance* – the sort of thing one associates with so many of C. P. Snow's characters who are realists in the sense of knowing their way around – on the other the more dangerous and exciting realism of *potentiality* – the realism involved in the ability to see the inner forces at work in a particular set-up. The one guides Defoe towards his unrivalled power of recording the surface of his world as it is. The other puts vitality and a sense of values into his book by making us see that world in terms of both its human deficiencies and possibilities.

The thesis of this short paper is that the development of Puritanism in the seventeenth century at first prevented but ultimately made possible the growth of the realistic novel. It is not easy for us at this distance to grasp the liberating power of Puritanism. We tend to think of the Puritan spirit in terms of restrictions: sexual prudishness, the Lord's Day Observance Society, Blake's chapel with 'Thou shalt not' writ over the door. Yet, for all its unsympathetic quality to the twentieth-century mind, Calvinistic Puritanism was able to fire the minds of aspiring people of the seventeenth century with a generous enthusiasm. This was primarily because Puritanism was a democratising force which preached a conception of value and moral order entirely different from that of feudal society and the medieval church. As Professor Haller puts it in his fine book *The Rise of Puritanism*:

Calvinism helped this movement [the democratisation of English society and culture] by setting up a new criterion of aristocracy [the 'elect'] in opposition to the class distinctions of the existing system. . . . It became difficult not to think that election and salvation by the grace of God were available to everyone who really deserved them. Moreover, once the Calvinist preachers admitted that the only true aristocracy was spiritual and beyond human criteria, they had gone a long way towards asserting that all men in society must be treated alike because only God knows who is superior.[5]

Calvinism, in fact, by its vivid insistence that all men were damned, had the paradoxical effect of insisting that all men were equally capable of being saved.

The seventeenth-century Puritans, everyone knows, were suspicious of fiction because it is not true. Yet two forms at least of Puritan literature undoubtedly contributed to the development of the novel: one was the allegory, of which more later; the other the spiritual autobiography. One might, indeed, go further and draw a general parallel between the development of a Puritan prose style and the growth of the sort of 'realism' which was to emerge in the style of the novelists. Just as one finds in seventeenth-century fiction and sub-fiction a distinction between the style of the courtly romance and that of plebeian realism, so is there also a distinction between the two main types of religious writing of the period. Whereas the prose of the defenders of the Anglican Church (the sermons of Donne, Andrewes and their successors) was of a style which contemporaries described as 'witty', rich in complex verbal play, learned allusion and rhetorical devices suitable to a highly educated audience, the style of the Puritan preachers had quite a different basis.

The Puritans demanded plain sermons, addressed to the understanding not of scholars but of ordinary men. The object of the Puritan preachers was not to impress, not to delight, but to convince. . . . Both pulpit orators and political pamphleteers had to cultivate the virtues of clarity and directness, straight-forwardness and simplicity.[6]

This type of preaching came to be described as 'spiritual' as opposed to 'witty', and it is interesting to notice how this demand for plainness links with the growing pressure of the contemporary scientists who, for their own purposes, were encouraging a more down-to-earth manner of writing. It is important to recognise that the growth of realism in almost all aspects of seventeenth-century writing was to a great extent a class matter. The demand for realism tallied with the underlying demand of the up-and-coming burghers and capitalist farmers for a sweeping away of the mystifications which they associated with attempts to perpetuate the feudal order.

The spiritual autobiographies were an important part of the literature of Puritanism and enjoyed a considerable vogue in the early seventeenth century. Many of the leading Puritan preachers wrote journals in which were expressed the private thoughts and experiences of the man seeking salvation and hoping to help others along the same road. Some were by members of the sects (Baptists, Quakers, Ranters) and it is not hard to see their links with Bunyan, for the interest of such books is not so much psychological (in the modern sense) as illustrative: they view the individual life as a kind of parable. Others were by more conservative figures (Presbyterians and Anglicans). The interesting thing is to see how the connection between the practical and the spiritual, the realistic and the allegorical, enters into the very prose of these writers. Oliver Heywood (1630–1702) in his *Autobiography* can write that one purpose of his book is

to inferre a good caution from the by-past for the remaining part of my life, that where I have seen danger of a shipwreck I may observe such rocks and quicksands and charge my owne hart with more jeolousy and watchfulness, and make a covenant with my senses, members, facultys, and know satans devices, and where my strength and weakness lyes: and what a helpful improvement may former experiences prove to future closewalking.[7]

Within such a passage the significance of a metaphor like a voyage or journey becomes very clear. For the writer there is very little distinction between the allegorical and the real.

Professor G. A. Starr has shown[8] how the spiritual biographies tended to become more secular so that by 1708 we have *An Account of Some Remarkable Passages in the Life of a Private Gentleman; with Reflection thereon. In Three Parts, Relating to Trouble of Mind, some violent Temptations, and a Recovery; in order to awaken the Presumptuous, and encourage the Despondent*, a work which has sometimes been attributed to Defoe himself. The *Private Gentleman* clearly marks a significant stage in the transition from spiritual autobiography to fiction, and one can see how the shape of such a book – the shape of a man's life – was to determine the typical shape of the eighteenth-century novel. And, again, the contrast between allegory and realism is seen to be less decisive than we often tend to think. In the *Private Gentleman* anecdotes and experiences are given the force of 'illustrations'. Which takes one straight to Fielding and the first sentence of *Joseph Andrews*: 'It is a trite but true observation that examples work more forcibly on the mind than precepts.'

The spiritual autobiographies gave more to the novel than the idea of a man's life as a basic form of literary organisation: they are brimful of a sense of life as struggle. This is one of the qualities that distinguish them from the content of the typical romance. The chivalric hero has many adventures and, often enough, battles. He may even be a kind of crusader; but his adventures are essentially straightforward. He fights the enemy a great deal but it is seldom that he has to fight himself. He may well carry his lady's favour, but he doesn't carry a burden. Whereas Puritan literature is full of a sense of struggle and conflict of the most intense kind – both physical and spiritual.

Defoe's novels – to take a somewhat formalistic view of them – link together the realistic, if episodic, tradition of the picaresque stories and the moral tensions of the literature of Puritanism. Robinson Crusoe, like Bunyan's Christian, sets out on a pilgrimage, and, though it is not an allegorical pilgrimage, it is a Puritan one. For Puritanism by the beginning of the eighteenth century has changed, or rather split. The split is indicated by the choice Defoe himself had to make as a lad at a Dissenters' Academy when he had to decide whether to become a minister or a business-man. Had he chosen the first career then he would have been faced, like Bunyan, with another choice – between giving up his faith and going to jail. Bunyan, after the Restoration, stuck to his guns and his people, the artisans and petty bourgeoisie of Bedfordshire, who, faced with the defeat of the Puritan Left, refused to compromise, were persecuted, jailed and driven underground. A persecuted minority is very likely to express and maintain its faith in allegorical rather than realistic terms, partly for tactical reasons, but also because its *thinking* will be in those terms.

Defoe, on the other hand, when he decided not to become a dissenting minister and took to public life and business enterprise in a big way, chose the opposite path to Bunyan's – the path of that section of the Puritan middle-class who *had* gòt something out of the seventeenth-century Revolution and were quite prepared to accept the 1688 compromise. These were people who were indeed now in a position of considerable strength and power. Freedom for them was a very *real* thing, associated with what they could now *do* (as opposed to the sects for whom freedom meant, above all, freedom to believe, to maintain, to cling onto the truth, a truth that was always — as far as its actual manifestation was concerned — in the future). The shift within Puritanism from the allegorical to the realist tradition is bound up with the growing material success of the bourgeoisie. Because the well-to-do Puritans were now to a considerable degree in control of their situation, their interest in conscience and morality became much more practical, more bound up with action, less inward and more outward; interest in the here and now as opposed to the future; therefore, in literary terms, more realistic.

There is at least one seventeenth-century book within the Puritan tradition that illustrates this development fascinatingly. I am thinking of Governor William Bradford's *History of Plymouth Plantation (1606–1646).*[9] Bradford was one of the Pilgrim Fathers who crossed the Atlantic in the *Mayflower* and was chosen Governor of Plymouth, New England, in 1621, and most years from then until his death in 1657. His *History* tells the story of the Pilgrims' departure, for conscience' sake, from England to Holland, and of the years of their settlement in Leyden and their decision not to stay there. Here the description of the close, harassed, conscientious community has very much of the tone of allegory, of the early preachers and of *The Pilgrim's Progress.*

After they had lived in this citie about some 11. or 12. years, (which is the more observable being the whole time of that famose truce* between that state and the Spaniards,) and sundrie of them were taken away by death, and many others begane to be well striken in years, the grave mistris Experience having taught them many things, those prudent governours with sundrie of the sagest members begane both deeply to apprehend their present dangers, and wisely to foresee the future, and thinke of timly remedy. In the agitation of their thoughts, and much discours of things hèar aboute, at length they began to incline to this conclusion, of remoovall to some other place. Not out of any newfanglednes, or other such like giddie humor, by which men are oftentimes transported to their great hurt and danger, but for sundrie weightie reasons. . . . And first, they saw and found by experience the hardnes of the place and countrie to be such, as

* This truce, signed 9 April, 1609, was to expire in 1621.

few in comparison would come to them, and fewer that would bide it out, and continew with them. For many that came to them, and many more that desired to be with them, could not endure that great labor and hard fare, with other inconveniences which they underwent and were contented with. But though they loved their persons, approved their cause, and honoured their sufferings, yet they left them as it weer weeping, as Orpah did her mother in law Naomie, or as those Romans did Cato in Utica, who desired to be excused and borne with, though they could not all be Catoes. For many, though they desired to injoye the ordinances of God in their puritie, and the libertie of the gospell with them, yet, alass, they admitted of bondage, with danger of conscience, rather than to indure these hardships; yea, some preferred and chose the prisons in England, rather then this libertie in Holland, with these afflictions.[10]

The vocabulary here is typical of the Puritan discourse of the time and is, in an interesting way, both concrete and abstract. 'The grave mistress Experience' is invoked and the advice she offers shows her to be concerned with practical considerations, above all with the fact that life in Leyden is really too difficult to be feasible since it puts off well-disposed people who might otherwise join the community. But the practical problems Bradford is discussing, though piquant enough, are not the core of his concern. The word 'transported', half way through the passage, is used metaphorically rather than literally, the 'dangers' which beset the community are spiritual (above all the danger of a disintegration of purpose). Bradford's people look on their moves as a pilgrimage, but because they are weighed down by their situation and can find little practical to do to improve it, they tend to think all the time in terms of metaphors and analogies. Liberty and bondage, in such a situation, become qualities dependent less on the ability to do this or that than on states of mind. Prison in England seems to some less oppressive than the 'free' conditions of life in Leyden. The sense of oppression and difficulty, in fact, tends to lead to allegorical rather than practical thinking. To maintain a spiritual integrity becomes the overwhelming consideration, and the pilgrimage, though it involves physical movement, is a spiritual pilgrimage, conceived essentially in the terms of allegory. The obvious comparisons, in considering this part of Governor Bradford's *History*, are with Bunyan's allegorical city of Mansoul in *The Holy War*. It is not just a question of language but of a whole mode of experience. The pilgrims need to see themselves in the terms of allegory in order to survive.

If we now turn to an episode in the same book some twenty years later, in 1638, after the same people have settled in New England, the contrast is most illuminating:

Amongst other enormities that fell out amongst them, this year 3. men were (after due triall) executed for robery and murder which they had committed; their names were these, Arthur Peach, Thomas Jackson, and Richard Stinnings; ther was a 4., Daniel Crose, who was also guilty, but he escaped away, and could not be found. This Arthur Peach was the cheefe of them, and the ring leader of all the rest. He was a lustie and a desperate yonge man, and had been one of the souldiers in the Pequente warr, and had done as good servise as the most ther, and one of the forwardest in any attempte. And being now out of means, and loath to worke, and falling to idle courses and company, he intended to goe to the Dutch plantation; and had alured these 3., being other mens servants and apprentices, to goe with him. But another cause there was allso of his secret going away in this manner; he was not only rune into debte, but he had gott a maid with child, (which was not known till after his death,) a mans servante in the towne, and fear of punishmente made him gett away. The other 3. complotting with him, ranne away from their maisters in the night, and could not be heard of, for they went not the ordinarie way, but shaped such a course as they thought to avoyd the pursute of any. But falling into the way that lyeth betweene the Bay of Massachusetts and the Narrigansets, and being disposed to rest them selves, struck fire, and took tobaco, a litle out of the way, by the way side. At length ther came a Narigansett Indean by, who had been in the Bay a trading, and had both cloth and beads aboute him. (They had mett him the day before, and he was now returning.) Peach called him to drinke tobaco with them, and he came and sate downe with them. Peach tould the other he would kill him, and take what he had from him. But they were some thing afraid; but he said, Hang him, rougue, he had killed many of them. So they let him alone to doe as he would; and when he saw his time, he tooke a rapier and rane him through the body once or twise, and tooke from him 5. fathume of wampam, and 3. coats of cloath, and wente their way, leaving him for dead. But he scrabled away, when they were gone, and made shift to gett home, (but dyed within a few days after,) by which means they were discovered; and by subtilty the Indeans tooke them. For they desiring a canow to sett them over a water, (not thinking their facte had been known,) by the sachems command they were carried to Aquidnett Iland, and ther accused of the murder, and were examend and comitted upon it by the English ther. . . . The Gov^{rt} in the Bay were aquented with it, but refferrd it hither, because it was done in this jurisdiction; but pressed by all means that justice might be done in it; or els the countrie must rise and see justice done, otherwise it would raise a warr. Yet some of the rude and ignorante sorte murmured that any English should be put to death for the Indeans. So at last they of the iland brought them hither, and being often examened, and the evidence prodused, they all in the end freely confessed in effect all that the Indean accused them of, and that they had done it, in the maner afforesaid; and so, upon the forementioned evidence, were cast by the jurie, and condemned, and executed for the same. And some of the Narigansett Indeans, and of the parties friends, were presente when it was done, which gave and all the countrie good satisfaction. But it was a matter of much sadnes to them hear, and was the 2. execution which they had since they came; being both for wilfull murder, as hath bene before related. Thus much of this matter.[11]

The moral concern in this passage is not less than in the earlier one, the Puritan tone no less pervasive. Yet the whole effect is quite different. The morality is of a pre-eminently practical sort. All sorts of very impure but highly relevant considerations enter into the judgements made. A sense of racial superiority has already asserted itself among the colonists. Arthur Peach's attitude to the Indian he kills has a terrifyingly authentic plausibility. So does the murmuring of the rude and ignorant sort who don't like the idea of Englishmen being punished for what they have done to an Indian. The Governor himself is impelled in his thinking by other considerations besides abstract justice. Politics has entered in and the need to cope with the complexities of a colonial situation.

If the first passage reminds us of Bunyan, the second takes us nearly all the way towards Defoe. We are told all we need to know about Arthur Peach and his friends with extraordinary economy, and all the time it is the practical detail, the significant fact, the tone of voice, that makes the point. No abstract morality; simply the way people live and act and talk. Verisimilitude, achieved by factual detail in itself (the precise measurements of the stolen goods) and by the telling, 'unnecessary' detail ('they had mett him the day before, and he was now returning') which in practice adds the very necessary sense of interrelationship, continuity, life. The naming of people and things and places is 'convincing' not because it provides 'evidence' but because it reflects the actual way people do relate and establish their identities and their stories.

This second passage contains, in fact, all the essential elements of the realistic novel. The style is the style of *Moll Flanders*, right down to the final sentence, dismissing an unpleasant episode as adequately coped with, necessarily recorded and best forgotten. All the tormenting, inner strain of the Leyden days is gone, replaced by other tensions, not less exacting, but acted out in the practical pilgrimage of establishing a new society rather than in the recesses of the individual conscience. Bunyan's Christian has become Defoe's Robinson Crusoe, Puritan still, but a reasonably successful administrator of his domain. The mountain in the sunlight has become the coasts and forests of the Atlantic seaboard. Allegory has become realism, not because the new tensions are more real than the old ones, but because Puritans like Bradford and Defoe have become part of that section of humanity which is in control of things. The whole history of realism a literary style seems to me to be bound up with this business of control and power.

Notes

1 Margaret Schlauch, *Antecedents of the English Novel, 1400–1600* (Oxford University Press, 1963).

2 A. A. Parker, *Literature and the Delinquent* (Edinburgh University Press, 1967).

3 F. W. Chandler, *The Literature of Roguery* (Constable, 1907), p. 225.

4 F. R. Leavis, *The Great Tradition* (Chatto & Windus, 1948).

5 W. Haller, *The Rise of Puritanism* (Harper & Row, 1957 edn), p. 178.

6 Christopher Hill, *The Century of Revolution, The History of England*, vol. 5 (Nelson, 1961), p. 183.

7 Ed. J. Horsfall Turner, 1881–3, Vol. i, p. 133.

8 G. A. Starr, *Defoe and Spiritual Autobiography* (Oxford University Press, 1965).

9 I have used the edition edited by William T. Davis and published in the series of *Original Narratives of Early American History*, 1908 (reprinted 1959).

10 See n. 9 above, p. 44.

11 See n. 9 above, pp. 344–6.

In defence of *Moll Flanders*

I

Professor Ian Watt's *The Rise of the Novel* is one of the works of literary criticism of the last decade that have added substantially and rewardingly to our ability to read eighteenth-century literature better. If this paper revolves around some disagreements with Mr Watt that is to be taken as a mark of gratitude rather than an attempt to denigrate. It is because *The Rise of the Novel* has a deservedly wide currency that it is worth examining what seems to be fundamentally wrong in Mr Watt's approach to Defoe.[1]

It is with *Moll Flanders* that I am concerned and I agree with Mr Watt that it is the key work in any estimate of Defoe's significance as a novelist. In *The Rise of the Novel* forty-two pages are spent on *Moll* and constitute the fullest discussion of the book I know. Towards the end of the discussion the conclusions are summarised:

> Defoe's forte was the brilliant episode. Once his imagination seized on a situation he could report it with a comprehensive fidelity which was much in advance of any previous fiction, and which, indeed, has never been surpassed . . .
>   How far we should allow Defoe's gift for the perfect episode to outweigh his patent shortcomings — weaknesses of construction, inattention to detail, lack of moral or formal pattern — is a very difficult critical problem.[2]

It is a problem, however, about which Mr Watt has left us in little doubt as to where he stands. The passage I have quoted is followed by a couple of pages of generous and perceptive appreciation of Defoe's genius, happily described as 'confident and indestructible'. But these pages cannot eclipse the thirty-five that have preceded them in which scepticism — peppered, it is true, with valuable observations and insights – has reigned. Mr Watt praises Defoe highly for verisimilitude and not for much else. The conclusion is clearly stated:

His blind and almost purposeless concentration on the actions of his heroes and heroines, and his unconscious and unreflective mingling of their thoughts and his about the inglorious world in which they both exist, made possible the expression of many motives and themes which could not, perhaps, have come into the tradition of the novel without Defoe's shock tactics . . .[3]

Blind, purposeless, unconscious, unreflective: the adjectives are damaging and lead us – for all Mr Watt's scrupulous reservations – in the same direction as Dr Leavis's 'brush-off' footnote in *The Great Tradition*:

Characteristic of the confusion I am contending against is the fashion (for which the responsibility seems to go back to Virginia Woolf and Mr E. M. Forster) of talking of *Moll Flanders* as a 'great novel'. Defoe was a remarkable writer, but all that need be said about him as a novelist was said by Leslie Stephen in *Hours in a Library* (First Series). He made no pretension to practising the novelist's art, and matters little as an influence. In fact, the only influence that need be noted is that represented by the use made of him in the nineteen-twenties by the practitioners of the fantastic *conte* (or pseudo-moral fable) with its empty pretence of significance.[4]

It is worth recalling that this footnote – which has, incidentally, along with a couple of others in the same work, had more influence in keeping students of English literature away from the eighteenth-century novel than any other pronouncement – is attached to a sentence which distinguishes as major novelists those who 'not only change the possibilities of the art for practitioners and readers, but . . . are significant in terms of the human awareness they promote: awareness of the possibilities of life'.

It is precisely on such grounds that I would claim that *Moll Flanders* is indeed a great novel.

II

Mr Watt uses, to pinpoint his doubts about Defoe's literary status the famous passage in *Moll Flanders* in which Moll doesn't steal the watch in the meeting-house.

The next thing of moment was an attempt at a gentlewoman's gold watch. It happened in a crowd, at a meeting house, where I was in very great danger of being taken. I had full hold of her watch, but giving a great jostle, as if somebody had thrust me against her, and in the juncture giving the watch a fair pull, I found it would not come, so I let it go that moment, and cried out as if I had been killed, that somebody had trod upon my foot, and that there was certainly pickpockets there, for somebody or other had given a pull at my watch; for you are to observe that on these adventures we always went very well dressed, and I had very good clothes on, and a gold watch by my side, as like a lady as other folks.

I had no sooner said so, but the other gentlewoman cried out, 'A pick-pocket' too, for somebody, she said, had tried to pull her watch away. When I touched her watch I was close to her, but when I cried out I stopped as it were short, and the crowd bearing her forward a little, she made a noise too, but it was at some distance from me, so that she did not in the least suspect me; but when she cried out, 'A pickpocket', somebody cried out, 'Ay, and here has been another; this gentlewoman has been attempted too.'

At that very instant, a little farther in the crowd, and very luckily too, they cried out, 'A pickpocket', again, and really seized a young fellow in the very fact. This, though unhappy for the wretch, was very opportunely for my case, though I had carried it handsomely enough before; but now it was out of doubt, and all the loose part of the crowd ran that way, and the poor boy was delivered up to the rage of the street, which is a cruelty I need not describe, and which, however, they are always glad of, rather than be sent to Newgate, where they lie often a long time; till they are almost perished, and sometimes they are hanged, and the best they can look for, if they are convicted, is to be transported.

Mr Watt's comments on this scene may be summarised as follows. It is very convincing: full marks for verisimilitude and prose. But (*a*) the tone is too laconic, the scene is not planned as a coherent whole; (*b*) the point of view of the narrator is not consistent; (*c*) the relationship of the passage to the rest of the book is suspect; (*d*) the passage suffers from a general fault of the book – repeated falls in tension between episodes. Let us examine these criticisms.

(*a*) Mr Watt complains that

Defoe gets into the middle of the action, with 'I had full hold of her watch', and then suddenly changes from laconic reminiscent summary to a more detailed and immediate presentation, as though only to back up the truth of his initial statement. Nor has the scene been planned as a coherent whole: we are soon interrupted in the middle of the scene by an aside explaining something that might have been explained before, the important fact that Moll Flanders was dressed like a gentlewoman herself: this transition adds to our trust that no ghost-writer has been imposing order on Moll Flanders' somewhat rambling reminiscences, but if we had seen Moll

dressed 'as like a lady as other folks' from the beginning, the action would
have run more strongly, because uninterruptedly, into the next incident of
the scene, the raising of the alarm.[5]

Surely the point Mr Watt objects to is an important part of Defoe's
intended effect. Moll isn't a novelist, planning ahead. She lives from
moment to moment; she suddenly remembers things she ought to
have said before; and she remembers them haphazardly, partly
because that is the way people do remember things, but also because
she is such an incurable self-deceiver, yet doesn't want to deceive
herself or other people. Moll wants to be honest – with herself, with
us, even with the woman she steals from – but of course she can't be.
And the confusion is expressed in the organisation and disorganisa-
tion of her prose. If Moll's consciousness is a disorganised and im-
promptu business, so is her life.

(*b*) Defoe goes on to stress the practical moral, which is that the gentlewoman should have 'seized the next body that was behind her', instead of
crying out. In so doing, Defoe lives up to the didactic purpose professed in
the 'Author's Preface', but at the same time he directs our attention to the
important problem of what the point of view of the narrator is supposed to
be. We presume that it is a repentant Moll, speaking towards the end of
her life: it is therefore surprising that in the next paragraph she should
gaily describe her 'governess's' procuring activities as 'pranks'. Then a
further confusion about the point of view becomes apparent: we notice that
to Moll Flanders other pickpockets, and the criminal fraternity in general,
are a 'they', not a 'we'. She speaks as though she were not implicated in the
common lot of criminals; or is it, perhaps, Defoe who has unconsciously
dropped into the 'they' he himself would naturally use for them? And
earlier, when we are told that 'the other gentlewoman' cried out, we
wonder why the word 'other'? Is Moll Flanders being ironical about the fact
that she too was dressed like a gentlewoman, or has Defoe forgotten that,
actually, she is not?[6]

This carries the same point further. Of course, there are inconsis-
tencies here. They are the very life's blood of the book. It is true that
Moll speaks as though she were not implicated in the common lot of
criminals. She doesn't think of herself as a criminal. When she
learns what the other criminals in Newgate think of her she is
morally outraged. Occasionally, for a moment, like Joyce Cary's
Sara, she catches sight of herself in some mirror and sees herself, surprised. And she *does* think of herself, in the episode under discussion, as a gentlewoman. What Mr Watt sees as Defoe's carelessness I
see as his imaginative absorption in his subject, a penetration into

the layers of self-deception of which a human being, even a relatively honest one, is capable. Sir Leslie Stephen's reproach, in the essay Dr Leavis admires so much, that Defoe's novels lack 'all that goes by the name of psychological analysis in modern fiction' makes sense only if one is concerned to blame Defoe for not being Proust. There is no need for formal analysis of Moll's psychological processes in the meeting-house. They are revealed in all their complex, awful, funny, human contradictoriness in the very texture of the scene. This is a triumph of art.

(c) The connection between the meeting-house scene and the narrative as a whole confirms the impression that Defoe paid little attention to the internal consistence of his story. When she is transported to Virginia Moll Flanders gives her son a gold watch as a memento of their reunion; she relates how she 'desired that he would now and then kiss it for my sake,' and then adds sardonically that she did not tell him 'that I stole it from a gentlewoman's side, at a meeting house in London'. Since there is no other episode in *Moll Flanders* dealing with watches, gentlewomen and meeting-houses, we must surely infer that Defoe had a faint recollection of what he had written a hundred pages earlier ...

These discontinuities strongly suggest that Defoe did not plan his novel as a coherent whole, but worked piecemeal, very rapidly, and without any subsequent revision.[7]

There is a confusion of critical method here. It may well be (and, as Mr Watt says, external as well as internal evidence suggests it) that Defoe worked piecemeal and that his novels therefore lack a certain planned coherence. But this is a general critical statement about the kind of book we are dealing with, relevant no doubt, but not to be confused with our judgement of artistic success. The passage Mr Watt refers to can be read equally well as a further example of Moll's difficulty of separating the false from the true and of the curious tricks of the extended conscience. She happens to connect watch-stealing with the meeting-house episode because that gave her a shock and imprinted itself deep in her memory; she may even have found it necessary, for her peace of mind, to transform her failure – with its uncomfortable accompaniment of the taking of the boy pickpocket – into a comfortable success. Certainly time has dealt interestingly with the episode. This may not have been Defoe's intention. But certainly the main *point* in the Virginia scene from which Mr Watt quotes is to illuminate the wry twinge of half-conscience, half-triumph that Moll by now feels. She has become complacent in a way which in former days, for all her conscience-blocking, she dared not be. Whether she is referring to the same watch doesn't matter. To suggest that it does would seem to reveal an attitude towards the novel and novel-writing not quite relevant to the sort of book Defoe offers us. I will return to this point.

(*d*) The question of fall of tension between episodes is a valid point of criticism. That opening sentence, 'The next thing of moment was etc.' does indeed betray a weakness, a technical problem unsolved. There is, it is true, the sense in which Moll does indeed see her life as a kind of inventory of episodes, with nothing much of note between them. There is also the sense in which the book proceeds from one moral warning to the next on the old beggar-book level, and there is no doubt that this aspect of his book tends all the time to conflict with Defoe's major concern – to show us what Moll Flanders is like (in the way that the remnants of the old *Hamlet* revenge-drama tend to conflict with Shakespeare's major concern in his play).

In his analysis of the meeting-house scene Mr Watt omits to discuss what is surely its greatest, most moving moment; the taking of the boy pickpocket. The effect here is not at all due to verismilitude or any of the qualities habitually, and rightly, granted to Defoe; it is almost entirely moral and psychological. The phrase 'and very luckily too' leads us into it. What is lucky for Moll is the lynching of the boy for whom she can afford no more fellow-feeling than a single use of the adjective 'poor' and the dubious consolation that lynching is better than hanging or transportation.

The effect that Defoe achieves here is one that is central to the nature of *Moll Flanders* as a work of art. Moll's reactions to the episode, humanly speaking, are quite inadequate. It is easy, therefore, to underestimate Defoe's art, which can look, at first glance, to be inadequate in the same way. The paragraph is a flat one, a disclaimer, a refusal to see what has happened. But the phrase 'a cruelty I need not describe' is an indication of cowardice not on Defoe's part but Moll's. Of course, she can't bear to dwell on the scene: it is too near the bone. But that last sentence of the paragraph is, objectively considered, all compassion. The phrase 'and sometimes they are hanged', the whole rhythm of the sentence, the toneless forcing out of facet after facet of horror, all these contribute to a marvellous effect. Moll is playing it all down; she can't do anything else, she who has put herself beyond the possibility of looking at such a scene

objectively. But Defoe allows *us* to see all round the situation even if
Moll can't. And a far more important link between this whole episode and the later reaches of the novel than the link represented by
the watch which turns up in Virginia is the connection between this
last sentence and the whole Newgate episode of the book. It is only
then that we get the full force of the word 'luckily'.

I stress the power of this paragraph because it illustrates very well
the nature of the moral organisation of *Moll Flanders*, a feature of the
book that Mr Watt, and almost everyone else, plays down.

III

The underlying tension which gives *Moll Flanders* its vitality as a
work of art can be expressed by a contradiction which is at once
simple and complicated. Moll is immoral, shallow, hypocritical,
heartless, a bad woman: yet Moll is marvellous. Defoe might almost
(though he wouldn't have dreamed of it) have subtitled his book 'A
Pure Woman'.

Moll's splendour – her resilience and courage and generosity – is
inseparable from her badness. The fair and the foul are not isolable
qualities to be abstracted and totted up in a reckoning, balancing
one against the other. The relationship is far more interesting. One
is reminded, perhaps, of Yeats's Crazy Jane:

'Fair and foul are near of kin,
And fair needs foul', I cried.
'My friends are gone, but that's a truth
Nor grave nor bed denied,
Learned in bodily lowliness
And in the heart's pride.'[8]

That is too metaphysical for Moll; she wouldn't say that fair needs
foul. But the contradiction Yeats is expressing and, in expressing,
resolving, is essentially the contradiction Defoe's book expresses.
And the phrase 'the heart's pride' is not inappropriate to Moll.

The episode in *Moll Flanders* which tells us most about the underlying pattern of the book is the one very near the beginning in which
Moll as a little girl talks of her fear of going into service and her
desire to be a gentlewoman. Mr Watt picks out this passage as one
of the few examples in the book of an irony that we can be quite sure
is fully conscious, and his fastening on the scene tells us that he is a

good literary critic. But he lets go much too quickly. This is an absolutely essential episode, as Mr Alick West, in the best analysis of *Moll Flanders*, I know, has well pointed out:

> The life the child wants — working for herself in freedom — is the contrasting background to the life the woman gets in a world where a gentlewoman does not live on the threepences or fourpences she earns by her own labour, but on riches of unexplained origin.[9]

This sentence not only shows what *Moll Flanders* is about but illuminates the specific artistic pattern of the book. It leads us straight to what makes Moll at the same time splendid and contemptible. What makes her splendid — a great heroine — is that she wants her independence, to work for herself in freedom. She is a woman who is determined to be a human being, not a servant, and the feeling of what it means to be a servant is what generates the impulses which carry her through most of the book, until she too has become a gentlewoman with servants, living on riches whose origin she likes to forget about or to confuse but which Defoe has only too clearly explained.

Unless we see Moll in history we cannot grasp her moral stature as a heroine. Instead, we will bring to her the flat and static sort of moral judgement which she herself (and one side of Defoe himself) brings when she is forced to enter the sphere she calls morality or religion. And here Virginia Woolf's feminist preoccupations offer a more central and artistically relevant approach to the book than any other. The examination of Defoe's social and economic attitudes that Mr Novak[10] has offered us is not, of course, irrelevant; nor are Mr Watt's observations on the significance of the criminal class at this period; but neither emphasis goes to the heart of the matter. Moll becomes a criminal because she is a woman, and it is not at all by a chance in the book's structure that she comes to her second career (that of a thief) by way of her first (that of a wife). Too little is known about the position of women in the eighteenth century, but the general outlines are clear enough and Mr Watt himself in the chapters on Richardson in *The Rise of the Novel* has notably contributed to our appreciation of many of the problems involved. So have recent emphases on the importance of arranged marriages and contemporary feelings about them in Restoration and eighteenth-century literature.[11] Such extra-literary confirmation is not irrelevant to a critical approach to *Moll Flanders* because only on the basis of a just assessment of the facts can we form an opinion as to whether Moll's childish fears about the consequences of not being a gentle-woman are justified – whether in fact they represent an amiable delusion or a naive but genuine moral insight. All the evidence points to the conclusion that Moll is right, that to become a maidservant in that period meant the end of any possibility that could conceivably be subsumed under the words freedom or independence, any possibility therefore of individual human development or flowering. The choice Moll makes is therefore one which, with whatever reservations, deserves our positive sympathy, and the moral tensions about which Defoe's novel is constructed are not trivial or arbitrary.

Not to stress this point is to prejudice artistic judgements. It is only within the social context that we can begin, for instance, to assess Defoe's treatment (or lack of it) of Moll's role as mother. Mr Watt writes:

> Here the conclusion about her character must surely be that, although there are extenuating circumstances, she is often a heartless mother. It is difficult to see how this can be reconciled either with her kissing the ground that Humphrey has trodden, or with the fact that she herself loudly condemns unnatural mothers, but never makes any such accusation against herself even in her deepest moments of penitent self-reprobation.[12]

This puts the cart before the horse. Surely the very point that Defoe has been making us understand is that Moll is *at the same time* unusually honest and extraordinarily dishonest, and that the significance of her situation (whether it be horror or irony) is that she dare not be any more compassionate than she is. What Mr Watt sees as inconsistency I see as profundity. Moll is genuinely sorry that she has been a heartless mother; but that is part of the price she pays *and has to pay* for her independence. The really dreadful aspect of the book lies in Moll's ultimate absorption, via her 'repentance', into the very way of life against which she has so vigorously rebelled.

The Newgate section of the book is an extraordinary achievement and not primarily on the level of verisimilitude. If Newgate is hell to Moll it is above all because it is a place where her habitual habits of self-deception cannot do their job, a real eighteenth-century *huis clos*. Newgate is reality, the eighteenth-century world with the lid off, the world from which Moll set out and to which she comes back, defeated, to emerge as a conformist.

IV

It is worth looking at *Moll Flanders* in its historical context in a
rather different sense from the one I have so far emphasised. Moll is
perhaps the first major plebeian heroine in English literature. The
Doll Tearsheets and Doll Commons of the Elizabethan drama are her
literary ancestors, but they are never right at the centre of the plays
they appear in, any more than the sensible peasant-bred servants in
Molière. Moll is unique. And throughout the eighteenth century
she remains so. For Pamela, precisely because she makes the opposite choice to Moll's, is not a heroine. She bears on her shoulders
none of the weight of human aspiration which heroism — including
the fictional kind — involves. Polly Peachum is nearer to being a
heroine; but the Polly of *The Beggar's Opera* needs Lucy Lockit to
complete her and together they do — also within the walls of Newgate — throw a great deal of light on the problems and emotions of
eighteenth-century plebeian women. Strictly speaking, however, it
is impossible to speak of a plebeian heroine after Moll until Jeannie
Deans, who is different because she is a peasant, not a townswoman.
If one looks further afield the important figure among Moll's successors is another peasant girl, Susannah (Mozart's even more than
Beaumarchais's), who is an anti-Pamela and a great advance on the
Molière servants.

V

We must see the place of *Moll Flanders* in total history if we are to
see it in literary history. The book is not to be judged as though it
were an imperfect forerunner of *Pride and Prejudice* or *What Maisie
Knew*. Behind almost all the unsatisfactory criticism of Defoe today
is a predisposition to judge his books in terms relevant to the novel
as it developed in the nineteenth century and to praise in Defoe
primarily those aspects of his art which point, so to speak, in that
direction. 'Dramatisation' (or what Percy Lubbock calls 'scenic' presentation), a conscious manipulation of 'point of view' and a moral
preoccupation of the sort one associates with, say, George Eliot:
these are assumed to be the elements of maturity in a novelist's development. 'Personal relationships' in the more analytical and isolable
sense of the term are seen as the proper, even the ultimate, subject of
the novel. And, of course, in an important sense, this is true. Novels

will always be about men and women in their living, and therefore
personal, relationships.

The trouble with Moll Flanders, however, is that by her very
mode of existence she is precluded from having personal relationships of the sort modern critics most value. Mr Watt seems to recognise this when he writes:

> ... it is certain that, at the end of the long tradition of the European
> novel, and of the society whose individualism, leisure and unexampled
> security allowed it to make personal relations the major theme of its
> literature, Defoe is a welcome and portentous figure. Welcome because he
> seems long ago to have called the great bluff of the novel – its suggestion
> that personal relations really are the be-all and end-all of life; portentous
> because he, and only he, among the great writers of the past, has presented
> the struggle for survival in the bleak perspectives which recent history has
> brought back to a commanding position on the human stage.[13]

But he is arguing here that Defoe's positive quality is his concentration on isolated individuals. I think this is a mistaken argument.
Moll's life is not an isolated life; she has as many personal relationships as anyone else. That she is unable to have full and satisfactory
personal relationships is due not to her individualism but to the
actual problems she is faced with. Moll is forced to be an individualist by her decision to try to be free in the man's world of
eighteenth-century England; but her impulse to her free is due not
to individualism but to a desire for better relationships with other
people than life as a servant will permit.

The whole nature of Defoe's book – its construction, its texture,
its detail, its vitality, its power to move us – is determined by his
awareness of the contradiction between Moll's human aspiration and
the facts of the human world she lives in. Because so much of the
contradiction was, in the year 1722, insoluble and yet had to be resolved, much of the resolution takes the form of ambiguous or ironical statement.

'It is interesting to compare Defoe's methods with those of a con-
temporary artist facing a comparable problem, the Italian novelist
Pier Paolo Pasolini in his impressive film *Accattone*. Accattone,
Pasolini's 'hero', is in many respects very like a twentieth-century
Moll Flanders. He is a feckless young man who lives as a ponce in
Rome, and the film treats his life episodically. There is one scene in
particular reminiscent of Defoe's novel. Accattone, needing money
to buy a present for his girl, steals a chain from the neck of his young

son, telling himself all the time what a swine he is. The moral impact of the film is in one sense much the same as that of *Moll Flanders*: we feel a deep sympathy for Accattone without approving of him, and we are shocked at the human inadequacies of the total situation that is revealed. Yet the similarities are scarcely less striking than the differences, of which perhaps the most important is that we know precisely where Pasolini stands: there is no moral ambiguity in *his* attitude. Accattone is presented to us clearly, objectively, as a product of contemporary society, and although he is not sentimentalised or excused, the social situation of which he is a part, and at least to some extent a victim, is implicitly condemned.

This is not a matter of chance. Pasolini knows very well that Accattone is unable to resolve his problems; but he also knows that, in the middle of the twentieth century, Accattone's problems are not insoluble. Whereas, to Defoe, at the beginning of the eighteenth century, Moll's problem is indeed insoluble and this inevitably affects the whole nature of his artistic handling of it.

The question 'How far is Defoe's irony intentional?' is not really a fruitful question. For one thing, it is impossible to know the answer for sure; for another, it oversimplifies the nature of artistic consciousness and indeed of all consciousness. Defoe's writing was presumably not *un*intentional, not *un*conscious. He knew what he was doing. But, of course, he will not have been aware of all the implications of what he was doing; no one ever is. It is true that Defoe's own comprehension of some of the most important implications of Moll Flanders's story must seem to us to be incomplete. He underwrites her own ultimate complacency, obviously taking her salvation much too much at its face value. But this limitation is far less important than that 'negative capability' which allowed him to reveal the humanity of Moll. What is important is that he tackled the big, central human problems of his time and went deep, revealing the contradictions as well as the surface qualities, and revealing them in a form which in itself illuminates their nature because it springs from them.

Notes

1 I should add, in fairness, that I am also concerned to correct what I now regard as inadequacies in my own approach to Defoe in my *Introduction*

to the English Novel, vol. I (London, 1951). For a realization of these in-adequacies I am indebted not only to time, with its gift of second chances, but, in particular, to Mr Alick West and to Professor Bonamy Dobree who was the first person I heard talk of Defoe with the right kind of enthusiasm.

2   *The Rise of the Novel* (London, 1957), p. 130.

3   *Ibid.*, p. 134.

4   *The Great Tradition* (London, 1948), p. 2.

5   *Op. cit.*, p. 97

6   *Ibid.*, p. 98.

7   *Ibid.*, pp. 98–9.

8   'Crazy Jane Talks with the Bishop', *The Collected Poems of W. B. Yeats* (2nd edn, London, 1950), p. 294.

9   *Mountain in the Sunlight* (London, 1958), p. 90.

10   Maximilian E. Novak, *Economics and the Fiction of Daniel Defoe* (California, 1962).

11   Especially C. Hill, 'Clarissa Harlowe and her times' (*Essays in criticism*, Vol. V, 1955, pp. 315–40) and P. F. Vernon, 'Marriage of convenience and the moral code of Restoration comedy' (*Essays in Criticism*, Vol. XII, 1962, pp. 370–87).

12   *Op. cit.*, p. 110.

13   *Op. cit.*, p. 133.

Dickens and the popular tradition

I

By *Socialist Realism*, in the field of literature, I assume we mean literature written from the point of view of the class-conscious working class, whose socialist consciousness illuminates their whole view of the nature of the world and of the potentialities of mankind. By *Critical Realism* I assume we mean literature written in the era of class society from a point of view which, while not fully socialist, is nevertheless sufficiently critical of class society to reveal important truths about that society and to contribute to the freeing of the human consciousness from the limitations which class society has imposed on it.

That the division between Critical Realism and Socialist Realism is a tricky business, which though basic is seldom clear-cut, should not surprise us, for the socialist revolution begins many years and even centuries before it can actually take place. As Lenin reminds us: between the bourgeois–democratic revolution and the socialist revolution there is no Chinese Wall. Which does not mean that between the bourgeois-democratic revolution and the socialist revolution there is no essential difference. What Lenin is warning us against is the expectation of a simple process, a black-and-white picture.

I should like to make two points about Critical Realism which I feel may be worth bearing in mind. One is that it covers a great deal of literature which varies very much not only in quality and subject-matter but also in the point of view from which it is written. To take one or two examples only from the field of English literature: Defoe, Fielding and George Eliot are all, I think correctly, described as critical realists, but though they all three adopt a point of view deeply critical of British bourgeois society the three points of view have *almost* as much that distinguishes them as they have in common and their individual contributions to the liberation of British consciousness, though not incompatible, are certainly very different. It is important therefore to define, within the general context of Critical Realism, the particular point of view of particular writers and of particular tendencies within this general picture.

My second general point is that when we speak of point of view in relation to creative literature we are referring to something somewhat different from a man's consciously held, or fairly easily abstractable, ideas. We all know from experience that a writer may have very curious, illogical and even reactionary opinions and yet be a pretty good writer, and conversely that there are writers whose philosophical and political opinions are enlightened and 'correct' and yet who are not very good writers. The explanation, of course, is not that the processes involved in the exploration of the world through art and those involved in the formulation of scientific laws are contradictory but that they are not as a rule the same. You may well have appreciated in general terms the correctness of a certain principle but not have understood very fully the actual ways that principle operates: or you may have a remarkable grasp of the way it operates in a specific case or area but yet fail to see its general significance. This can happen to scientists as well as artists. I am not, heaven knows, trying to press some great general distinction between Science and Art or between the make-up of the Scientist and the Artist; but it seems that, just because he is dealing with human material of an exceptionally high degree of complexity, it is particularly possible for the artist to have very valuable specific insights without being able to transform them into general or theoretical ones. To cut short a complicated and difficult (though to me fascinating) subject, I think we should remember that when we refer to the point of view of a writer and use the adjectives 'socialist' or 'critical', we are using adjectives which, though valid and necessary, are normally used in contexts in which the texture of thought is rather more abstract and theoretical than the habitual processes of art. The words 'socialist' and 'critical' are never of course to the Marxist *purely* abstract words. Marxism, which teaches us that reality is more basic than what we think about it, must itself always be a counteracting force to any tendency to 'pure' abstraction, 'pure' theory. Yet − to oversimplify a bit − when in everyday life we refer to a man as 'socialist' or 'critical' we are usually referring to his formulated *opinions*, whereas the important thing about an artist is not his opinions (on that level) but his *sensibility*, his all-round apprehension and comprehension of things. I am not for a moment meaning to pose the concept of sensibility *against* that of intelligence or reason or science. This is a fatal error in much bourgeois thinking. But I am suggesting that it may be useful to remind ourselves that when we refer to a writer's point of view in the artistic sense we are referring to his sensibility rather than to his opinions or intentions, though of course both these are relevant factors.

That is why I am presuming to use in this paper the term 'popular' more often than the term 'critical'. Within the general movement of Critical Realism, it seems to me, there are certain writers who – though certainly critical of bourgeois society – remain in their overall sensibility essentially attached to the ways of thinking and feeling of that society. I would put Charlotte Brontë, Mrs Gaskell, Thackeray and George Eliot within that category. They are honest writers, they have many insights and attitudes highly inconvenient to the ruling class: I do not want to underrate their value. But their sensibility, for all its progressive aspects, seems to me in the end to be exercised, however critically, within the confines of petty-bourgeois feeling: it does not, even in the case of George Eliot (the best of them), burst the buckles of bourgeois consciousness, though it certainly strains them. Whereas, in a basic and essential way, Emily Brontë and Dickens and Hardy *do* burst the buckles. The view of the world they express, the feelings they generate, are not socialist but they are more than what is generally meant by critical. And it would seem that the essential difference between these two groups of critical realist writers is that the latter write from a point of view which can be described not merely in somewhat negative terms as critical but in positive terms as popular, that is to say expressive of the sensibility of progressive sections of the people other than the petty-bourgeois intelligentsia. Hardy is a popular writer in this positive sense because his sensibility is essentially a peasant sensibility. Emily Brontë and Dickens reflect, as it seems to me, that great popular alliance of working class and petty bourgeoisie which *might* – up to about 1848 – have succeeded in giving the bourgeois-democratic revolution in Britain a different and more revolutionary content and thereby in bringing the socialist revolution very much nearer. The might-have-beens of history are, of course, mere speculation. To the literary critic and cultural historian, however, they have a sort of reality, for he is concerned with the expression of forces which, though they may in the actual power-struggle be for the time defeated, yet remain powerful and fruitful. Dickens was not a Chartist, but he could not, I think, have been the novelist he was without Chartism, and in the 1850s and 1860s Dicken's novels carry forward the spirit of Chartism and in some ways even deepen it and bring it nearer the spirit of Socialism.

II

There is a striking contrast between Dickens's general reputation, by no means confined to Britain, as one of the great writers – one of the dozen or so writers of the world whom almost every literate person knows something about – and his treatment by literary specialists in his own country and America. Even among critics who have taken the novel seriously there has been little disposition to recognise him as a supremely great writer, a writer in the category of Shakespeare and Chaucer. The most serious modern English academic literary critic, Dr Leavis, can find no central place for him in his great tradition of the English novel. And even though in the last thirty years – thanks largely to the work of Professors Edgar Johnson, Sylvère Monod, John Butt and Kathleen Tillotson and the admirable pioneering monograph of T. A. Jackson – the position has improved somewhat, there is still nothing like a general recognition in 'respectable' literary circles of Dickens's stature.

Even among those who have done something to fight for the novelist's reputation one has the uneasy sense of the right thing being done for the wrong reason. We must all be grateful for Mr Edmund Wilson's famous essay 'The Two Scrooges', which made it impossible for the sentimental-hearty view of the great writer to be maintained, yet it has to be said that one of the chief effects of Mr Wilson's essay was to provide the stuffy, respectable Dickens-figure with a few good sadistic neuroses very much to the taste of the post-Freudian western reader. And much as one must welcome the debowdlerising of the Dickens legend which Georgina Hogarth and the Dickens Clubs had for long succeeded in maintaining, there has been a tendency for recent biographical work simply to replace the image of Dickens the Victorian fuddy-duddy by that of the Edwardian sugar-daddy. Among the highbrow literary critics the

situation has not been much better. It is now fashionable to refer to
the novels as 'symbolic' and certainly this often reflects a more serious and rewarding approach than that of a few decades ago; but
'symbolic' is a word which has at best to be used with the greatest
care and can more easily lead away from than towards a just assessment of Dickens's art, especially if its use betrays − as it so often
does − a preoccupation with Jungian metaphysics.[1]

Why is it that twentieth-century Western literary criticism has so
singularly failed to come to terms with Dickens's art? I think the
reason has little to do with objective artistic merit but is almost
entirely a matter of the historical development of capitalist society
over the last hundred years and of the position of the intellectual
within that society.

To say that Dickens was very unlike a twentieth-century intellectual is, in a sense, to say something all too obvious, yet it is perhaps worth saying because it explains at least in part why so many
twentieth-century intellectuals have either despised Dickens or
praised him for off-centre reasons. Specifically, to catalogue the
dissimilarities, one might say that Dickens, unlike most twentieth-
century western literary intellectuals, was very vulgar, very practical and very optimistic. Perhaps it should be added that, though
habitually living beyond his income, he was, by professional middle-
class standards, very rich. Also that he was in the more formal, academic sense, quite unintellectual.

None or all of these qualities, of course, however admirable, in
themselves make Dickens a great writer; but they do involve his
being, when we come to take stock of him, a great writer of a particular and − by modern standards − peculiar kind. And if I use the
word 'popular' to describe the kind I do so with my eyes open.

III

There are various reasons for using the word 'popular' in connection
with Dickens's novels and some of them, though by no means irrelevant, are not, in my opinion, among the conclusive reasons.

(i) In the first place there is the fact that Dickens was, and has on
the whole continued to be, very widely read. There had never been
anything like the success of *Pickwick*. And the public that read
Dickens was, from the first, remarkably wide, ranging from the
aristocracy (including later on the dear Queen herself) to countless

not highly educated working-class people. It is improbable that any subsequent serious British novelist, even George Eliot at the height of her fame, had so large or so wide-ranging a reading public, though a contemporary best-seller like John Braine's *Room At The Top*, with its vast Penguin printing, might come within a comparable distance. But though a large circulation over a long period must be seen to be in the end a *sine qua non* of popular literature, yet the obverse is not true and I think it essential to insist that a satisfactory use of the word 'popular' cannot permit of its identification with circulation. It is indeed precisely this identification that has led to the debasing of the word 'popular' in a country like Britain where it is most often used as a synonym for 'commercially successful'.

(ii) More important, perhaps, is the question of Dickens's *relation* with his public. There is no doubt that, both as an adherent of serial publication and as Editor of *Household Words*, Dickens enjoyed an unusually close relationship with his readers. We all know about the letters begging him to spare Little Nell and it is all too easy to see only the ridiculous side of this kind of thing. Professor John Butt has put the matter into perspective very effectively in *Dickens at Work*:

To the author [serial publication] meant a larger public, but also a public more delicately responsive, who made their views known during the progress of a novel both by writing to him and by reducing or increasing their purchases. Through serial publication an author could recover something of the intimate relationship between story-teller and audience which existed in the age of the sagas and of Chaucer; and for an author like Dickens, who was peculiarly susceptible to the influence of his readers, this intimate relationship outweighed the inherent disadvantages of the system.[2]

This point deserves emphasis, for it involves something important in any consideration of a genuine popular tradition – an attitude to art in which the audience is seen neither purely as consumer (the commercial relationship) nor as a superior group of like-minded spirits (the highbrow relationship) but in some sense as collaborator. It involves of course a rejection of the extreme individualist attitude in which 'self-expression' as opposed to the organisation of social experience is seen as the object of art and in which the whole importance of communication is played down.

(iii) A further point which has undoubted relevance to the position of Dickens in a popular tradition is his relationship to existing forms of popular culture of various sorts. Too little detailed work has yet been done on this subject, but it is not difficult to sense a number of profitable lines of exploration. There is the absorption, for instance, of the fairy-tale imagination. Quilp and Fagin, to say nothing of Squeers or Krook, are ogres; Betsey Trotwood (not to mention Brownlow or John Jarndyce) is a fairy godmother; Miss Havisham partakes of the tradition (given of course a sharp twist) of the sleeping beauty. The novels are full of witches and wicked uncles and Cinderellas and babes in the wood.

It is perhaps worth making the point that such traditional elements in folk culture do not have to be turned into 'archetypes' in order to gain significance and interest. The prevalence of the wicked uncle is quite easily explained in historical terms rather than as the manifestation of some abstract psychological pattern. In a society in which inheritance and primogeniture are important it is naturally uncle, father's younger brother, who has a particular temptation to do the babes out of their rights. Ralph Nickleby needs no Jungian pedigree. The little lost boys of Dickens are an all too natural product of a situation in which the maternity death rate was still something like twenty per cent. Twentieth-century readers are happy to see Dickens's concern with the Little Em'lys and Nancys as evidence of some kind of unresolved personal obsession; in fact his very sensible interest in Miss Burdett Coutt's attempts to do something practical for prostitutes shows that he saw the problem as an objective, though difficult, social one. If many of the typical recurring figures and episodes in Dickens's novels partake of an older popular tradition it is because he moved, both in life and imagination, so deep in the actual experiences of the people, which do indeed recur and form definable and typical patterns, the expression of which in fantastic terms is the basis and function of folk art.

I am not trying, of course, to suggest that Dickens was himself without his psychological problems, eccentricities and worse. He was a complex and in some ways deeply unhappy man. But his acceptance of an active practical and public life, his thorough-going commitment not, in the twentieth-century intellectual's manner, to certain *ideas* about reality but to reality itself, to facing the world and changing it, counteracted to a profound extent his personal frustrations.[3] What I would insist is that the sensibility behind the novels is essentially sane, balanced and un-neurotic; the traditional description of Dickens as a comic novelist, though it has sometimes veiled his greatness, is right; the elements of violence and extremity in the books – which are immensely important – involve no more than an imaginative penetration into the realities of the life he knew. If they are not 'nice' books it is because he did not live in a nice world. I think the fairy-tale tradition greatly helped Dickens to encompass artistically (perhaps fantastically is a richer word) the life he was faced with and one of the marks of his triumphant absorption of this tradition is the fact that he has himself added so many characters and episodes to popular mythology. You do not have to read *Martin Chuzzlewit* to know the significance of Mrs Gamp.

Then there is his closeness to contemporary manifestations like the melodrama and the music-hall. Lady Dedlock is, in one sense, a stock figure of nineteenth-century melodrama. She is an ancestress of the heroine of *East Lynne* and of the smart bad women with a 'past' who move in and out of the plays of Pinero and Oscar Wilde. Dickens's own passion for the theatre and his love of acting were not mere sidelines or exhibitionism. It is hard to imagine any twentieth-century major novelist visiting the provinces for the sheer love of it in some ephemeral contemporary farce. And it is just as hard to imagine a modern author describing *in the same tone* George Rounce-well's visit to Astley's Music Hall in *Bleak House*:

He stops hard by Waterloo Bridge, and reads a playbill; decides to go to Astley's Theatre. Being there, is much delighted with the horses and the feats of strength; looks at the weapons with a critical eye; disapproves of the combats, as giving evidences of unskilful swordsmanship; but is touched home by the sentiments. In the last scene, when the Emperor of Tartary gets up into a cart and condescends to bless the united lovers by hovering over them with the Union Jack, his eyelashes are moistened with emotion.[4]

The point here is that the tone is neither ironical, patronising nor sentimental though there is a whiff of both the first and last, a whiff which it is easy to blow up into a gale, but which represents, it seems to me, an *acceptance*, neither an ignoring nor a sophisticated savouring, of George's experience. It has nothing in common for instance with Mr T. S. Eliot's self-conscious discovery of the significance of Marie Lloyd.

(iv) Associated with this point one should mention the interesting fact, brought only recently to general notice by the success of Mr Emlyn Williams's 'readings', that the best *milieu* for the appreciation of Dickens is reading *aloud*. The novelist's own performances, so phenomenally successful in his later years, have been used by recent critics to illustrate elements of his personal desperation (his need for money to maintain his extravagant way of life; the psychological need he is alleged to have tried to satisfy by the repeated reading of the blood-curdling murder of Nancy) rather than to illuminate the nature of the novels. Public readings of the sort Dickens himself went in for are of course a special case, involving careful pruning and choice of subject-matter, but they do usefully remind us that novels *can* be read aloud and indeed were. In fact this habit of reading aloud, which Victorian families went in for much more than their descendants of the television age, needs to be considered seriously by anyone trying to define the level of communication at which Dickens was aiming. It also underlines, incidentally, the dilemma involved in the need to avoid bringing a blush to the cheek of the young person. I would suggest that the texture of Dickens's prose is, whether through conscious effort or not, perfectly adapted for reading aloud. At this level his wit, which is apt, in the demanding silence of private reading, to seem a bit heavy-handed, the repetitiousness and underlining which the more sophisticated reader often finds tiresome, turn out to be just right. I think this is an observation worth making because it throws light on the rather basic question of the level of sensibility on which Dickens was working. Before we speak of the effects of a scene like the death of Jo in *Bleak House* as 'crude' – let alone 'sentimental' – we need to remind ourselves of two things: in the first place that, just as the texture of dramatic dialogue is bound to be, for the sake of immediate comprehension, less subtly suggestive than, say, the conversations in a Henry James novel, so will the semi-dramatic medium of a public, or fireside, reading impose on the author a style in which the effects are likely to be somewhat 'broad'. In the second place the very adjective 'public' has important implications: it involves communication, not just on a writer's own terms, but on the terms of the outside world. The tendency of modern Western criticism is to resent any such intrusion on the idealised communication between the individual artist and the perfectly attuned reader and to feel the need to explain away as a conscious 'concession' any broadening of effect which an admired artist goes in for. It is time we realised that Dicken's vulgarity – though no doubt it raises its problems – is on the whole an incomparable element of strength.

I have mentioned a number of points – the width of his reading public, his attitude to it, his closeness to what remained or had been adapted after the industrial revolution of an older folk culture, his implicit attitude to art as a public activity – all of which, I believe, inevitably lead us to the word 'popular' when we consider Dickens's art; but I do not think any or all of these considerations, however important, is the chief reason for calling Dickens a great popular writer. For that we must look at the actual nature and content of the novels themselves. By this I do not mean of course simply their subject-matter – the material *on which* Dickens worked – but the total complex that he created, which includes inextricably subject-matter (abstractable only in the sense that the fantastic world of a novel can and must *in the end* be related to the real world), organisation, rhetoric, and the writer's personal, controlling point of view. While insisting that art is not life I do not think that we should take at all a purist attitude to the question of subject-matter. I do not think it fortuitous that the greatest English writer of the mid-nineteenth century should have written about London, slums, prisons, railways, factories, dustheaps, the docks, workhouses, and law-courts, as well as about well-to-do mansions, financial speculators and comfortable middle-class homes. I do not doubt that the novelist who deals really well with a relatively small and even un-promising social area (like Jane Austen) is of more value in every important sense than one who (like Disraeli) deals trivially with a much larger one; but to extend this thought to a defence of limita-tion almost for its own sake is not, I think, helpful, and I do not doubt that the sheer breadth of Dickens's social interests and his passionate concern with what an historian must call the major issues of his day are one of the essential elements of his greatness.

His novels are fantasies, a series of images, complex but clear, difficult and at the same time simple, of significant areas of life in mid-nineteenth-century England, of human situations within that area which combine into a total situation or pattern or image which is the book. Sometimes the book is dominated by a single visualised image to which all else adheres – the image of the Law (made con-crete in the Court of Chancery) in *Bleak House*, of the prison in *Little Dorrit*, of the Thames in *Our Mutual Friend*. Sometimes the image is best described in more abstract terms – the title of *Great Expectations* or *Hard Times* is self-revelatory, bearing as much consideration as the visual pattern of a picture. The content of each book can be thought of only in terms of the total image or pattern which fuses all the component parts which go to make it up – subject-matter, style, the author's controlling point of view. The total image or pattern of a

Dickens novel is always concrete not theoretic, many-sided not flat, developing not static, historical not metaphysical. And the content is popular.

IV

It is necessary to indicate as clearly as possible the sense in which the words *people* and *popular* are used in these pages. It will not be easy to do so within a short space, without laying oneself open to the charge of a somewhat abstract dogmatism. Fortunately Dickens himself has given us a good starting-point. In a well-known passage which concludes a speech given at the Annual Inaugural Meeting of the Birmingham and Midland Institute on 27 September 1869, he announced that he would discharge his conscience of his political creed 'which is contained in two articles, and has no reference to any party or persons' and proceeded: 'My faith in the people governing, is, on the whole, infinitesimal; my faith in The People governed, is, on the whole, illimitable.'[5]

The remark caused, at the time, quite a rumpus, especially among Liberals who, assuming that by 'the people governing' Dickens was referring to Mr Gladstone's government, thought Dickens must have turned Tory. The novelist himself did his best to clarify his meaning by insisting on a small 'p' for the first people and a capital letter for the second and returned to the subject next time he was in Birmingham, adding for good measure an interesting quotation from Buckle's *History of Civilisation in England* which develops the theme that 'lawgivers are nearly always the obstructors of society rather than its helpers'.[6]

That contemporary politicians and political theorists should have misunderstood Dickens's statement, despite his clear denial that he was referring to any party or persons, is not surprising, for what he said by-passes in two sentences the essential assumptions on which the political thinking of bourgeois democracy is based. The bourgeois democrat, who believes that the British parliamentary system as developed since 1832 is the apogee of democracy, cannot accept that there is a fundamental and insuperable division in his society between those who govern and those who are governed. For, after all, he will argue, the governed *elect* those who govern them. If the People choose as their rulers people who rule against them, or those whose interests are different from their own, then either they are very foolish (and probably not fit to govern anyway) or else they will discover their error and in the course of time correct it. That they *cannot* correct it within the framework of political assumption imposed by the socio-economic system as at present operating is to the average bourgeois democrat literally unthinkable, for it involves passing beyond the very assumptions on which his own thinking is based. For the theory of bourgeois democracy of the type developed in Britain in the last hundred and fifty years is in fact dependent on the contention that there are within that society no *insuperable* class divisions, that is to say no basic divisions of interest which cannot, within the existing social order, be modified to the point of elimination. To put it another way, the bourgeois democrat cannot (without ceasing to be a bourgeois democrat) accept the proposition that the ruling class in his society, by virtue of its ownership of the productive forces and its control of the state and propaganda apparatus of society, is able to rule against the interests of the overwhelming majority of the People, despite the democratic rights the people have won.

The force of Dickens's statement of his political creed lies precisely in the recognition implicit in it of two separate and conflicting forces: the people governing and the People governed. That he was quite well aware, on a pretty deep level of political understanding, of what he was saying and doing is made clear by a letter he wrote to James Fields, a few days after his second appearance at Birmingham in January 1870:

I hope you may have met with the little touch of Radicalism I gave them at Birmingham in the words of Buckle? With pride I observe that it makes the regular political traders, of all sorts, perfectly mad. Sich was my intentions, as a grateful acknowledgement of having been misrepresented.[7]

Now the recognition of a fundamental division between People and rulers does not necessarily imply an analysis of the class basis of this division of the sort that Marx and Engels, contemporary citizens of Dickens's England, developed. Dickens was not a systematic political thinker. The very speech which ended with his profession of Radical faith reveals an extraordinary mixture of paternalism, radicalism, belief in self-help, religious idealism, anti-clericalism and straightforward practical business-sense. The ambiguous attitudes towards philanthropy, embedded so deep in *Bleak House*, and

expressed so interestingly in the complexities of his actual relationship with Miss Burdett Coutts, exemplify the sort of dilemma
which was never resolved in his life. One would not wish to give the
impression that Dickens was an unconscious Marxist or even a pre-
Marxian socialist. He was, as he himself recognised, a Radical, with
a good deal of the ambiguity that word implies in the mid-nineteenth century. But we are less interested in Dickens as a political
thinker than in Dickens as a novelist. It is the emotional force and
the imaginative imagery behind his confession of political faith
rather than its abstract significance or its precise connection with
Buckle's (or Carlyle's) philosophy that is important. And the test of
Dickens's status as a popular writer lies not in his opinions but in his
novels. If one stresses, then, this particular political statement it is
because it does so remarkably draw together a number of threads,
impressions and emphases which, especially in the later novels,
become more and more dominant.

Dickens, then, sees the People not as a vague or all-inclusive term
– an indiscriminate 'everybody' – but as a specific force in contradistinction to those who rule. And he sees them hopefully, confidently. That is all. But it is enough, both for his purpose as a
creative writer and for a general clarification of the use of the word
'popular'. That capital letter on which he set so much store is indeed
of great significance. For what it indicates is a recognition of the
People not simply as a passive mass but as an active force. This is
fundamental. The People, in a society in which the essential property and power is in the hands of a small exploiting class, are those
who are exploited as opposed to those who exploit them. There is, of
course, no absolute merit in being exploited; but there is a specific
de-merit in being an exploiter, because the maintenance of the exploitation by which you live is bound, whatever your personal
character or motives or auxiliary good deeds, to lead you to actions
and attitudes and ideas which hold back the necessary development
of human beings as a whole. In a class society like modern Britain
the virtue of the People is that, unlike the ruling class, they are
capable of solving constructively the fundamental problems with
which society as a whole is faced and in doing so are able to raise
themselves and the whole society to a new level of achievement and
potentiality, to a new freedom. This advance is neither automatic
nor inevitable, except in the general sense that history shows that up
till now human beings as a whole have in fact (with whatever dif-

ficulties, setbacks and errors) tended to choose to solve their essential problems and to develop rather than to deteriorate. The struggle for power in modern British society is to be seen therefore not just as a struggle between two main and morally equal class groupings, of which the chief virtue of the larger is that it comprises more numbers than the smaller, but as a struggle between people and anti-people. The concept of the People, in fact, is inextricably bound up with questions of value and questions of value can be discussed only in relation to the People. Since there are no values but human values (the whole concept of what is valuable meaning what is good for human beings) it is impossible to judge or evaluate any manifestation of human culture, whether it is *Bleak House* or the latest television serial, except in terms of its part in, and contribution to, human development. To state this general principle is not, of course, to imply that one has done more than to state a general principle. The problems of its application are extremely complex and certainly defy dogmatic treatment. But the principle is nevertheless true and it is for this reason that the question of Dickens's attitude to the People is so closely associated with the value of his novels.

'Popular' does not – if we are to use the word thoughtfully – mean simply pertaining to the people in a passive sense. On the contrary, to use the word in such a sense is to debase it, and, in doing so, further debase the people. To refer to the *Daily Mirror* as a 'popular' paper or a trashy television serial as 'popular' culture is a betrayal not only of words but of human dignity itself, for it implies that the worst is good enough for the People. Of course millions of men and women read the *Daily Mirror* and of course the act of buying it is, strictly speaking, voluntary. So no doubt was the act of the Indian women who used to commit suicide when their husbands died and of tens of thousands of young Germans who enlisted in the Nazi armies. If the pressures are strong enough people can be conditioned to take almost any action willingly. Human progress consists in the slow and often painful overcoming of those pressures and attitudes which, however widely accepted and even gloried in for a time, in fact prevent human beings from enlarging their realm of freedom. Popular culture, if the phrase is not to become a mockery, is the culture which helps and strengthens the people, increases their self-confidence and clarifies their problems and potentialities.

A popular tradition in literature implies, then, a literature which looks at life from the point of view of the People seen not passively but actively. Such a literature will not, of course, except at its peril, gloss over the weaknesses, the corruptions, the unpleasantness or the degradation of the People: it will not, except at its peril, see life as it *wants* to see it. If its spectacles are rosetinted it must be with the reflection of Blake's rose, not the rose on the chocolate box. Blake's or Dickens's London is not the less terrible for being seen from the point of view of the People, nor is Hardy's Oxford or Sholokhov's Ukraine. The essential characteristic of a popular tradition is not that it should be optimistic but that it should be true: and because it is true it will in fact be optimistic. But these large and generous words like true and optimistic are not as a rule the best to use in discussion and analysis. More modest ones serve us, on the whole, best. To use as a touchstone for the products of a popular tradition the question: is it true? may be in practice less helpful and have less to do with truth than the question: does it serve the People? And though this touchstone, too, like any other, can be abused, its abuses are at least more discussable and therefore more corrigible than the sort of inhumanity which defends itself in terms of high abstractions and absolute values.

V

I should like to demonstrate from *Bleak House* what I mean when I suggest that it was the popular point of view from which Dickens's novels were written that determined their essential nature and significance as works of art. I shall have time only to mention three points but perhaps they will serve to show what I am trying to get at.

(i) The central importance of the Law in Bleak House *and Dickens's point of view in relation to it.*
At the heart of *Bleak House* is the Court of Chancery. It is, most obviously, at the centre of the plot of the novel, for it is the case of Jarndyce and Jarndyce that links the various essential characters and groupings of the book and brings them into contact. But it is also the dominating image of the book, the very core of its pattern, sensuous and intellectual. It is the heart of the geography of the novel in the sort of way that London is at the centre of modern industrial England, and the Court of Chancery is embedded in London. It is presented with complete concreteness as a man-made institution physically and economically bound up with the development of a

particular society, and the insinuating fog, so famously and graphically called up in the opening paragraphs of the book, creeps deep into the very texture of the novel, not merely colouring it but extending its dimensions. For the fog in *Bleak House*, like that of T. S. Eliot's *Prufrock* and indeed a real London fog, has a many-sided physical presence, cruelly pinching the toes and fingers of the shivering little 'prentice boy; and though, through the image of the megalosaurus, it recalls a past of primitive mud, barbarism and uncontrol, it combines this vision with the actual soot-flakes of the coal age so that the fog becomes associated at once with early Victorian London and with how much and how little man has made of man.

Everything in *Bleak House* is linked together by the Law. It is the Law that has ruined Miss Flite and Gridley and will ruin Richard. Tom-All-Alone's, the foul slum which spews up Jo, is 'in Chancery of course'. Lady Dedlock's sin and Esther's stigma is to have offended the Law at a point in which legal and social sanctions come together, for Esther is *illegitimate*. The Law brings almost nothing but misery and it is revealed as being inextricably bound up with the British state, and that state is shown (though Dickens himself would not have used the phrase) as an organ of class domination. To indicate how far Dickens's view of the state had developed by 1852 it is only necessary to compare *Oliver Twist* with *Bleak House*. While *Oliver Twist* is a novel which attacks certain abuses within bourgeois society, *Bleak House* strikes at the very foundations of that society.

The Law then in *Bleak House* is revealed as a vital and integral part of the social fabric as a whole. It is continuously associated in extremely complex but entirely concrete ways with money and power. The poor, like Jo, are at its mercy because they are poor; and it is the power of money that gives Mr Tulkinghorn his hold, via the Smallweeds, over an upright man like George Rouncewell. The Law is, in fact, a business: Mr Vholes is the extreme instance but by no means an isolated one. And Dickens makes his general point when he writes: 'The one great principle of the English Law is to make business for itself. There is no other principle distinctly, certainly and consistently maintained through all its narrow turnings. Viewed by this light it becomes a coherent scheme, and not the monstrous maze the laity are apt to think it.'[8] The Law is administered by people who are at best, like Conversation Kenge and Guppy, absurdly, at worst, like Tulkinghorn and Vholes, wickedly inhuman. Mr Tulkinghorn may not have a very coherent personal motive

for his vendetta against Lady Dedlock but the point is that he
is the agent of an impersonal system more potent and more sinister
in its motivation than any expression of personal spite or hatred.
Lady Dedlock implies this when she describes him to Esther as
'mechanically faithful without attachment, and very jealous of the
profit, privilege and reputation of being master of the mysteries of
great houses'.[9] It is this very impersonality that makes Mr Tulkinghorn so formidable. It is not his personal wickedness that Lady
Dedlock is up against any more than it is the personal kindliness of
the Lord Chancellor that determines the workings of the Court of
Chancery. This sense of the Law as a force in itself, an independent
business, self-perpetuating within its own closed circles of privilege
and procedure, is basic to the meaning of *Bleak House*.

And yet it is also basic that the Law is not in the last analysis independent. It has, like every bureaucracy, its inner circular logic, an
almost infinitely frustrating image which breaks the spirit of those
who get trapped in it; yet this apparent self-sufficiency is in the end
illusory. Mr Tulkinghorn's power is great but it is dependent on the
great houses which employ him. He is Sir Leicester Dedlock's man.
That is why the old baronet is so furious when he is killed. In *Bleak
House* it is Sir Leicester, despite his personal anachronistic honour-
ability, who is shown as the fountain-head of the Law. The Law is
Sir Leicester's Law, the law of the ruling class. To present it in this
way was possible to Dickens only because his own artistic point of
view was diametrically opposed to Sir Leicester's. Because he saw
British society from the point of view of the People, *Bleak House* is
conceived and constructed in the way it is.

(ii) The presentation of character in Bleak House
The characters in *Bleak House* are conceived and presented in relation
to the central pattern of the book – the revelation of the working of
the Law. Dickens habitually gives his characters *general* characteristics, associated with their work, their social position, the sort of lives
they lead, before he establishes their more individual features or
endows them with their individual, idiosyncratic note or rhetoric.
Notice the first presentation of Lady Dedlock: '. . . there is this
remarkable circumstance to be noted in everything associated with
my lady Dedlock as one of a class – as one of the leaders and representatives of her little world; she supposes herself to be an inscrutable being, quite out of the reach and ken of ordinary mortals.

. . .'[10] There is, of course, no contradiction between this general presentation of a character as a type and his presentation as a unique and even eccentric individual. Those readers who think that such a phrase as 'my lady Dedlock as one of a class' denotes in the author a lack of respect for the individual peculiarity of a character are in fact themselves victims of the illusion from which Lady Dedlock suffers. She thinks she is inscrutable but in fact it is she who is most deceived.

It is usual to talk of Dickens's novels as though the characters, so rich and individual as they are, were simply invented casually, if prodigally, with no purpose beyond the expression of their own idiosyncratic vitality. But in fact in *Bleak House* there is scarcely a single character who does not contribute to the central pattern of the book. One or two, like Mr and Mrs Bayham Badger, with whom Richard lodges, do seem to be thrown in gratis for sheer good measure, but they are the exceptions. Take for instance a figure like Mrs Pardiggle, the lady who takes Esther and Ada to the brickworkers. At first it might seem that her sole functions in the novel are to provide a necessary link in the plot and, incidentally, an amusing extra figure. But in fact Mrs Pardiggle is an essential specimen in the exhibition Dickens has prepared. She, the Puseyite philanthropist, not only contrasts with and sets off the significance of Mrs Jellyby but contributes to the consideration of the whole question of philanthropy which is one of the main themes of the book. John Jarndyce's tolerance of the ghastly Mrs Pardiggle becomes a comment on his own philanthropy and quality of feeling, just as his toleration of Skimpole, which at first seems an amiable generosity, in fact nullifies his efforts to help Jo and redeem his connection with Tom-All-Alone's. And, at the same time, Mrs Pardiggle's religious affiliations do more than add a side to her personal character; they contribute to the working-out of the connection between religious bigotry and the working of an unjust Law which is a central theme of the novel. It is the religious fanaticism of Lady Dedlock's sister which, allied to the legal stigma of illegitimacy, sets in motion the story of Esther. Mr Chadband (connected by marriage with Esther's aunt and through Mrs Snagsby with the world of the Law) contributes also to this important theme.

What I would wish to emphasise here, besides hoping to stress the tightness and consistency of the organisation of *Bleak House*, is that the attitude which such a treatment of character involves is something quite outside the province of a bourgeois sensibility. The superb *individuality* of Dickens's creations should not lead us to imagine that his approach to them is an *individualist* one. On the contrary it is because he sees the workings of capitalism as the determining and significant factor in the lives and personalities of his individual characters that he is able to allow them so much freedom of development. It is because a figure like old Beau Turveydrop is so firmly conceived as a *social* phenomenon, an anachronism surviving from the Regency period, that his idiosyncrasy is so rich. It is because the horrible Smallweeds are indeed seen as part of a system, parasites of the oppressive Law, that they can be at the same time repulsive and funny, degraded human beings yet still human. I think this is very important. Because Dickens's artistic point of view is truly popular it is able to be truly inclusive. Even the most degenerate characters in *Bleak House* preserve a quality which makes the reader not ashamed to laugh. It is not quite a case of Baudelaire's '*hypocrite lecteur, mon semblable, mon frère*' (a sentiment which despite its apparent sense of equality and humility has in fact still a suspect residue of individualism); but somehow in a Dickens novel we are all, including the reader, equals. Because there is no exclusion there is no contempt and no superiority. We look degradation in the face and see humanity there. So that we can judge and enjoy at the same time. Our partisanship enlarges our comprehension and our inclusive sympathy strengthens our partisanship. To understand all is to pass beyond limiting class judgements, but it is not to pardon all. This is the sort of thing I mean when I stress the effects of Dickens's popular point of view.

(iii) Imagery

One of the key scenes and images in *Bleak House* is the famous 'spontaneous combustion' episode in which Krook, the horrible old 'Lord Chancellor', is found dead.

It is an astonishing scene, of a power and intensity which anyone reading *about* it, as opposed to reading it in context, must find hard to imagine. Naturalistically, of course, the idea of the old man literally burning himself out is absurd and it was foolish of Dickens to have attempted a defence of it in such terms. But in terms other than the purely naturalistic the conception of the scene is completely right. It 'works' as infallibly as Gloucester's fall from the cliffs or

Don Giovanni's confrontation by the *commendatore*. It is, in the first
place, most carefully prepared for: the final sentence of the first
chapter of the novel with its image of Chancery burnt away in a
great funeral pyre opens up the idea. Then the presentation of Krook
as the 'Lord Chancellor' is done with a wealth of detail of the most
convincing sort. The oppressiveness, physical as well as psychological, of that ghastly house with its limitless junk, its sacks of human
hair, its creaking staircase and the wicked old cat, is established
with tremendous realistic as well as imaginative force. There is a
wonderful moment when Jarndyce notices that Krook is trying with
great difficulty to teach himself to read and write and suggests that
it might be easier for him to be taught by someone else. 'Ay, but
they might teach me wrong!'[11] is the old man's immediate reply. In
that second the almost schizophrenic horror of the *Bleak House* world
is glimpsed. At the most obvious level Krook's reply is wonderfully
funny, off-centre, full of eccentric 'character': but beneath the
laughter there opens up an abyss of alienation which is far more than
eccentric. The horror is not that Krook's distrust should have
reached such a point but that he is, in an awful sense, quite right. In
the world of Chancery in which every human being fights every
other with any weapon of deceit and cunning he can muster, there
is no security, no possibility of common trust. Language itself becomes a mode of deception and prevarication; the lawyer is there to
catch you out. It is only those like John Jarndyce who withdraws
from the whole set-up, or Mrs Bagnet, who lives in a different
world, who can risk the human emotions of trust and generosity.
The rest are like Mr Guppy whose language is indeed self-
expression.

It is entirely right that it should be Mr Guppy who discovers
what has happened to Krook. The pages leading up to the discovery
are technically superb in their building up horror and suspense. A
detailed analysis of them would show both the depth and the nature
of Dickens's debt to Shakespeare. *Macbeth* is obviously the source of
much of the imagery and treatment, especially the scenes around
Duncan's murder and its discovery. But if Dickens has learned from
Shakespeare, he has learned well, transforming as well as using, so
that there is nothing derivative in the limiting sense about the
scene. Indeed the climax of it is so uncompromisingly Dickensian
and raises so sharply so many of the issues which divide those who

admire and those who dislike Dickens that one cannot well avoid a
rather long quotation.

They advance slowly, looking at all these things. The cat remains where
they found her, still snarling at the something on the ground before the fire
and between the two chairs. What is it? Hold up the light.

Here is a small burnt patch of flooring; here is the tinder from a little
bundle of burnt paper, but not so light as usual, seeming to be steeped in
something; and here is – is it the cinder of a small charred and broken log
of wood sprinkled with white ashes, or is it coal? Oh, horror, he is here!
and this, from which we run away, striking out the light and overturning
one another into the street, is all that represents him.

Help, help, help! come into this house for Heaven's sake!

Plenty will come in, but none can help. The Lord Chancellor of that
Court, true to his title in his last act, has died the death of all Lord Chan-
cellors in all Courts, and of all authorities in all places under all names
soever, where false pretences are made, and where injustice is done. Call
the death by any name Your Highness will, attribute it to whom you will,
or say it might have been prevented how you will, it is the same death
eternally – inborn, inbred, engendered in the corrupted humours of the
vicious body itself, and that only – Spontaneous Combustion, and none
other of all the deaths that can be died.[12]

The spontaneous combustion image, examined in the cold light
of day, can be seen to express very completely the peculiar quality of
the view of British society which is embodied in *Bleak House*. It has
three essential features. In the first place it is an image dependent on
natural processes as opposed to metaphysical concepts. The process
that finishes Krook may not be scientifically accurate but it is nevertheless conceived in scientific, not mystical, terms. The corruption
that destroys him is presented not as some quality of being but is
specifically associated with dirt, gin, grease and old paper; with rags
and bottles; with sordid acquisitiveness.

In the second place the spontaneous combustion image is a revolutionary image, as opposed to a reformist one. No one could cure
Krook; he could not have been saved by charity or even by social
services. The whole implication is that processes are involved which
can culminate only in explosion and that such explosions are not
exceptional and unnatural but the inevitable consequences of the
processes themselves.

Thirdly, the image emphasises spontaneity as opposed to planned
action. No specific act has caused the explosion. No match has been

struck, no chain of power prepared; indeed no outside agent is involved.

It does not take much perspicacity to see the general significance of all this. The death of Krook, the Lord Chancellor, represents in *Bleak House* the extreme possibility, the ultimate culmination of the processes at work at the very core of the novel. It is in this sense absolutely central to the novel's meaning and nothing that happens afterwards does in fact cancel or even modify the significance of the episode. It is the high point of what is best described as the revolutionary feeling of the book and this quality is not peripheral to *Bleak House* but at the very heart of its power and profundity.

Yet it is a revolutionary feeling of a curious kind, for, though *Bleak House* is in this deep undeniable sense a revolutionary novel, there are no revolutionaries in it. Obviously this contradiction corresponds to the actual contradiction in Dickens's own attitude to capitalism. He hated it and wanted to see it destroyed but had very little idea as to how this could be done. And so in *Bleak House*, having expressed half way through the book with unforgettable power the revolutionary implications of his vision, he is faced with the problem of what to do with a real Lord Chancellor whose habits of life make spontaneous combustion less imaginatively plausible than in the case of old Krook.

The second half of *Bleak House* is by no means a failure, but it undoubtedly lacks something of the controlled intensity and relaxed artistry of the earlier reaches of the book. The murder of Tulkinghorn, brilliantly effective as it is on the theatrical level, is, compared with the death of Krook, a bit of a fraud; for whereas there is, despite the naturalistic implausibility of the means, a deep artistic inevitability in Krook's death, the manner of Tulkinghorn's removal is arbitrary, dictated only by the needs of the plot. And because there is no adequate motivation for Mademoiselle Hortense's action the affair is reduced to a 'mystery' in the detective-story sense and Inspector Bucket takes over. And though in one sense the Inspector is a good deal more plausible as *deus ex machina* than the process of spontaneous combustion, in a more important sense he is a good deal less adequate.

The world of *Bleak House* does not, like Krook himself, go up in smoke. The case of Jarndyce and Jarndyce, it is true, burns itself out and the fiasco of it destroys Richard. And the case of Lady Dedlock, too, smoulders relentlessly on to the inevitable, tragic flare-up, destroying not only the lady herself but Sir Leicester and all he stands for. And around these central tragedies the stage is littered with subsidiary corpses, some dead indeed like Jo and Gnadley, some metaphorically dead like Beau Turveydrop and the Chadbands and Harold Skimpole who are destroyed within the book as inexorably as Miss Flite is deprived of her wits. Each of these characters becomes a sort of living horror: when Mrs Pardiggle walks into a room humanity is squeezed out of it; the ancient Smallweeds live on, but the degradation they embody is more appalling than any death.

The imagery and significance of the spontaneous combustion episode embody both the strength and the limitations of Dickens's sensibility and correspond to the strengths and weaknesses of the popular forces in 1852.

VI

I have placed a good deal of emphasis on the Birmingham speech in which Dickens defined his attitude to the people because it seems to me to give an important clue to his significance as an artist. It ties up, so to speak, the gathering impressions made by his later novels and illuminates the essential unity between his artistic and his personal point of view. It shows that, for example, the linking of utilitarianism with the interests of the capitalist class, of Gradgrind with Bounderby (an insight far less obvious in the 1850s, when the Benthamite tradition of philosophic radicalism still wore progressive colours, than it is today), was no casual hunch; that the devastating exposure of the Law as an institution of class domination in *Bleak House* was what Dickens in every sense *meant*; it shows that the revelation of the character of acquisitiveness in *Great Expectations* and of the whole force and horror of Podsnappery in *Our Mutual Friend* were indeed no side-issues but central artistic insights. As I hope I have demonstrated from an analysis of *Bleak House*, it is from his popular point of view that the actual overwhelming artistic energy of the books springs.

Perhaps the most remarkable of the many extraordinary things about *Bleak House* is that it should have been begun in 1851, the year of the Great Exhibition, that symbol of expanding capitalism and of the economic boom which succeeded the miseries of the forties. It is not astonishing that the appalling conditions of the thirties and forties and the strength of the great popular Chartist movement should have produced in this period not only novels like *Oliver Twist* but *Sybil* and *Mary Barton* and *Alton Locke*. What is more remarkable is that *Bleak House* should go on from where *Oliver Twist* left off and that in the fifties and sixties the tone of Dickens's novels becomes ever more uncompromising. It is interesting that whereas the socialist Charles Kingsley was much impressed by the Great Exhibition in the Crystal Palace, Dickens loathed it. And he loathed it, fundamentally, because he hated nineteenth-century capitalism even more when it was working successfully than when it was working badly.

This is a point which repays the deepest consideration, for it reveals the nature of Dickens's moral and artistic sensibility in contrast to that of almost all his contemporaries among the writers. He was not less outraged than a Kingsley or a Mrs Gaskell by the conditions of life of the poor, not less touched in ways which it is no shame to call humanitarian; but in his humanitarianism there was less tinge of superiority, less tendency to look on the people as 'less fortunate than ourselves' with the reservations such a phrase applies. The condition of the poor aroused in Dickens not just pity, but indignation, and his indignation was based on something more solid than a general sense that such things must not be. Dickens was not uttering an empty phrase when he talked about his illimitable confidence in the People: he was expressing the very quality of mind that made it possible for him to be not just a good but a supreme writer.

It is not by chance that in the very speech at Birmingham in which he defined his attitude to the people he had already had occasion to express his views on 'materialism'. What had, apparently, particularly riled him was a sermon, delivered only a few days previously, by Dr Francis Close, Dean of Carlisle, who had delivered himself of the sentiment that 'There is no question that there is in the present day an evil spirit of the "bottomless pit" rising up among us, . . . and he was bound to say he laid a large portion of it at the door of science.' Dickens took up the point with splendid gusto:

I cannot forbear from offering a remark which is much upon my mind. It is commonly assumed – much too commonly – that this age is a material age, and that a material age is an irreligious age. I have been pained lately to see this assumption repeated in certain influential quarters for which I have a high respect, and desire to have a higher. I am afraid that by dint of

constantly being reiterated and reiterated without protest, this assumption
– which I take leave altogether to deny – may be accepted by the more un-
thinking part of the public as unquestionably true; just as certain cari-
caturists and painters professedly making a portrait of some public man,
which was not in the least like him, to begin with, have gone on repeating
it and repeating it, until the public came to believe that it must be exactly
like him, simply because it was *like itself*, and really have at last, in the
fullness of time, grown almost to resent upon him their tardy discovery
that he was not *like* it. I confess, standing here in this responsible situation,
that I do not understand this much-used and much-abused phrase a
'material age'. I cannot comprehend – if anyone can; which I very much
doubt – its logical signification. For instance, has electricity become more
material in the mind of any sane, or moderately insane, man, woman or
child, because of the discovery that in the good providence of God it was
made available for the service and use of man to an immeasurably greater
extent than for his destruction? Do I make a more material journey to the
bedside of my dying parents or my dying child, when I travel there at the
rate of sixty miles an hour, than when I travel thither at the rate of six?
Rather, in the swift case, does not my agonized heart become overfraught
with gratitude to that Supreme Beneficence from whom alone can have
proceeded the wonderful means of shortening my suspense? . . . When did
this so called material age begin? With the invention of the art of printing?
Surely it has been a long time about; and which is the more material object,
the farthing tallow candle that will not give me light, or that flame of gas
that will?[13]

I have quoted the speech at length, not only because it is in some
of its incidental aspects so splendidly Dickensian, but because it reminds us that Dickens, unlike so many of his contemporaries and
successors, was not an intellectual Luddite. And this, as C. P. Snow
has recently emphasised, is something significant. An important
aspect of the rise of a 'highbrow' as opposed to a popular culture in
the last hundred years has been the sharp division among intellectuals between a scientific and a literary culture. Literary intellectuals
have, by and large, been not only ignorant of science but have
adopted an attitude of self-conscious superiority to it. This attitude
is, I feel certain, due less to the increasing complexity and special-
isation involved in modern scientific knowledge (though obviously
this is a real problem), than to what is at bottom a fear of losing a
privileged position. The modern literary intellectual is afraid of
science for the same reasons that he is afraid of the people: both
threaten, though in different ways, his security as a member of an
élite. The nature of the sensibility developed by the literary intelligentsia of the western world during the last hundred and fifty years,
their ideas about freedom, their most sacred and most deeply in-

grained modes of feeling, the assumptions of value so deeply assumed that a questioning of them is too agonizing to be even seriously considered: all this is a consequence of a fundamental division between People and ruling class. The significance of the passage from Dickens I have just quoted is that in it he boisterously and yet carefully avoids so many pitfalls. Science he sees not as a danger but as a blessing: it is its potentialities 'for the service and use of man' that attract him, and his illustrations have all the homely practical effectiveness of a man used to thinking not in terms of abstraction but in those of the real world in which theory and practice have to be united.

Even more significant is Dickens's attitude to the word 'material' and his refusal to be drawn into a way of thinking which sees 'material' and 'spiritual' as opposites. This is not, it must be stressed, a mere matter of verbal juggling. It is, as far as the development of a unified popular culture is concerned, an absolutely essential issue. For idealism, the refusal to recognise that spiritual values have a material basis, is in its various forms the mental sustenance of class division. The modern intellectual's posing of spiritual values in some sort of opposition to material values often proceeds (as far as his subjective development is concerned) from a humane and healthy reaction against the actual operation of capitalist society in which spiritual and human decencies are indeed subordinated to mercenary considerations and the perpetuation of class domination; but the posing is nevertheless fatal, for by removing spiritual values or indeed 'thought' of any kind into some kind of 'special' realm so that they become the property of the 'enlightened', their actual application in practice is made more difficult. For it is only when intellectuals have a *respect* for material reality that they are able to help change anything, material or spiritual.

Dickens had such respect for material reality. And because he had it he was able to develop a sensibility that was in so deep a sense popular. I am not suggesting that Dickens's sensibility was completely unified, that there were no areas of weakness, no loose ends or unresolved conflicts in his make-up. But I am suggesting that – perfection excluded – he had an astonishingly unified sensibility – an ability to face, absorb and cope with a remarkably wide area of reality, certainly a good deal wider than that of any succeeding British writer. And I am not posing width here against depth. His art is deep because it is broad and tough and balanced.

He was able to achieve this unified sensibility because he looked at life from the point of view not of the ruling class or of some sort of intellectual *élite*, but from that of the people. One of the sources of his artistic greatness is his capacity to look degradation in the face and see humanity there. This was possible because he looked not from above but from the level. It is easier for an artist in class society to share the People's aspirations in a general, somewhat abstract, way than for him to share their way of looking at life. Dickens was not without his complacencies, but they did not include the basic complacency of evolving an outlook 'better' than the People's or of imagining – as even the most sincere and tormented of middle-class reformers imagine – that the world will be changed by the middle class. The very vulgarity of him, his enjoyment of the material pleasures, the lack of what the petty-bourgeois sensibility calls 'good taste': all this is not a limitation but a colossal strength, a product of an inclusiveness of sympathy which is the opposite of insensitivity.

Looked at in artistic terms this meant that his point of view and hence his artist's poise, his capacity to release and control and organise artistic energy was not only inclusive but at once sufficiently firm and sufficiently flexible to permit of continuous growth and development. When one calls him a popular writer what is primarily involved is not his opinions or his success but the quality of his sensibility.

I have tried, in my analysis of *Bleak House*, to show in concrete terms how this quality of sensibility asserts itself in art. If one were to attempt to summarise in a more general sense the principal features of that sensibility one would have to say that it was:

(i) realistic (in the sense that the fantasy-world which the artist creates bears a humanly helpful relation to the real world, i.e. makes us see the real world more realistically when we look at it again and thereby helps us to cope with the real world),

(ii) critical (as opposed to a view which accepts and records passively. The popular novelist, just because his point of view is popular, sees art actively as a challenge. He is not afraid of being accused of propaganda, for he knows that all writing has an effect and he knows the sort of effect – a strengthening of the people – he wants to make),

(iii) non-abstract (as compared with the work of the 'Condition-of-England' novelists or of the Godwinian Radicals who were in certain respects Dickens's ancestors),

(iv) non-metaphysical (in the sense that the characters are not seen as metaphysical entities but as interdependent social creatures, historically placed, and that there is no tendency towards an underlying metaphysical pattern or interpretation),

(v) inclusive (seeing society from below rather than from above and thus avoiding the exclusiveness of the ruling-class or *élite* sensibility),

(vi) optimistic (basically confident of the capacity of men and women to make their world better),

(vii) historically and linguistically based in existing manifestations of popular culture. Necessarily therefore national (as opposed to cosmopolitan) and linked with the folk-imagination of the peasantry under feudalism.

Dickens is a supreme realist artist. To describe him as a critical realist rightly emphasises his critical relationship to the bourgeois society he inhabits; to insist on his place in a popular tradition elucidates the nature and quality of his critical realism.

Notes

1 A good example of the sort of thing I mean are some recent interpretations of *Great Expectations* by Dorothy Van Ghent (in *The English Novel, Form and Function*) and G. R. Stange (*College English*, Vol. XVI, October 1954), admirably commented on by Julian Moynahan in *Essays in Criticism*, Vol. X, No. 1, January 1960.

2 John Butt and Kathleen Tillotson, *Dickens at Work* (1957), p. 16.

3 Dickens's capacity to turn to objective use material, often very deeply felt, from his own life is most impressive. *David Copperfield*, the most autobiographical of the novels, is one of the most balanced, certainly the tenderest. An episode like the discovery of Mary Beadnell, about whom he had nursed deeply romantic illusions, is used in *Little Dorrit* with remarkable poise and control.

4 Ch. XXI.

5 *The Speeches of Charles Dickens* (ed. K. J. Fielding, Clarendon Press, 1960), p. 407.

6 *Ibid.*, p. 411.

7 *The Letters of Charles Dickens* (1893), p. 735.

8 *Bleak House*, Ch. XXXIX.

9 *Ibid.*, Ch. XXXVI.

10 *Ibid.*, Ch. II.

11 *Ibid.*, Ch. XIV.

12 *Ibid.*, Ch. XXXII.

13 *The Speeches of Charles Dickens*, pp. 403–4.

Our Mutual Friend

Most people today who take Dickens seriously as a writer would probably agree with what was, in 1937, the minority view expressed by T. A. Jackson when he wrote, referring to the later novels:

> Dickens sought, by means of the incident-plot of his novels, to achieve a moral-plot indicative of and symbolizing a politico-ethical criticism of the social-life of his time.[7]

There may be, perhaps, from the metaphysicians and myth-critics a certain jibbing at 'politico-ethical' and even 'social', but even from such quarters there will be agreement that Dickens's plots are 'more than' plots and that the later novels, especially, embody a more complex and profound level of organisation and significance than most early literary criticism of Dickens, however 'enthusiastic, recognised.

This is not to suggest that there is anything abstract or even allegorical about the conception of a novel like *Our Mutual Friend*. About *Hard Times* and even *Great Expectations* there is indeed a certain recognisable background of abstract thinking which emerges, interestingly, in their very titles; but by and large the images around and through which Dickens worked are not conceived in at all an abstract way. What he mostly thought about was, indeed, his plots and characters; but to get these plots and characters 'right', to satisfy the essential, not necessarily fully formulated, end he was after, required, as he went on, their more and more careful subordination to a whole, and in that whole a moral view and purpose is predominant.

More critical notice has been taken of the grammar of the title of *Our Mutual Friend* than of its significance. This is not altogether surprising, for a consideration of Dickens's titles is not always rewarding. It is hard to make much of *Martin Chuzzlewit* as a title and *Little Dorrit* is a good deal less interesting than its rejected alternative *Nobody's Fault*. Yet it is perhaps significant that in this big, ambitious, eminently serious novel Dickens should have underlined in his title the role of John Harmon. It is of course obvious that in the incident-plot (hereinafter referred to simply as plot) John Harmon, alias Handford, alias Rokesmith, is the kingpin. It is his inheritance and his supposed murder that sets the whole thing going; he is indeed the Beginning of the story, 'the man from nowhere'. But, without overdoing Harmon/Rokesmith's significance (he doesn't really bear too much loading with that commodity) I think it is worth noticing that his part in the moral-plot (hereinafter the pattern) is also important. For his function within the novel is to link not only diverse characters but diverse areas. Not least important is the actual topographical link he supplies, for it is he who brings the mounds or dust-heaps into relation with the river and this, as we shall see, is fundamental to the imagery of *Our Mutual Friend*. But there is another respect, thematic rather than concrete, in which Harmon/Rokesmith forms a vital link. He connects the area of wealth with the area of poverty. And this is fundamental to the conception of the novel. T. A. Jackson puts it quite correctly: 'Class-contrast and class-antagonism, class-hatred and class-contempt are woven into the innermost texture of *Our Mutual Friend*.'[2]

The idea of mutuality as involving more than the isolable *personal* relationships of individual characters is, of course, very deep in Dickens. There is a deeply-felt moment in *Bleak House*, more important in the pattern of that book than is generally recognised, when Esther Summerson tries to sum up her feelings and Ada's about their first ghastly visit, with Mrs Pardiggle, to the brickmakers' cottage:

We both felt painfully sensible that between us and these people there was an iron barrier, which could not be removed by our new friend (Mrs Pardiggle). By whom, or how, it could be removed we did not know; but we knew that. (Ch. 8).

All Dickens's novels might be described on one level as explorations into the human effects of this iron barrier and the ways of removing it, and *Our Mutual Friend* is perhaps the most profound and consistent of these explorations. What underlies Mr Boffin's description

of Harmon/Rokesmith as 'our mutual friend' (he is talking to Mrs
Wilfer) is that character's part in bridging and, in a sense, loosening
up the class-relationships of the whole world of the novel. For not
merely does Harmon/Rokesmith connect the Boffins with the Wilfers
but he is also the unwitting means of introducing Eugene Wrayburn
to Lizzie Hexam, a connection just as important to the pattern of
Our Mutual Friend.

In the Boffin—Wilfer relationship class-antagonism as such does
not arise, though there is a great deal of caste-antagonism and caste-
contempt. Mrs Wilfer is every bit as snobbish as Lady Tippins, but
the joke is, of course, that her snobbery has no real social basis: she is
a tragedy-queen out of a tenth-rate repertory company. And Bella's
mercenariness, though almost fatal, is in an important sense unlike
the mercenariness of Podsnappery, based on shares and exploitation;
hers is a working-class mercenariness, not much different in essence
from that of Richardson's Pamela, based simply on the bitter experience of what not having money involves. What is fought out in the
Boffin—Rokesmith—Wilfer area of the novel is a moral battle which
is a class-battle in the quite fundamental sense that it hinges on
class-values. Is the way out of poverty the way of Podsnappian
acquisitiveness? Bella at first thinks it is. She learns better through
the example of the apparent corruption of Mr Boffin.

This episode, which has often been objected to as improbable or
clumsy, seems to me one of Dickens's happiest inspirations. It serves
a double purpose, not in the facile sense of getting two effects for the
price of one but in the rarer way of revealing simultaneously two
sides of the same coin. Bella is tested and changed by her experiences, graduating in the school of nineteenth-century heroines from
the status of a Dora (in *David Copperfield*) to somewhere approaching that of a Nora (in *The Doll's House*); and at the same time the
possibilities of corruption inherent in the Boffin-situation are triumphantly revealed. Dickens gets it both ways: the alternative possibilities before Boffin are both dramatised and the degrading horror
of the one throws into relief the humane excellence of the other.
These alternative possibilities of corruption and human decency are
underlined meanwhile within the Boffin area of the book by the respective paths of Messrs Wegg and Venus. The relationship between
Boffin and Wegg seems to me extraordinarily well done. Not only
Wegg's meanness but Boffin's own vulnerability emerge in episodes
as psychologically subtle as they are funny. There is more than a

touch of the nastier kind of unease in Boffin's naïve dealings with his literary man. Because he is in the position of patron he begins behaving like a patron – he who so hates patronage (it is a recurring theme of consideration throughout the book). One understands Wegg's irritation, even though his basic reactions are of course unforgivable. And it must also be said that Dickens's plot, towards the end of the Boffin–Wegg strand, gets him into one of those rare situations in which he is not quite on top of things. Boffin's dissimulation is fair enough in relation to Bella, but when the golden dustman has simultaneously to unravel the complicated machinations of Wegg and Venus it is not always clear in which persona he is performing or who is leading whom up the dust-heap or why.

The question that both Bella and the Boffins have to face is whether, given the opportunity, they want to 'rise', i.e. emerge morally from the working-class world into the world of Podsnap the bourgeois. This, it is worth stressing, is the real issue, an issue not of money as such but of values. The corrupting force in *Our Mutual Friend* is not money but bourgeois attitudes to it. That is why critics who take the superficial view that class is simply a matter of birth or level of income can make little of the pattern of *Our Mutual Friend* and are likely to end by presenting an image of Dickens as a comfortable middle-class do-gooder with vulgar tastes and a soft spot for the deserving poor.

The question that both Bella and the Boffins have to face is the Hexams' and the Veneerings' problem as well as the Wilfers' and the Boffins'. One of the central aspects of the problem is – as in so much Victorian literature and thinking – that of education. Almost the first thing Mr Boffin does when he gets his money is to employ Wegg to improve his education. Again, one recalls the importance of books in preserving David Copperfield's integrity and the wonderful moment in *Bleak House* when old Krook is found teaching *himself* to read and write because he cannot trust anyone else to teach him right. To insist that Dickens was keen on education is to miss half the point. What he also recognised was that in a class-divided society education itself has a double tendency, to corrupt as well as to liberate. At the school where Charley Hexam learns and Bradley Headstone teaches – a 'temple of good intentions' Dickens calls it – 'an exceptionally sharp boy exceptionally determined to learn, could learn something' (Bk. II, Ch. 1.) and the worth of that something is not underestimated. But the *values* which Charley Hexam imbibes

are also part of his education and they, of course, are not merely
snobbish in the more superficial sense, making him socially contemptuous of Lizzie and her friends, but infected at the core with
anti-working-class attitudes, especially the idea of 'getting up in the
world'. The imagery used to describe Bradley Headstone's mind is
extraordinarily telling:

> From his early childhood up, his mind had been a place of mechanical
> stowage. The arrangement of his wholesale warehouse, so that it might be
> always ready to meet the demands of retail dealers — history here, geo-
> graphy there, astronomy to the right, political economy to the left ... this
> care had imparted to his countenance a look of care. (Bk. II, Ch. 1)

Not only is the educational system as such here linked with the
processes of capitalist economy, but Headstone's own personal
neuroses connected organically with the socio-intellectual system of
which he is a cog, a system which is revealed as inhuman not only in
its underlying values — commercial and mechanical — but in its division of knowledge and experience into isolated compartments. In a
single sentence Dickens is indeed, in terms entirely relevant to the
personal situation he is depicting, producing a profound humanist
critique of the modern British educational system.

'Rising' is a desperate danger in the world of *Our Mutual Friend*,
for to 'rise' is to enter the sphere of the Podsnaps and the Veneerings. Charley Hexam does not enter that sphere financially but spiritually he does, and his spiritual corruption is inseparable from his
social ambitions, his undeviating, fanatical determination to make
himself 'respectable in the scale of society'. And when, in his nausea-
ting complacency, he finally turns on the wretched Headstone, his
tone and language are those of Mr Podsnap. Charley's final judgment on his sister (Bk. IV, Ch. 7) and Podsnap's (Bk. IV, Chapter
the Last), though made from socially different positions, are inter-
changeable. For level of income is not the determining feature of
Podsnappery and an increase in income is not the same as 'rising'.
Lizzie Hexam will not be corrupted by becoming Mrs Eugene Wrayburn any more than Mrs. Boffin is spoiled by her innocent enthusiasm for Fashion and her frank enjoyment of the pleasures of
wealth.

Does this mean that Dickens makes a simple division between
'good' and 'bad' characters and that the 'good', irrespective of social
status or class position, resist corruption while the 'bad' are drawn

under, like Rogue Riderhood drawn under the treacherous waters of the Thames? I do not think such an assessment stands up to a thoroughgoing examination. Obviously Dickens is not, in a crude sense, a social determinist; he does not imply that the social 'background' of a character is inescapable. Lizzie and Charley Hexam grow up in the same house, subjected to the same general social influences, but turn out quite differently. Lizzie, so to speak, moves upstream, Charley down. But Charley's deterioration is bound up, not just with 'character' in an isolated, unchanging sense, but with specific social choices, including Lizzie's own ambitions for him as opposed to her lack of ambition for herself. We understand why Lizzie wants to get Charley away from the riverside and we respect her for it, but we are forced to recognise, as she herself never quite does, that she has, in all innocence, made a frightful error in judgement, an error which, faced with a temptation of her own, she manages to avoid. Lizzie refuses to be drawn into corruption, just as Jenny Wren and Mr Riah and Mr Venus do, and though the refusal costs each of them something, what is maintained is moral independence. These people, despite their poverty, decline to 'rise' by grasping 'opportunities' that will undermine their humanity.

This is the significance of the Betty Higden episode which is all too easily seen as merely a bit of doubtless well-intentioned propaganda against the workhouses and their 'honourable boards', a not very relevant return to the preoccupations of *Oliver Twist*. In naturalistic terms old Betty is no doubt overdone (rather in the way Firs, the old servant in *The Cherry Orchard*, can be felt to be overdone), yet her uncompromising and obsessional determination to be beholden to no one, even the undemanding Mrs Boffin, is an important, and I think necessary, strand in the pattern of Dickens's presentation of the problems of poverty and working-class morality. To accept patronage is to lose independence, to drift into the arms of the 'honourable boards' is to accept human degradation. It is notable that in *Our Mutual Friend* it is not the idea of social services that is attacked: Dickens goes out of his way to praise the children's hospital and to show that old Betty's suspicions of it are groundless. He is not holding up Mrs Higden's sturdy independence as something preferable to the acceptance of a decently conceived system of planned social welfare. What he is underlining is a moral embedded deep in this novel: that a genuine emancipation or even amelioration involves the maintenance of their moral independence by working-class people and that such independence is incompatible either with 'rising' or with the acceptance of the sort of charity which has bourgeois strings attached.

For of all of Dickens's novels this is the one most deeply and consistently impregnated with a consciousness of the power of the bourgeoisie. How essential the 'society' chapters – set in the homes of the Podsnaps and Veneerings – are to the basic conception of the novel is emphasized by the nature and positioning of Chapter the Last, which is very different from the usual final chapter of a Victorian novel, tying up loose ends and adding more or less irrelevant information about the future careers of the characters. 'The Voice of Society' it is called and it is clear that Dickens is using the word 'society' with deliberate and effective ambiguity; for though the voice referred to is in fact 'society' in the narrower sense of those who people the 'society columns' of the newspapers, it is the implication of the whole novel that their voice is the one which dominates society as a whole and that their values are in a precise sense the ruling values of the world of *Our Mutual Friend*. These values get their fullest and most insistent symbolic expression in the novel in the recurring emphases on dust and shares. The dust-heaps are the dominant visual image of the accumulation of wealth and power; but it is a feature of that power that it operates not openly but mysteriously, through bits of paper: wills, promissory notes, the offer of reward which Rogue Riderhood clutches, above all, through shares.

As is well known to the wise in their generation, traffic in Shares is the one thing to have to do with in this world. Have no antecedents, no established character, no cultivation, no ideas, no manners; have Shares. Have Shares enough to be on Boards of Direction in capital letters, oscillate on mysterious business between London and Paris, and be great. Where does he come from? Shares. Where is he going to? Shares. What are his tastes? Shares. Has he any principles? Shares. What squeezes him into Parliament? Shares. Perhaps he never of himself achieved success in anything, never originated anything, never produced anything! Sufficient answer to all; Shares. O mighty Shares! (Bk. I, Ch. 10)

Such a passage, quoted out of context, may give the impression of an aside, a perhaps not quite legitimate intrusion of one of Dickens's hobby-horses. In fact it is fully integrated into the structure of the novel. The immediate occasion of it is the approaching marriage of the Lammles, one of the minor triumphs of the book and a brilliant advance on Thackeray's treatment of a similar theme in the 'how to live on nothing a year' part of *Vanity Fair*, because the emotional nature of the Lammles' impasse is suggested in a way Thackeray cannot reach. But it is not simply the Lammles' career that the passage touches: it is the whole operation of Podsnappery, from the honourable boards that terrify Betty Higden and the honourable debt that almost ruins Mr Twemlow to the whole marvellously funny career of the Veneerings who emerge from nothing and disappear into nothing, but take in a seat in Parliament on their way, people from nowhere, spreading a sort of doom.[3]

It is, I suppose, the uncompromising nature of this insight, so fundamental to *Our Mutual Friend* of the null and friendless nature of the Podsnap world, that has led, as much as anything, to the underestimating of this novel. Henry James's unfavourable contemporary review in *The Nation*, though it does its author less than justice (the later James would have been more generous, though whether he would have been as frank is perhaps more doubtful), centres on this very question.

What a world were this world if the world of *Our Mutual Friend* were an honest reflection of it! ... Society is maintained by natural sense and natural feeling. We cannot conceive a society in which these principles are not in some manner represented. Where in these pages are the depositories of that intelligence without which the movement of life would cease? Who represents nature?[4]

The tone of sophisticated outrage is arresting and straightway illuminates the gap between the worlds of, say, George Eliot, Matthew Arnold, and Henry James on the one side and Dickens on the other. Who represents nature indeed? One recalls Mr Squeers's rich philosophical aside to the effect that nature is a rum'n. Or perhaps the simplest reply is to ask: whose nature? It is of the very essence of *Our Mutual Friend* that Podsnappery does represent a significant area of nature – bourgeois nature – and that for 'natural sense and natural feeling' this particular area of aspiration, to use an expressive phrase of the Artful Dodger's, 'ain't the shop'.

The Jamesian shift, in the passage just quoted, from 'natural sense and natural feeling' to 'depositories of intelligence' is in itself interesting. Clearly it is because he is unable to see the Boffins as the depositories of the kind of intelligence which he, Arnold-like, associates with those whose destiny it is to set standards for society and spread sweetness and light, that Henry James cannot even recognise their natural sense and natural feeling. James sees the Boffins as eccentrics. Whereas to Dickens it is they, above all, who are the representatives of the sort of nature he was most interested in – popular nature in the true nineteenth-century sense of popular, expressive of the worth and potentiality of the People as opposed to those who rule and exploit them.[5]

The two most important concrete visual images in *Our Mutual Friend*, as everyone recognises, are the mounds and the river. It is worth emphasising that they are not, in any abstract or schematic sense, symbols, but straightforward poetic images, embodying in the richness of their relevant qualities and the manifold 'rightness' of their relationship to one another, the central content and meaning of the novel. Several critics, especially perhaps Humphry House, have helped us to see the full importance of the dust-heaps, not merely as historical phenomena, actual outcrops on the face of Victorian London and specific examples of capital accumulation and speculation, but in the nature of their content of waste and even excrement.[6] The mounds get their effect in the novel in a number of ways working simultaneously. Visually they are huge, ugly, barren, man-made, yet in their operation there is a kind of perverse fertility about them, the fertility of manure and – the connection is not arbitrary – dividends. They keep the system going. To own them is not merely to be rich but to control the processes of social continuity. And the poor live within their shadow and their stench.

The mounds are connected with the river in several ways. Visually or geographically they rear up as a sort of artificial Primrose Hill, overlooking North London. In terms of the plot it is, as I have already suggested, Harmon/Rokesmith who links the two areas and a subsidiary link is provided by the ludicrous romance of Mr Venus and Pleasant Riderhood. An interesting associative connection has been suggested in the form of the Houses of Parliament ('the national cinder-heap') which stand by the river.[7] But though this may be a trifle far-fetched, the main relationship is clear. It is the filth of London, itself one vast fog-infested dust-heap, that pollutes the river and turns it from a pleasing and refreshing stream into a flowing sewer of filth and refuse. There is indeed a grim and significant parallel between the image of old Harmon (and Silas Wegg) fishing his wealth out of the dust of commercial London and Gaffer Hexam fishing his sordid living out of the polluted waters of the chartered Thames.

Rivers nowadays always seem to tempt the Jungians to their most

absurd excesses and no one familiar with the ways of twentieth-
century American criticism especially will be surprised to find the
Thames of *Our Mutual Friend* saddled with every conceivable kind of
ritual significance. Unfortunately for these interpretations, on the
only occasion really conducive to such an emphasis – the rescue and
revival of Rogue Riderhood – Dickens goes out of his way to laugh
at any such idea as the restorative power of drowning. Pleasant
Riderhood is visited by

> some vague idea that the old evil is drowned out of him, and that if he
> should happily come back to resume his occupation of the empty form that
> lies upon the bed, his spirit will be altered. In which state of mind she
> kisses the stony lips, and quite believes that the impassive hand she chafes
> will revive a tender hand, if it revive ever.
> Sweet delusion for Pleasant Riderhood . . . . (Bk. III, Ch. 3)

It is quite true of course that Eugene's conversion follows his
immersion in the river; but here the point is no more 'mythic' than
in the case of the unconverted Riderhood. The reason that Eugene
has to be rescued in that particular way is simply that this is the
sphere in which Lizzie, the female waterman, is uniquely capable of
achieving such a rescue.

Not that one would wish to under-emphasise the importance of
the Thames in *Our Mutual Friend*. It is, in the early reaches of the
book and the lower ones of the river, the very mainstream of corruption and wretchedness. This is a persistent image in Dickens's work.
The prostitute Martha in *David Copperfield* is drawn towards the
river:

> 'I know it's like me!' she exclaimed. 'I know that I belong to it. I know
> that it's the natural company of such as I am! It comes from country places,
> where there was once no harm in it – and it creeps through the dismal.
> streets, defiled and miserable – and it goes away, like my life, to a great sea
> that is always troubled – and I feel that I must go with it.' (Ch. 47.)

Even here, though, the corruption and wretchedness are not in the
least mysterious, let alone metaphysical. The filth is the actual filth
of London, the wretchedness is poverty. Almost all the poor
characters of *Our Mutual Friend* live around the river, and when
Charley Hexam is trying to persuade Lizzie to marry Headstone and
get away from the house in Smith Square he argues that she 'would
at last get quit of the river-side and the old disagreeables belonging
to it' (Bk. II, Ch. 15).

Even the upper reach of the river, the idyllic Berkshire valley, takes on a sinister colour when the inhabitants of the corrupted lower river, Riderhood and Headstone, invade it. But by and large it is a place of sweet contrast and it is obviously not fortuitous that the model factory should be placed here or that Betty Higden should escape westwards in her flight from the honourable boards. It is to Chertsey, Walton, Kingston, and Staines that Betty goes.

In those pleasant little towns on Thames, you may hear the fall of the water over the weirs, or even, in still weather, the rustle of the rushes; and from the bridge you may see the young river, dimpled like a young child, playfully gliding away among the trees, unpolluted by the defilements that lie in wait for it on its course ... (Bk. III, Ch. 8)

If one is to talk of 'waste-land' imagery in connection with this novel it must be in a very naturalistic and precise sense.

Between the mounds and the river the complex, cunningly interwoven dramas of *Our Mutual Friend* are worked out, merging into a single drama in which the values of humanity struggle against those of Podsnappery. That it is the profoundest sense a class struggle would be clear even if the 'moral' were not underlined in the final chapter where, with the greatest analytical candour, the personal relationships involved in the plot are examined and judged in the light of the moral preoccupations which control the novel's pattern. The bourgeois class delivers its judgment on the marriage of Lizzie and Eugene, and Mr Twemlow, the dim little aristocrat, who has learned at any rate something from his dealings with the Lammles and Fascination Fledgeby, dissociates himself from it, standing up even to the veiled threat of Podsnap to tell Lord Snigsworth of his class-apostasy. Perhaps the most significant moment of the whole scene is the judgment of 'the Contractor, of five hundred thousand power':

It appears to this potenate * that what the man in question should have done, would have been to buy the young woman a boat and a small annuity, and set her up for herself. These things are a question of beef-steaks and porter. You buy the young woman a boat. Very good. You buy her, at the same time, a small annuity. You speak of that annuity in pounds sterling, but it is in reality so many pounds of beefsteaks and so many pints of porter. On the one hand, the young woman has the boat. On

---

* Cf. Mr Venus's early description of Pleasant Riderhood: 'She is worthy of being loved by a Potentate.'

the other hand, she consumes so many pounds of beefsteaks and so many pints of porter. Those beefsteaks and that porter are the fuel to that young woman's engine. She derives therefrom a certain amount of power to row the boat; that power will produce so much money; you add that to the small annuity; and thus you get at the young woman's income. That (it seems to the Contractor) is the way of looking at it. (Bk. IV, Chapter the Last)

It is particularly telling, not only because of the brutal connections it reveals between the Contractor's morals and his social position, but because it echoes Eugene's own cynical morality of his unregenerate days. Then he was able to say to Jenny Wren:

'I think of setting up a doll, Miss Jenny.'
'You had better not,' replied the dressmaker.
'Why not?'
'You are sure to break it. All you children do.'
'But that makes good for trade, you know, Miss Wren,' returned Eugene. 'Much as people's breaking promises and contracts and bargains of all sorts, makes good for *my* trade.'
'I don't know about that,' Miss Wren retorted; 'but you had better by half-set up a penwiper, and turn industrious and use it.'
'Why, if we were all as industrious as you, little Busy-Body, we should being to work as soon as we could crawl, and there would be a bad thing!'
'Do you mean,' returned the little creature, with a flush suffusing her face, 'bad for your backs and your legs?'
'No, no, no,' said Eugene; shocked – to do him justice – at the thought of trifling with her infirmity. 'Bad for business, bad for business. If we all set to work as soon as we could use our hands, it would be all over with the dolls' dressmakers'.
'There's something in that,' replied Miss Wren; 'you have a sort of an idea in your noddle sometimes.' Then, in a changed tone: 'Talking of ideas, my Lizzie,' they were sitting side by side as they had sat at first, 'I wonder how it happens that when I am work, work, working here, all alone in the summer-time, I smell flowers.' (Bk. II, Ch. 2)

I think this is a most interesting and subtle passage, revealing very strikingly the profundity of Dickens's moral control of his plot. Here the essential conflict of values at the heart of *Our Mutual Friend* is expressed simply, yet in the most richly complex terms. Eugene's attitudes emerge in all their crudity. The doll is obviously Lizzie, though its 'setting up' can also imply the bribing of Jenny, and Eugene has no hesitation in discussing the whole affair in terms of the morality of trade. But even he is shocked when Jenny puts the working-class case in equally crude and personal terms, associating her own infirmities with her class position. And Jenny herself is forced to acknowledge that, in the competitive world she lives in, 'there's something in' Eugene's cynical morality. But she is unconvinced and turns to Lizzie (who seems, incidentally, to understand nothing of the implications of the conversation) with her thought about smelling flowers, a theme that is then developed at sufficient length to associate Jenny's dreams and her morality with the nature-imagery of the upper-Thames sections of the book. What Jenny is granting in this passage is the short-term expediency of the Wrayburn-Contractor morality, while clinging to a scale of values and aspiration not only more humane but altogether more 'natural'. And it is only when Eugene himself comes to accept those values – the popular values of those who work with their hands, as opposed to the ruling-class values of Podsnappery – that the conflict within the novel can be resolved and Mortimer Lightwood can fare to the Temple, gaily.

It is only those who, like George Orwell, wear blinkers which prevent a recognition of what Dickens is saying and of what class-conflict really is, who fail to see the profundity and consistency of the artistic structure of *Our Mutual Friend*. I think Jack Lindsay is doing the novel no more than justice when he describes it as one of the greatest works of prose ever written, a work which finally vindicates Dickens's right to stand, as no other English writer can stand, at the side of Shakespeare.[8]

Notes

1   T. A. Jackson, *Charles Dickens: The Progress of a Radical* (1937), p. 203.

2   *Ibid.*, p. 204.

3   Mr Hillis Miller, in an interpretation of *Our Mutual Friend* which strikes me as being, by and large, of almost ludicrous irrelevance, makes an excellent point when he refers to the 'nullity' of the Veneerings (*Charles Dickens, The World of his Novels*, 1958, p. 297).

4   *The House of Fiction* (ed. L. Edel, 1957), p. 255.

5   Dickens's clearest expression of his conscious commitment to the 'popular' side in precisely this sense is to be found in the famous speech at Birmingham, 27 September 1869 (*The Speeches of Charles Dickens*, ed. K. J. Fielding, 1960, p. 407).

6   *The Dickens World* (1942 edn), pp. 166 ff.

7   Edgar Johnson, *Charles dickens, His Tragedy and Triumph* (1953), p. 1030.

8   *Charles Dickens* (1950), p. 308.

Felix Holt the Radical

Felix Holt the Radical begins magnificently. We are taken right into history, into the England of 1832, after the passing of the Reform Bill. But there is nothing musty about the history, no sense of a retreat into the past. On the contrary, by choosing as her subject an England thirty-five years gone, George Eliot's instinct, as in *Middlemarch*, may well have been wise. It is not easy for a highly self-conscious and responsible novelist to absorb quite contemporary experience with the kind of assurance which ultimately creates good art. Such a writer often does best with the material he has stored from his youth; then recollection in tranquillity brings forth a freshness of emotion which has yet passed, unselfconsciously, through the toughening of experience. That George Eliot was able to draw on the memories of her Midland childhood and youth no doubt helped avoid a repetition of the conscientious but rather arid sort of history behind *Romola*: that she should have chosen a period and a subject so closely interwoven with the England of 1866 prevents — at the outset at least — any loss of urgency, for to understand 1832 was, after all, an essential part of understanding 1866.

For the England in which George Eliot was writing was itself on the brink of a new Parliamentary reform, and one which raised far more immediately than the Bill of 1832 the question of working-class suffrage, one of the preoccupations of *Felix Holt*. To appreciate how contemporary a book this was one has only to see George Eliot's novel in association with non-fictional works like Bagehot's *English Constitution* (1867), Matthew Arnold's *Culture and Anarchy* (1869), and the *Studies in Parliament* (1866) of R. S. Hutton, who himself reviewed several of her novels for *The Spectator*. *Felix Holt* was published in the year that Robert Lowe — himself the author of the 'revised code' for the administration of education under which Matthew Arnold operated as a school inspector – warned the House of Commons: 'Once give working men the votes, and the machinery is ready to launch those votes in one compact mass upon the institutions and property of this country.' Arnold's fear of the cultural attitudes of the populace, symbolised for him by the tearing down the Hyde Park railings in 1866, is closely connected with Lowe's famous remark, after the passing of the 1867 Reform Bill, that it was essential to 'prevail on our future masters to learn their letters', and it was in this context that George Eliot brought Felix Holt out of fiction into actual public life by publishing the 'Address to Working Men by Felix Holt' in *Blackwood's* in January 1868.

The triumph of the opening chapters of *Felix Holt* is threefold: the general evocation of post-Reform Bill Britain (especially in the Introduction and Chapter 3, but permeating the whole enterprise); the vivid and remarkably intense and finely dramatised presentation of a number of personal relationships and tensions; and the linking of the two – the general and the particular – by the revelation of certain patterns which are at once private and public, personal and typical. In a sentence that has become well known, George Eliot showed her consciousness of what she was doing:

These social changes in Treby parish are comparatively public matters, and this history is chiefly concerned with the private lot of a few men and women; but there is no private life which has not been determined by a wider public life, from the time when the primeval milkmaid had to wander with the wanderings of her clan, because the cow she milked was one of a herd which had made the pastures bare. (Ch. 3)

It is a sentence we shall return to.

The sketching-in of the general social situation is extremely well done. George Eliot, like Hardy, looks at a landscape historically and sees the social forces behind the visual changes, and this, as in a Breughel picture, is what gives the visual effect its point and significance. The changes brought about by the Industrial Revolution – the coal mines, the canals and their consequences – are most effectively suggested. (It is interesting to compare the use of similar material by another Midlands novelist, Lawrence, in *The Rainbow*.) Before these changes the social separation in Treby between the County aristocracy and the well-to-do traders and richer farmers had been complete. The Debarry and Transome families owned the estates and supplied the rectors, while the prosperous middle class

'played at whist, ate and drank generously, praised Mr. Pitt and the
war as keeping up prices and religion, and were very humorous
about each other's property' (Ch. 3). Now, as Treby Magna

> gradually passed from being simply a respectable market-town – the heart
> of a great rural district, where the trade was only such as had close relations
> with the local landed interest – and took on the more complex life brought
> by mines and manufactures, which belong more directly to the great cir-
> culating system of the nation. (Ch. 3)

the old divisions alter. On the one hand landed and industrial
interests begin to come into open conflict; on the other the nature of
the working people changes. Trebian Dissent alters its character.
Political Radicalism becomes an urgent issue. 'There were Dissenters in Treby now who could not be regarded by the Church people
in the light of old neighbours to whom the habit of going to chapel
was an innocent, unenviable inheritance' (Ch. 3). Radicalism is seen
here by George Eliot not simply as a set of opinions: it is a social
force arising out of basic economic changes.

The return to Treby of Harold Transome after fifteen years of
successful money-making in the Middle East and of Felix Holt after
a period of study in Glasgow opens up the personal interest of the
novel. Harold Transome is heir to the estate of Little Treby. His
return home is a superb scene. His mother, weighed down by the
burdens of an incapable husband, a dissolute elder son, and a series
of ruinous law-suits, has kept the estate going. She is proud, energetic, intensely Tory, intensely bitter – and the bitterness is grad-
ually revealed to be bound up with her secret: that her son Harold
was fathered, not by her feeble husband, but by a bold and able
young lawyer named Matthew Jermyn. Now, the hated elder son
dead, Harold comes home, rich, to take over the estate. Mrs Transome, uncompromising in so much, has built up over the hard and
lonely years a powerful compensatory illusion: when Harold comes
back everything will be well. Not only fortune will come back to
Transome Court, but honour and joy. And then Harold comes and
he is his father's son, an energetic, insensitive second-rater. He
brings with him foreign habits, a little son of dubious parentage,
plenty of ambition but no sense of the past, in which his mother
lives. He is not consciously unkind nor especially unscrupulous, but
he has no understanding whatever of the kind of person Mrs Transome is. And to cap her humiliation he announces that he intends to
stand in the forthcoming election as a Radical.

Felix Holt is also a Radical, but of a quite different kind. His
father has been a relatively successful quack doctor, so that he could
afford to study, but his whole *milieu* is in entire contrast to Transome Court – plebeian, Dissenting, respectable. He too disappoints
his mother: for he insists, on getting back to Treby, that they will
not live on the proceeds of quack medicine, which he believes to be
fraudulent, but on the money gained by honest work as a watch-
maker. Felix, indeed, takes his Radical stand on the fundamental
question of class allegiance: he is a worker and will remain one.
'Why should I want to get into the middle class because I have some
learning?'[1] he asks. Advance must come through the raising of the
working class as a class, and for that he feels an intense responsibility, and he will not compromise, either in his personal life or in
his principles, with the rich. 'I want the working men to have
power' he is to tell the Nomination-Day crowd (Ch. 30).

Harold Transome's Radicalism is, of course, something quite different from this. He is a Radical because the future looks that way,
because

nothing was left to men of sense and good family but to retard the national
ruin by declaring themselves Radicals, and take the inevitable process of
changing everything out of the hands of beggarly demagogues and purse-
proud tradesmen. (Ch. 2)

And he wins an important round by gaining the support of his old
Tory clergyman uncle with the assurance, 'I am a Radical only in
rooting out abuses':

'That's the word I wanted, my lad!' said the Vicar, slapping Harold's knee.
'That's a spool to wind a speech on. Abuses is the very word.' (Ch. 2)

It is this contradiction between two kinds of Radical, the ruling-
class kind, who is in fact just about as revolutionary as Disraeli's
Tory Democrats, and the working-class sort, who is wanting a
fundamental change in social organisation, that is the real core of
George Eliot's novel. And it is a marvellously promising subject, for
not only is the contradiction at the heart of it a real one historically,
bearing the closest and most searching general consideration, but it
also opens up in its personal aspects an enormously rich and fruitful
field of human observation, dramatically and psychologically, as the
early sections of *Felix Holt the Radical* indicate.

I have said that the triumph of the opening chapters of the novel is threefold. The general evocation of England in 1832, which it is inadequate to describe as 'background' (personal lives are not acted out against a backcloth of social life; the interdependence is closer and subtler than that), has been touched on. So has the magnificent presentation of a personal situation, that of Mrs Transome, her son, and the lawyer Jermyn. What is rather more difficult to establish – chiefly, I think, because our tools and vocabulary of analysis are either too 'literary' or not literary enough – is the nature of the artistic pattern of the book at this stage.

I have said that the core of George Eliot's novel is the contradiction between two kinds of Radical, that this is indeed a novel *about* Radicalism. I think this is shown by (*a*) the title of the novel, with its gratuitous emphasis on Felix's politics, (*b*) the direction of emphasis in the general historical passages, (*c*) the way, at the end of Chapter 3, Felix Holt is introduced as a contrast-cum-parallel to Harold Transome, with their relationship to their respective mothers as well as their Radicalism stressed, and (*d*) the development in the early structure of the book, of two main contrasting areas of interest – the Transome-Jermyn area and the Holt-Lyon area – with other episodes and characters subsidiary to these two. This general view of the pattern of *Felix Holt* is, it seems to me, borne out by the passages of detailed analysis of the formal organisation of the novel by Barbara Hardy in her interesting book, *The Novels of George Eliot*.[2]

Harold Transome's Radicalism is not presented simply as a personal opinion: the operation of it involves a whole area of social life – the support of the clerical uncle, the bringing into play of a 'machine' run, though scarcely controlled, by Jermyn and his satellites. Similarly, Felix Holt, though a strongly individualistic and non-conforming character, is presented as a part of the whole Dissenting community: his relationship with the Lyons, the Dissenting minister and his daughter, is as socially inevitable and firmly grounded as Transome's relations with Matthew Jermyn. All this produces, in the first hundred or so pages of *Felix Holt*, a deepening sense that the personal stories within the novel are not subsidiary to (that would give a false impression), but, to use George Eliot's own word, essentially determined by the wider public life of Treby. She makes the point explicitly in the sentence:

There could hardly have been a lot less like Harold Transome's than this of the quack doctor's son, except in the superficial facts that he called himself a Radical, that he was the only son of his mother, and that he had lately returned to his home with ideas and resolves not a little disturbing to that mother's mind. (Ch. 3)

The problem about this sentence is whether the word 'superficial' is used ironically. As W. J. Harvey has remarked, 'These facts, of course, turn out to be anything but superficial',[3] and there would not, one might assume, be any point in stressing the parallels which give the book its peculiar structure unless they were in fact significant. But I think there is an ambiguity here, and am not sure that George Eliot's use of the word is really ironical.

It is necessary to stress this point because it is my argument that George Eliot fails to develop or fully realise the pattern which is the core of her book. The obvious retort, of course, is that it evidently isn't really the core of the book, that George Eliot's intention and preoccupation is somewhat other than I have suggested, and that I am not only foisting my own pattern on the novel, but unreasonably blaming the author for not sticking to it. I agree that this would be a silly thing to do. The point at issue is not, it should be added, precisely what George Eliot consciously intended to do or not to do. One can scarcely ever measure the exact degree of self-consciousness of an artist, or anyone else. The important thing about a work of art is not what its author may at some point or other have intended, but what is there.

What happens in *Felix Holt* is that George Eliot, having made clear what her novel is about, having revealed its incipient pattern, then fails to fulfil the promise she has hinted at.

I have already suggested that the developing pattern of the book, even in its early stages, is not without its ambiguities. Though the central theme is expressed primarily in the historical terms already discussed, there are, right from the start, indications that within George Eliot's mind other and perhaps contradictory forces are at work.

An example of what I have in mind comes at the end of the Introduction. The general line and tone of the writing has, in the first pages, been historical. The use of the coachman as a kind of choric figure, at once character and *compère*, permits George Eliot a degree of irony which is immediately 'placed' by the reader within an objective context. The processes of social change are thus rendered and commented on in a way which is at the same time personal and impersonal: the historical forces evoked are envisaged in terms of actual living people and their individual destinies. Abstraction is thus avoided and an objectivity at once concrete and intimate achieved. Then, in the last two paragraphs of the chapter, we notice a change of method, accompanied by a significant change in tone, a certain hushed intensity which tells us that the author's feelings are in some way peculiarly engaged.

Sampson the coachman has been hinting that

> some 'fine stories' lie behind the public fortunes of the Transome family. And such fine stories often come to be fine in a sense that is not ironical. For there is seldom any wrong-doing which does not carry along with it some downfall of blindly-climbing hopes, some hard entail of suffering, some quickly-satiated desire that survives, with the life in death of old paralytic vice, to see itself cursed by its woeful progeny – some tragic mark of kinship in the one brief life to the far-stretching life that went before, and to the life that is to come after, such as has raised the pity and terror of men ever since they began to discern between will and destiny. But these things are often unknown to the world; for there is much pain that is quite noiseless; and vibrations that make human agonies are often a mere whisper in the roar of hurrying existence. There are glances of hatred that stab and raise no cry of murder; robberies that leave man or woman for ever beggared of peace and joy, yet kept secret by the sufferer – committed to no sound except that of low moans in the night, seen in no writing except that made on the face by the slow months of suppressed anguish and early morning tears. Many an inherited sorrow that has marred a life has been breathed into no human ear.

Readers will, I think, be divided in their reactions to such a passage. To some the shift into an emotionally-charged tone raptly generalising upon the secret sufferings of humankind will bring a sympathetic sense that here at last the true depths are being sounded. George Eliot has moved, such readers will feel, from the relative superficies of material development to the deeper mysteries of the human heart and its sorrows. This, they will feel, is the real thing.

Other readers will note the change with a certain suspicion as a move from a controlled objectivity to a vaguer and perhaps self-indulgent expression of an attitude of mind not altogether free of abstract generalisation and the preacher's tone of voice. I do not want to attempt to adjudicate between two hypothetical reactions; but I think the texture of the writing here is worth examining. What gives the prose its curious density is not simply the piling up of a multiplicity of issues and images, many of which are somewhat mystifying to anyone reading the book for the first time; there is also a slipping into a characteristic rhythm based on deeply-held convictions about the unchanging sadness of the human lot. George Eliot's artistic intentions in *Felix Holt* seem to me rather basically unresolved. Is this to be a novel about Radicalism or a novel about Mrs Transome? The logic and structure of the book point in one direction, the emotional engagement of the author in the other.

This is why, despite some excellent things in the later part of the novel, the promise of *Felix Holt* is not really fulfilled. The area in which Mrs Transome appears is never less than distinguished;[4] and Mrs Transome extends to the other characters closest to her personal tragedy — Harold, Matthew Jermyn, even her poor husband — a dimension of artistic vitality they do not always have in other parts of the book. But it has to be said that this consideration of the Transome situation — fine and moving as it is — is not linked organically with the rest of the novel. Even the Transomes' relations with Esther in the part of the book in which she is living at Transome Court have little of the conviction one associates with most of the scenes in that house and the increasing tendency of the author to fall back into a 'sweet Esther Lyon' rhapsody tells its own tale. The political part of the book too is almost incidental to the Transome drama, the essence of which could have been achieved without the introduction of the theme of Radicalism as anything but a relatively trivial matter. The development of Harold's relations with Jermyn and the whole bitter humiliation of Mrs Transome need not have been significantly different if Harold Transome had stood as a Tory candidate.

Clearly, with Mrs Transome George Eliot had got hold of a situation which engaged her deeply. Put in general terms, this has something to do with the position of woman *vis-à-vis* men; but chiefly it involves the question of moral responsibility and the sense — so deep in George Eliot — that we get nothing on the cheap in this severe world and no past action can be obliterated. Mrs Transome, like Mrs Alving, is trapped by ghosts. The revelation of her situation is done with fine artistry, great psychological insight and dramatic power; but it remains peripheral. As Leslie Stephen remarked years ago, one would really need to know a little more about that early love-affair to have the sense of even Mrs Transome's story being fully explored. As it is, even the presentation of this, the finest, area of the latter part of the novel suffers from the nature of the plot.

Felix Holt the Radical begins clearly to deteriorate from the time (about the twelfth chapter) when the complexities of the plot start to take over control and to undermine the development of the wide and significant conflicts which George Eliot has earlier established. This plot is excessively tortuous and involves not only two mysteries of parentage, but a most formidable paraphernalia of legal detail over which the author (assisted by the eminent Positivist lawyer, Frederic Harrison) was excessively conscientious. Its most obvious disadvantage is that it is almost impossible on a first reading to be quite clear as to who knows what about whom. But this would not really matter very much if the plot were doing its job in reinforcing the main image or pattern of the novel. The plot of *Bleak House* is, we recall, enormously complex and dependent on a number of chances – to say nothing of legal complications – which no one demanding naturalistic probability could be likely to accept. Yet the plot of *Bleak House* triumphantly serves the total design and meaning of Dickens's novel, while that of *Felix Holt* continuously detracts from the seriousness of George Eliot's.

Why is this? In literary terms, because the forces brought into play in the unravelling of the plot do not correspond with those which have been set in motion by the statement, in the opening chapters, of what the novel is about. This is to be a novel about the personal fortunes of people whose lot is organically bound up with the condition of England, with class-conflicts and the moral problems involved in social advance, with the two faces of Radicalism and what political responsibility implies. Yet it is all worked out in terms of legal niceties, unexpected inheritances and complex intrigues in which little or no conflict of principle arises. The law, which dominated the plot, is never itself given any serious moral or historical consideration. It is simply there. Compared with the consideration of the law in *Bleak House*, that in *Felix Holt* is superficial and inadequate. Jermyn, as a 'convincing character' abstracted from his place in the novel, may be superior to Tulkinghorn, who exists primarily as a visual image reinforced by an idiosyncratic rhetoric; as a significant figure in an achieved work of art he is greatly inferior.

That Felix should be imprisoned for his part in a riot he has tried to quell is a fact conveyed by George Eliot without a breath of irony;[5] the whole episode is treated entirely in terms of individual characters' motives and consciences. The trial scene has no more moral profundity and almost as much conventional melodrama as the one in *Mary Barton*. A certain irony is directed upon the stupid Mrs Holt, who is convinced that the gentry can get her son off if they feel so inclined. Yet when this in fact happens the episode is

treated entirely unironically and its moral and social implications
ignored, not only by the morally uncompromising Felix, but by the
omniscient author, who is not averse to moral reflection in other
moments of the book.

There is, indeed, almost no resolution to this novel at all – and
such as there is comes near to seeming a mockery in the light of the
issues that have been raised, the depths sounded. Esther, it is true,
marries Felix, putting behind her the vanities on which she has fed
herself; but her moral choice, as has been truly said, does not carry
the conviction of a tragic ordeal.[6] This is not only because too much
self-interest is involved, but because at the trial, as throughout
almost all the latter part of the novel, the actual implications of
Felix's Radicalism are lost sight of. It is to his 'nobility' that Esther
testifies at his trial, not his principles: what she gives him is a high-
grade character-reference. And her ability at the end to provide 'a
little income for your mother, enough for her to live as she has been
used to living; and a little income for my father, to save him from
being dependent when he is no longer able to preach' (Ch. 51), this
not merely softens the end of the book, leaving it in a comfortable
glow of cosy compromise, but undermines the whole moral position
on which Felix has originally taken his stand. Why it should be
better to accept Esther's money than his father's is not revealed.

What would seem to be involved in all this is a failure on George
Eliot's part to face, morally or artistically, the problems she has set
in motion in undertaking this particular novel. W. J. Harvey has
drawn attention[7] to the rather odd abandonment, in the course of
the book, of the projected debate between Mr Lyon and the curate,
Mr Sherlock. The episode as it stands is so disproportionate to any
furthering of the plot achieved by it that it is hard to believe that
George Eliot had not originally intended an actual confrontation.
Why did she draw back? Our suspicions of something incompletely
realised have, of course, been aroused even in the excellent early
reaches of the book by the presentation of Felix himself and the lack
of 'bite' in the Holt-Lyon sections as compared with the Transome-
Jermyn ones. There is something dangerously near a musical-
comedy, *Quaker Girl* atmosphere about the whole conception of
Esther. Yet there is also in the early chapters that involve Felix and
Esther a good deal of strength. The tendency to idealise is counteracted by much that is shrewd and true. The presentation of Felix
at this stage seems to me, despite the warning lights, successful, the

rather absurd and even repulsive aspects of him — the priggishness and pedantry — are, by and large, 'placed', and a genuine strength and simplicity emerges. And the tendency to idealisation does not matter much in this context where the pattern of the book is firmly established. The most important thing about Felix and Esther at this stage is that they should be there at all, embodying a way of life firmly contrasted with the Transomes'. And though the realisation of Mr Lyon is weak compared with that of, say, Mark Rutherford's Dissenting ministers, I cannot feel that Dr Leavis's dismissal of him as a bore is the last word. [8]

I am arguing, it will have become apparent, that the basis of George Eliot's failure in this novel is a drawing back from certain of the realities of the social situation which the book is about. Of these the most important is the nature of the common people and their problems, particularly in the light of the new possibilities of democratic advance. She is sympathetic. She sees clearly enough the limitations of Transomian Radicalism and she feels deeply the necessity for something different. She recognises indeed that a more genuine Radicalism must be based, not on the fears of the ruling class, but on the aspirations of the working people; and this recognition gives what strength it has to her presentation of Felix. But the weakness of the recognition is that it is so theoretical and idealistic. And this is why the idealisation of Felix becomes *in the end* a serious artistic flaw.

Felix cannot, of course, be, for George Eliot's purposes, a typical working man. The typical working men in *Felix Holt* are crude, brutal, and stupid. They are incapable of any real foresight, let alone idealism. It would be a mistake to write off George Eliot's picture as simple middle-class prejudice, though one might well accuse her of not seeing the trees for the wood. But the brutalisation of whole sections of the working class is not just the invention of a too-refined imagination; it is a fact of the times and had to be reckoned with. George Eliot, however, does not reckon with it: she accepts it as a fact and turns away. Again, this would not matter (for the novel is not *about* working-class life in the way that *Mary Barton* or *Alton Locke* is) if Felix himself were conceived differently. His weakness as a hero is not that he is not just like the miners he meets at the 'Sugar Loaf' at Sproxton. A working-class leader is never a typical worker in the sense of being an average one. Felix's necessary part in the book is not to be an average representative of the working people:

his part is to be a Radical, a leader. And it is here that the element of
idealism in George Eliot's conception of her hero is fatal. For Felix is
not allowed to be a leader; he is not allowed to grapple in a serious
way with the actual problems of popular leadership, and his very inadequacies in this respect are paraded as virtues. It is *because* he is an
ineffectual idealist that Esther respects him. George Eliot did not in
the final analysis want a hero that could be a hero.

Experience of misunderstanding leads me to wish to emphasise
that my criticism of the presentation of Felix is not based on some
kind of irrelevant personal disagreement with the principles with
which his author endows him. I am not trying to rewrite George
Eliot's novel for her. Felix is an inadequate hero simply because he
does not in fact play a hero's part in the novel, though it is essential
to the structure and conception of the book that he should do so.
Unless what Felix stands for as a Radical emerges as more convincing than what Harold Transome stands for, the conflict between them becomes, artistically, an unfruitful conflict and Esther's
choice a mere matter of personal preference. By disarming Felix as
an effective moral agent, George Eliot commits the blunder of disarming him as an effective force in the book.

George Eliot cannot really plead ignorance or historical limitation
for her failure here. It is true, of course, that it was more difficult to
be an effective Radical in 1832 than a few years later, when the
Chartist Movement was in full swing. But Chartism did not arise
overnight, and it is worth noticing that in Chapter 30 of *Felix Holt*,
the Nomination Day scene, a Radical speaker is allowed to put
forward, eloquently enough, the Chartist demands for universal
suffrage, annual Parliaments, secret ballot and equal electoral dis-
tricts, and advises the workers to use their influence on behalf of
Transome, even though he doesn't have much faith in liberal aris-
tocrats. It is at this point that Felix gets up and makes a critical
speech denouncing the demand for the franchise.

His arguments are not silly, and it is not the mere mouthing of
them that disqualifies Felix from carrying forward effectively the
pattern of George Eliot's book:

'I should like to convince you [he says] that votes would never give you
political power worth having while things are as they are now . . . .' (Ch.
30)

As late as 1871 George Eliot's Radical friend, Frederic Harrison,
was arguing against universal suffrage on the grounds that in a class-

divided society the ruling class can bribe, confuse, and nullify the voting power of the masses. And this is indeed a real problem and one which, especially in the early days of democratic aspiration, was bound to give the strategists of social change serious pause. Felix is obsessed by the thought that the people have been so deeply corrupted that any change that is less than fundamental – a change of heart – merely perpetuates in differing forms existing corruptions. But such thinking can, of course, have more than one implication. Frederic Harrison in 1871 was arguing in the context of the defeat of the Paris Commune, with which he felt a deep sympathy: what he was feeling towards is a more thorough-going revolutionary analysis of the nature of the State than Radicalism could provide. Whereas what Felix Holt offers as an alternative to the vote is defined only in the vaguest and least practical terms. His chief concern is lest the drunken and stupid seventy per cent should be in a position perpetually to outvote the sober and thoughtful thirty – an argument which reflects a rather fundamental lack of confidence, not simply in the franchise, but in any possibility of social change at all, especially when the alternative to the Chartist programme is seen, not as some sort of non-Parliamentary revolutionary action, but simply as the changing of 'public opinion'. Felix is a 'moral force' man: but here again George Eliot gives him less than a fair chance. For the actual division in the 1830s and 1840s between those Radicals who put their faith in 'moral force' and the 'physical force' men was *within* the Chartist Movement, and the 'moral force' advocates were those who had most, not least, faith in Parliamentary action.

By depriving him of faith in both Parliamentary action and the creation of a popular, revolutionary 'mass movement', George Eliot ensures that Felix by the end of the book is not only an ineffectual Radical, but a deficient hero.

What Felix is in fact left with is not much more than a vague hope in the powers of good books and personal example – and his own clear conscience. All that has happened in the course of the novel is that Harold Transome has failed to win a seat in Parliament; Mrs Transome's secret has been revealed; Jermyn has been ruined; and Felix and Esther have settled down to a life of modest good works and high moral principles, a culmination which George Eliot invests, not only with approval, but with a novelettish kind of coy cosiness.

And lest there should be any doubt as to what has happened to the great human issues raised so impressively in the early pages of the

book there is included in the Epilogue, for those who like their tale
to have a moral, the following paragraph:

As to all that wide parish of Treby Magna, it has since prospered as the rest
of England has prospered. Doubtless there is more enlightenment now.
Whether the farmers are all public-spirited, the shopkeepers nobly independent, the Sproxton men entirely sober and judicious, the Dissenters
quite without narrowness or asperity in religion and politics, and the
publicans all fit, like Gaius, to be the friends of an apostle – these things I
have not heard, not having correspondence in those parts. Whether any
presumption may be drawn from the fact that North Loamshire does not
yet return a Radical candidate, I leave to the all-wise – I mean the newspapers.

Perhaps one should not pause too long on such a passage, remembering that, in rounding off her novel, George Eliot felt herself
trapped in a convention she did not relish. Yet I think it is quite a
significant paragraph. The first sentence, in its unembellished irony,
its rather grim simplicity, goes to the heart of George Eliot's
dilemma. England has prospered: the successful 1850s and 1860s
have succeeded the unstable 1830s and 1840s; but nothing has been
solved. She can neither accept nor reject the word 'prosper' and her
ambiguous attitude invests the word with interest. But neither can
she close with this bare, rich statement. The sentences that follow
have a different tone, apparently more explicitly ironical, actually
nearer in flavour to cynicism than to a fruitful irony. The paragraph
as a whole is tired writing, weary and dispirited, without the vitality of a controlled despair.

I do not want to labour or belabour the weaknesses of *Felix Holt*,
but I think the sort of failure indicated here, and the artistic failure
to create a figure commensurate with the needs of her central theme,
is bound up with George Eliot's whole position in relation to the
England of the 1860s and the future of democracy. Felix is conceived not historically as a figure of the 1830s expressing the tensions and dilemmas of a Radical at that stage of English history, but
rather as the author of the 'Address to Working Men' which George
Eliot was to publish in 1868.

One of the striking features of that 'Address' is how very unhis-
torical it is in its approach. The argument is conducted almost
entirely in terms of general principles and attitudes and an emotional conviction of 'the supreme unalterable nature of things'.[9] The
principles invoked are very much the same as those which Matthew

Arnold was at the same time formulating in *Culture and Anarchy*, and the two works make an illuminating example of the strengths and weaknesses of the high-minded mid-Victorian intellectual. In certain respects they represent a genuine liberation of the sensibility – especially in their critique of the characteristic attitudes and opinions of the aristocracy and middle class. But when it comes to the question of change, of tackling the real problems implicit and explicit in the democratisation of British society, what stands out is a fear of the 'mob' – the sinister people who tore down those Hyde Park railings – which incapacitates both writers from facing creatively the very issues which on one level of consciousness they recognize to be the essential ones. Raymond Williams puts the point well when he notes that when George Eliot 'touches, as she chooses to touch, the lives and the problems of working people, her personal observation and conclusion surrender, virtually without a fight, to the general structure of feeling about these matters which was the common property of her generation, and which she was at once too hesitant to transcend, and too intelligent to raise into any lively embodiment. She fails in the extension which she knows to be necessary, because indeed there seems "no right thread to pull" '.[10] And I feel sure that Mr Williams is right in associating this inadequacy particularly with 'the fear of a sympathetic reformist-minded member of the middle classes at being drawn into any kind of mob-violence'.[11]

I am not, of course, primarily concerned with George Eliot's social and political attitudes as such. Nor would I wish to dismiss her fear of violence as an incomprehensible lapse without any objective basis, though I think it has to be said that she finds it easier to excuse or ignore the use of violence if it is associated with the defence of an established order. What concerns me, in discussing *Felix Holt*, is to try to isolate the quality of sensibility which seems to lie behind the successes and weaknesses of this particular book; to try, in other words, to answer the question: Why does this novel, which begins so well, peter out into so weak an ending? I do not think we can answer this question, which is an aesthetic one, without exploring issues which may seem at first to have little to do with aesthetic values. And central to the whole question, I believe, is the tendency of the writers of the 1860s – including George Eliot and Matthew Arnold, but not, significantly, Dickens – to look at life more and more from the point of view of the modern middle-class intellectual with his own peculiar mixture of high-mindedness and blindness, social conscience and irresponsibility, realism and idealism, his contradictory support and fear of democracy, his contempt for privilege and wish for privilege.

If *Felix Holt the Radical* did not give evidence, in its early reaches, of so rich an apprehension of central nineteenth-century dilemmas, an attempt to analyse the causes of its collapse would be merely tiresome. As it is, this flawed but often impressive book does indeed tell us a good deal about the nature of Victorian Radicalism, its very failure as an historical novel reflecting a deeper and perhaps more interesting failure, the inability of George Eliot to see herself as a character in history.

Notes

1 (Ch. 5.) Bernard J. Paris, in his *Experiments in Life, George Eliot's Quest for Values* (Detroit, 1965), p. 199, says that Felix Holt 'feels bound by heredity to the working class'. But though George Eliot, like most Victorian novelists, is in general very conscious of heredity, this is scarcely the issue here. Felix's allegiance is based on *values*, not heredity.

2 Two passages (pp. 89–93, 137–9, 1959 edn) are particularly relevant.

3 *The Art of George Eliot*, p. 174.

4 The best appreciation of this part of the book is in F. R. Leavis, *The Great Tradition* (Chatto & Windus, 1948), pp. 52 ff.

5 What Barbara Hardy refers to as 'narrative irony' (*Novels of George Eliot*, p. 93) operates only by implication. We may see the irony in the plot, but George Eliot makes little or nothing of these possibilities. It is interesting that in her chapter on 'The Ironical Image', in which Mrs. Hardy examines the deeper and more telling irony of George Eliot, *Felix Holt* is not mentioned.

6 *Ibid.*, p. 62.

7 *Op. cit.*, p. 134.

8 *Op. cit.*, p. 52.

9 From 'An Address to Working Men, by Felix Holt' in *Essays of George Eliot*, p. 429.

10 Raymond Williams, *Culture and Society 1780–1950* (Chatto & Windus, 1958), p. 109.

11 *Ibid.*, p. 104.

Beauchamp's Career

Meredith published *Beauchamp's Career* in 1876. Like several of his novels, it is a deeply political book – not merely in the more super-ficial sense that its main characters are politicians, but in the more important one that it is conceived in political terms: the human issues it discusses, even when they are personal and private in form, are presented as fundamentally political ones. The characters of the novel are all, though the setting is contemporary, seen as characters in history: they are individualised men and women, but they are always presented – consistently and insistently – as, in Aristotle's sense, political animals, social creatures inconceivable in any social setting save that of England of the 1870s. And England itself is seen, as few nineteenth-century English novelists see it, as part of Europe: an eccentric part, no doubt, with the British Navy (in which Lieutenant Beauchamp serves) turning the Channel into something more than a moat, but concentric too, never wholly isolated by those fogs and mists with which Dickens and Emily Brontë only too plausibly shroud their more insular island.

Behind *Beauchamp's Career* lie two specific events, as well as a longer train of development. One is a by-election at Southampton in 1867 in which Meredith had spent two months working for his friend, F. A. Maxse, recently retired from the Navy, who was stand-ing as Radical candidate. Maxse was beaten and Meredith was con-vinced that the principal cause was bribery, direct or oblique:

It is a very corrupt place. It has been found by experience of the enlarged franchise that where there are large labouring populations depending upon hire (especially in a corrupt and languishing town like Southampton) they will be thrown into the hands of the unscrupulous rich. . . . This is one of the evils we have to contend against until the poor fellows know . . . where their own interests lie and the necessity for their acting in unison.[1]

The other event is the Paris Commune, to which Meredith, like other positivist Radicals of the day (Frederic Harrison is perhaps the classic example), responded with a deep sympathy for the Communards, clearly expressed by Maxse when he wrote (in a lecture published in 1872) of

> that terrible week in May, when an ignorant soldiery entered Paris, on behalf of religion and order, and rioted in the bloodshed of Paris workers and their families, while the clerical journals hounded them on to massacre; and one of them indignantly demanded why only 40,000 Communists had been killed . . .
> We may dragoon, sabre and shoot down democracy in the manner they have been doing recently in Paris; we may invent any hideous epithet wherewith to deprecate those who labour for the collective improvement of mankind, still . . . will men be found, some madly but others wisely, to devote themselves to an incessant struggle for radical change.[2]

I have quoted the passage at length because of its direct relevance to *Beauchamp's Career*, and because it breathes the very spirit of what in Britain in the 1870s was meant by the word 'Radicalism'. For Nevil Beauchamp, the hero of Meredith's novel, is a Radical, and his career, though not, of course, in literal detail, is clearly based on that of F. A. Maxse.

Beauchamp's Career is an extraordinarily brilliantly conceived novel. E. M. Forster has called Meredith the finest contriver that English fiction has ever produced:[3] but contrivance is not an adequate word to do justice to this book. For though the plot is a very different sort of thing from that of, say, a Dickens novel, such as *Bleak House*, a matter essentially of a number of carefully planned and well-prepared scenes, it has the merit of all good plots – that of being beautifully at one with the novel's total meaning.

Beauchamp's Career is not, of course, the only novel of this period whose subject is Radicalism. We have only to cast our minds over a decade either way to recall *Felix Holt* (1866) and *The Princess Casamassina* (1886). Yet to compare the effect of Meredith's with George Eliot's novel is immediately to be aware of an essential difference. *Felix Holt* is about Radicalism, but what we tend to remember is not so much its 'subject' as the personal stories of Mrs Transome and Harold, of Esther and Felix, and the two centres of interest, the personal and the political, never quite unite, except in the very opening chapters. With *Beauchamp's Career* there is no such duality. Whether one says that the novel is about Radicalism or about Beauchamp makes little difference, for the two elements within the conception of the book, the general and the particular, the politico/social and the personal, are inseparable. Nevil Beauchamp is interesting because he is a romantic Radical: romantic Radicalism as a human and historical phenomenon is interesting because the presentation of Nevil Beauchamp's career makes it so.

It might be inferred from this that Meredith's, as opposed to George Eliot's, is in a narrower sense a political novel, that unity is achieved by a process of abstraction more thorough-going so that non-political irrelevances are not allowed to creep in. But the inference would be false. The canvas of *Beauchamp's Career* is not narrower than that of *Felix Holt*, the conception of politics not less broad, the characters not less concerned with the most varied problems of moral, personal and intellectual life. Although the title speaks of Beauchamp's career, it is not a political career in the specialized sense that is implied. Beauchamp's career is not one aspect of his life, but his life itself.

Meredith has left us his own account of his intentions in the novel:

It is philosophical-political, with no powerful stream of adventure: an attempt to show the forces round a young man of the present day, in England, who would move them, and finds them unutterably solid, though it is seen in the end that he does not altogether fail, has not lived quite in vain. Of course, this is done in the concrete. A certain drama of self-conquest is gone through, for the hero is not perfect.... And I think his History a picture of the time – taking its mental action, and material ease, and indifference, to be a necessary element of the picture.[4]

It is a surprisingly objective description. 'An attempt to show the forces round a young man' gives a good idea of the sort of book this is. Meredith is very conscious – as conscious as Disraeli – of 'forces' in the historical sense. But he tackles the problem of their representation in concrete terms on a far more serious artistic level than Disraeli had any conception of. Nevil Beauchamp is a young aristocrat. The 'forces' round him work both externally and internally. He is a character in history, coming to consciousness in a specific situation – against the background of the French scare whipped up by Palmerston in 1858, the Crimean War, and the extension of the franchise in Britain. He starts as a romantic nationalist patriot and becomes a Radical democrat and republican under the impact of external influences: the Crimean War itself, the reading of Carlyle, the condition of the poor, the influence of the Radical Dr Shrapnel. At the same time the development of his personal, as well as his public life is revealed, largely through his relations with three women: the French aristocrat, Renée, the *bourgeois* Tory heiress, Cecilia Halkett, and the Radical Dr Shrapnel's ward, Jenny Denham, who is not much of a Radical but something of an intellectual.

Meredith on the whole succeeds remarkably well in achieving a sort of continuous interplay of public and personal forces. It is the revelation of corruption and inefficiency in the Crimean War, the utter division between the ideal and the actual, that directs Beau-champ's high-principled romanticism into Radical political chan-nels. But he remains at this stage romantically enraptured with the aristocratic Renée. All Meredith's resources are brought into play for the achievement of an appropriate glamour: the original meeting in Venice could not be more propitious, for the gallant Beauchamp has saved the life of the young woman's military brother. The conflict between chivalrous romance and the unromantic realities of feudal marriage-arrangements is fought out against a backcloth of the sun-tipped Alps on the Adriatic. The glamour is highly theatrical and, on the level on which Meredith is working, effective. Nevil Beau-champ's progress is dramatised in a series of significant scenes and episodes, linked together by a certain amount of connecting narra-tive and observation, the point of which is to provide the reader with necessary background information. The first chapter – the farcical episode of the young man's personal challenge to the insolent French upstarts – establishes the high-flown romanticism which is Beau-champ's starting-point and also the nature of his relationship with Rosamund Culling, the lady whose position in his uncle's household is to be the focal-point of such plot as the novel has. A fuller insight into the romantic Beauchamp is provided by the longer Venetian episode, his capitulation to the brittle, aristocratic but vivacious charms of Renée, who is able to combine (since she is French) the classic attractions and rigid social standards of the feudal damsel in distress with the high sophistication of an anti-Puritan culture. Renée is lost, not because Beauchamp is insufficiently romantic, but because the family ethic of the landowning French aristocracy is too strong for him. But because his romanticism remains untarnished, albeit unsuccessful, he retains the glamorous idealisation of Renée in his heart.

Between the episode in Venice and the next major episode, the wooing of Cecilia Halkett, comes the development of Beauchamp's Radicalism, the seeds of which have already been sown by the disenchanting experience of actual war (an interesting reversal of the situation described in Tennyson's *Maud*) and the reading of Carlyle. At first his Radicalism is almost purely romantic – the outraged response to the shattering of his ideal conceptions of honour and integrity against the material world of British *bourgeois* philistinism. 'Manchester', the embodiment of the nightmares of his uncle, the Whig landowner, is for Beauchamp, too, the villain of the piece. At first his attack on 'Manchester' is from the point of view of an idealised feudal past:

The inflated state of the unchivalrous middle, denominated Manchester, terrified him (iii, 24).[5]

But under the influence of the Radical Dr Shrapnel it changes. Shrapnel attacks 'Manchester' from a different standpoint:

. . . The people are the Power to come. Oppressed, unprotected, abandoned; left to the ebb and flow of the tides of the market, now taken on to work, now cast off to starve, committed to the shifting laws of demand and supply, slaves of Capital – the whited name for old accursed Mammon
. . . .
'. . . Now comes on the workman's era' (xxix, 271, 273).

Beauchamp casts in his lot with Shrapnel and becomes the Radical candidate for Bevisham (Southampton).

The chapters (xviii, xix) on election canvassing in *Beauchamp's Career* are something of a *tour de force* on Meredith's part, an extremely difficult, directly political episode, carried through with a good deal of *brio* and insight. But the centre of attention in the part of the novel which involves the election is Beauchamp's simultaneous personal crisis – his relations with Cecilia Halkett and his response to Renée's peremptory summons to her château in Normandy.

Cecilia Halkett is rich, beautiful (her 'English' beauty is remarkably well evoked) and a Tory. She likes and admires Nevil Beauchamp, but is repelled by his ideas. He admires her beauty and respects her quality of mind, a respect which Meredith's presentation admirably reinforces. Cecilia is not 'converted' to Beauchamp's Radicalism, but she is considerably affected by it. When she has to choose between his, to her, mistaken integrity and the unprincipled manœuvring of her father's Tory friends, she is on Beauchamp's

side. For a time it seems as though she may 'come over', and it is one
of Meredith's achievements to convey the complex interpenetration
of ideas and feelings in this relationship. It is not a simple matter of
a conflict between 'love' and 'reason'. Meredith, for all his tendency
to conceive his situations somewhat abstractly, knows very well that
life is more complex and richer than that. Cecilia's 'ideas' are also
'feelings': her Toryism is largely instinctive and class-determined,
nor can her affection for Nevil be separated from the 'ideas' involved.
If Nevil were ignoble, she would not wish to love him; and the revelation (through personal experience) that Radicalism is not ignoble must affect her judgment of its intellectual and moral validity.
From Beauchamp's side the interplay of public and private attitudes
is also complex. He recognises that the charm of Cecilia is linked
with her way of life, her wealth. In a splendid passage, unmatched
in its way in Victorian fiction, he watches Cecilia's yacht, the
Esperanza, carry her on the Solent:

He was dropped by the *Esperanza's* boat near Otley ferry, to walk along the
beach to Bevisham, and he kept eye on the elegant vessel as she glided
swan-like to her moorings off Mount Laurels park through dusky merchant
craft, colliers, and trawlers, loosely shaking her towering snow-white sails,
unchallenged in her scornful supremacy; an image of a refinement of
beauty, and of a beautiful servicelessness.
    As the yacht, so the mistress: things of wealth, owing their graces to
wealth, devoting them to wealth – splendid achievements of art both! and
dedicated to the gratification of the superior senses.
    Say that they were precious examples of an accomplished civilization;
and perhaps they did offer a visible ideal of grace for the rough world to
aim at. They might in the abstract address a bit of a monition to the un-
cultivated, and encourage the soul to strive toward perfection in beauty:
and there is no contesting the value of beauty when the soul is taken into
account. But were they not in too great a profusion in proportion to their
utility? That was the question for Nevil Beauchamp. The democratic spirit
inhabiting him, temporarily or permanently, asked whether they were not
increasing to numbers which were oppressive? And further, whether it was
good for the country, the race, ay, the species, that they should be so distinctly removed from the thousands who fought the grand, and the grisly,
old battle with nature for bread of life. Those grimy sails of the colliers and
fishing-smacks, set them in a great sea, would have beauty for eyes and soul
beyond that of elegance and refinement. And do but look on them thoughtfully, the poor are everlastingly, unrelievedly, in the abysses of the great
sea . . . (xv, 129–30).

It is a passage which well illustrates Meredith's method. My
immediate point is to note how uncompromisingly he breaks

through the *bourgeois* convention that the private and the public life are separable and that emotion is properly the province of one, 'reason' the other. The Beauchamp–Cecilia love relationship, the Radical–Tory political relationships and the popular–*bourgeois* class relationship entwine themselves into an inseparable fusion, expressed most successfully in images like that of the yacht and the colliers in which visual and social significance are united.

Beauchamp's failure with Cecilia is due to reasons altogether more complex than his failure to win Renée. The immediate cause may be Cecilia's conviction that she cannot replace the French girl in his heart, but the underlying reasons are subtler and more important. Fundamentally, Cecilia cannot draw herself sufficiently out of her class life. Like Renée, she submits to her father's social attitudes, superficially in order not to hurt him, more basically because they are her attitudes too. And here Meredith establishes a subtle point. Had the battle been simply between Beauchamp and his cousin Baskelett (a Tory candidate) and such representatives of Toryism as Grancey Laspel (the renegade Liberal) or even her father, Beauchamp might well, on the strength of his superior integrity, have triumphed. But there is another Tory in the picture, Sumner Austin, and it is he who most influences Cecilia, providing through his intelligent cynicism a haven of enlightenment within the ruling-class camp. 'Austin's a speculative Tory, I know, and that's his weakness' (xxxvii) is Colonel Halkett's comment when he learns that his friend has been putting forward to Cecilia views which give Nevil Beauchamp credit for sincerity and treat his Radicalism with respect. Halkett thinks Summer Austin is selling out to the enemy, but in truth the old lawyer is wiser from the Tory point of view than the true-blue Colonel. For it is he who gives Cecilia the strength to resist Beauchamp.

The decision, however, is not entirely Cecilia's. If she is drawn into marriage with the sound, dull Blackburn Tuckham, it is not simply her own lack of moral courage that is to blame. For there have been reservations about the relationship on Beauchamp's part too, and it is these reservations which not quite consciously lead him to postpone his proposal of marriage until it is too late. For he from his side clearly recognises the conflict between Cecilia's attachment to Tory ideas and his own Radical aspirations, and lacks full confidence that he could in fact carry her with him. The fact that he wants money to start a Radical newspaper and that Cecilia has money increases his scruples. And the attraction of Renée – now married to an elderly French *roué* – though less important by this time than Cecilia imagines, remains in Beauchamp's mind a compelling force, an incompletely subdued area of romantic irresponsibility.

How compelling it can be is illustrated by the episode of the sudden summons to France which Beauchamp, in the midst of the election campaign, chivalrously answers, thereby decisively contributing, through the ensuing scandal which his opponents are able to imply, to his defeat at the polls. Beauchamp responds unhesitatingly to Renée's call of distress, only to find that it was, rather, a whistle to a faithful dog, a display of power and a result of boredom. But again Meredith's contrivance is of unusual subtlety, for he suggests very successfully the real distress, the actual desperation which the Frenchwoman's triviality of life conceals. So that the episode at Tourdestelle, while it has the effect of underlining for Beauchamp the impossibility of reconciling Renée and Radicalism and of undermining – still unconsciously rather than overtly – his romanticism, also enables Meredith to develop further his image of the anachronistic decadence of the aristocracy and to prepare the ground for his next great episode for Renée, her flight to England.

By the time Renée is sufficiently desperate to throw herself upon Beauchamp's chivalry Beauchamp has changed. This episode – the arrival of the Frenchwoman in London, the high comedy involved in the averting of scandal, the realisation by Beauchamp that he no longer wants what he has romantically built up over the years, the consequences in pain and humiliation for Renée herself – all this is carried through triumphantly and tied up by one of Meredith's most brilliant strokes: the marriage of Beauchamp's uncle, Everard Romfrey, now Lord Avondale, to his lady housekeeper, Rosamund Culling.

This marriage is precipitated by the conjunction of a most complex series of events and motives. It represents at once the old aristocrat's revenge on his erring nephews – Beauchamp and Baskelett – his appreciation of the quality of Mrs Culling's devotion to his interests, the triumph (and at the same time frustration) of her efforts on behalf of her beloved Nevil, and the culmination of the social game that has been played with such sophistication around the flight, and return to conjugal humiliation, of Renée. To see such a moment primarily in terms of Meredith's unique technical skill with a plot is to do the novelist much less than justice. The moment is, technically, a triumphant one precisely because the strands of the plot have represented and involved so many real and relevant forces – psychological and social – which do indeed unite to form an episode of a significance which, like all good artistic images, is at once as complex as life itself and as concrete.

So complex indeed (though not troublesome or fussy) is the structure of this novel that there has meanwhile been going on, alongside the development of the Beauchamp–Renée relationship, another development equally important, which involves Cecilia, but in which Renée is not implicated – the baiting and horse-whipping of Dr Shrapnel.

Shrapnel is a slightly absurd and not wholly sympathetic figure, even though he represents the Radical point of view which is throughout the novel the political standpoint from which Meredith writes. The good doctor is a windbag. He has absorbed more of Carlyle than his critical ideas. And besides being a crank and a bit of a bore, he is hopelessly out of touch with many political realities, so that one of the problems of the Bevisham Radicals is to keep him out of the way during the election. But at the same time Shrapnel's integrity and the nobility and essential rightness of his ideas are emphasised; so that when Everard Romfrey, representative of the old world of feudal ideas, egged on by the unscrupulous Cecil Baskelett, and half-unwittingly encouraged by Rosamund Culling herself, is persuaded (quite falsely) that his lady housekeeper has been insulted by Shrapnel and takes his horsewhip into Bevisham, the full horror of the half-farcical episode comes home. It would be hard to find a better example of the strength of Meredith than the whole conception of this episode. Everything about it is magnificently integrated. The assault itself is not described. We see Romfrey departing for Bevisham, whip in hand; at once Beauchamp's view of the old Radical is reiterated, he is planning to take Dr Shrapnel for a voyage for the sake of his health; we hear of what Romfrey has done through Colonel Halkett's telling Cecilia, a method which allows us at once to grasp, through Cecilia's horrified comprehension, all its appalling implications, and at the same time to record the Colonel's complacent approval. A fuller description of the assault comes almost immediately, through a minor character, 'an Admiral of the Fleet and ex-minister of the Whig Government', who gives what might be called the public, ruling-class view of the outrage (xxxii, 303).

Meanwhile, Beauchamp is still ignorant of what has happened, and the next time we see him is when he arrives at Steynham to face his uncle.

What makes the episode so striking, so much more than an ingenious melodramatic contrivance, is its *rightness* on so many levels. As a symbolic illustration of the conflict between past and future, this particular encounter of Beauchamp's two guardians is magnificently right. A horsewhip has for centuries been an emblem of class-domination, as a famous Marx Brothers' joke ('If I had a horse I'd horsewhip you') reminds us. Everard Romfrey's motives are chivalrous, his action barbarous and his understanding entirely erroneous. He allows himself to be misled because of his political prejudices, and the misleading is itself wonderfully convincing, for though it is Cecil Baskelett, the conscious mischief-maker, who lights the trail, it is Rosamund Culling, sincere and conscientious, who has laid it. The whole description of Mrs Culling's reactions to Dr Shrapnel, her deep class prejudices, her desire to prevent Nevil from falling into the old man's clutches, her half-conviction that she has been insulted, her horror on the discovery of what her self-deception has led to, all this is superbly done. One is reminded, perhaps, of E. M. Forster's treatment of the Adela Quested part of *A Passage to India*: but a comparison leads to conclusions so much in Meredith's favour that one is surprised that so scrupulous a writer as Forster should not seem more aware of his own great debt to the older novelist.

The horsewhipping of Dr Shrapnel emerges with a kind of high artistic inevitability out of the main general themes of *Beauchamp's Career* as well as out of the detailed personal relationships of its plot. It symbolises, as I have suggested, the underlying conflict between the old ruling class and the groping popular movement, and does so with remarkable justice because the personal psychological basis of the episode corresponds so exactly to the general social movements involved. As a central, climactic situation, it poses to the individual characters involved choices which are at the same time private and public, personal and general: each is forced to take a personal moral position which involves in practice a class position. For some of the principal contenders the first choices are simple, spontaneous. Everard Romfrey's ruling-class friends, Whig or Tory, rally instinctively to his side, even though some, like Summer Austin, see the folly and brutality of his action. And to Beauchamp and the Radicals, Dr Shrapnel's entourage, there is no conflict of loyalty whatever: the moral issue is simple – as indeed objectively it is. The two people most agonised by the situation are the two women who love Beauchamp, but belong by birth and feeling to the ruling-class party – Cecilia Halkett and Rosamund Culling; and Meredith's account of their reactions is masterly. Once again it is not, with either of them, a simple conflict of 'feeling' *versus* 'reason' or 'love' *versus* 'prejudice'. Because Cecilia values Beauchamp she cannot see the assault on Dr Shrapnel as her father sees it, retribution richly deserved. To her it is barbarous; she is in no doubt about that. Where she falters is in her judgment about its fundamental wrongness, its total dishonourability:

Grieved though she was on account of that Dr Shrapnel, her captive heart resented the anticipated challenge to her to espouse his cause or languish (xxxii, 306).

Cecilia stands by Beauchamp, but with reservations. She goes with him to Bevisham, but stays outside when he visits the sick Shrapnel. Her heart is captive, imprisoned by her class allegiance, which is stronger than her feeling for Beauchamp or her respect for truth.

Rosamund Culling is, within her limitations, more courageous, for she, unlike Cecilia, feels a personal responsibility for the shameful assault, and this leads to an examination of conscience, meticulous and sincere, which has, most convincingly, the effect of raising her whole moral stature and – a brilliant touch this – of making Everard Romfrey see her differently and, indeed, marry her. The marriage involves a move into the final reaches of the book, in which Romfrey and Shrapnel are, personally, reconciled. It is Rosamund who restores honour to the Romfreys, rather in the way (though the means are utterly unlike) that in *Bleak House* honour comes back to Sir Leicester Dedlock in his defeat.

The closing chapters of *Beauchamp's Career* are, in terms of the story the book has told, almost arbitrary. Renée and romantic irresponsibility have been rejected; Cecilia has married her dull Tory dog; Rosamund Culling has brought about the reconciliation of Romfrey and Shrapnel; Nevil Beauchamp has recovered from an almost fatal illness. How is his career to develop now that the conflicts which have served to express its essence have been, in some sort at least, resolved? We are left with a series of images, none of them as fully developed as the central scenes and conflicts of the book: the image of Beauchamp's marriage to Jenny Denham, an unromantic but apparently happy one, of his cruising around the Mediterranean studying Plato and rejecting Dr Shrapnel's compulsive insistence to return to the political fray, and, finally, of his jumping into the Solent to save a boy from drowning and in doing so drowning himself. The final image is clearly intended as, in the least ambiguous sense, symbolic. A working-class child's life is saved at the expense of Nevil Beauchamp's:

> This is what we have in exchange for Beauchamp!
> It was not uttered, but it was visible in the blank stare at one another of the two men who loved Beauchamp, after they had examined the insignificant bit of mudbank life remaining in this world in the place of him (lvi, 527).

This is evolution, the survival of the fittest, the way the world progresses.

That final page of Meredith's novel recalls, perhaps, the close of two other novels, one written fifty years before *Beauchamp's Career*, the other fifty years later. In Stendhal's *Armance*, the young Byronic hero, Olivier, believing himself to be impotent, dives to death in the Aegean. The hero of Erich Kästner's novel, *Fabian*, 1931 a name which also tells its story, lives impotent through the chaotic, cynical, doomed days of the dying Weimar Repulic and the novel ends with him jumping into the river to save a child from drowning:

> The little boy swam ashore, howling. Fabian sank.
> Unfortunately, he had never learned to swim.

One remembers, too, the end of Jack London's *Martin Eden*, and the actual death of Hart Crane, and the significance of Madame Sosostris's advice to fear death by water deepens.

Beauchamp's Career is, I have hoped to suggest, a novel of remarkable interest and one greatly underrated in current literary criticism. I am also conscious that, in writing about Meredith's book, I have given the impression of its being better than it actually is. This is because the conception of the book considered in general terms, the idea behind it and the ideas involved in it are in fact more impressive than the book itself. It is, one might almost say (though this would be unfair), a better book to talk about than to read.

It is not easy to substantiate this view except on the basis of the rather unsatisfactory, subjective assertion that one does not sufficiently care about anything that happens in *Beauchamp's Career*. For all the interest it evokes, one is seldom touched. There are,.it must be added, important exceptions to this statement. The whole presentation of Rosamund Culling seems to me admirable; the canvassing episode at Bevisham is brilliantly done; the rejection of Renée is genuinely moving. And yet, by and large, what one admires about the novel is, I think one has to say, more fully expressed in the word 'conception' than 'achievement'; so that Forster's own word, 'contrivance', does have, even in this — one of Meredith's undoubted successes — a certain pejorative force, even though it seems to me so much less than just.

I would suggest that the reason why *Beauchamp's Career*, for all the qualities I admire in it, does not move or delight me as much as I feel it ought to, lies in a failure in style rather different from the sort of thing Forster indicates in *Aspects of the Novel*. One might put it this way: a novelist (whatever the particular quirks or intricacies of his vision or his philosophy) always has to present his situations either from the inside or from the outside. This is a social as much as a literary matter. I do not say he may not be able to do both, and I am not passing any value-judgement as to the relative merits of the two methods. Jane Austen among English novelists pre-eminently represents the one method, Fielding the other. I do not think Meredith manages either approach. He does not get so deep and close, so far *within* a situation, that it dramatises itself, so to speak, convincing us utterly of its authenticity by making us share the vibrations of the characters who are acting it out. We very seldom (in this context) know sufficiently what his characters *are*; the precise quality of their feelings at the lived moment is not conveyed to us. We never really know, in that sense, what Beauchamp feels about Renée any more than (to change novels) we know what Lucy feels when Richard Feverel leaves her stranded at Cowes. For social reasons, Meredith cannot allow himself to work from inside.

Now this wouldn't matter at all if he had found some other way to bring his people fully to life, to give to a situation that breath of living significance (or significant living) which convinces us of artistic authenticity. But unfortunately, having opted for the 'outside' method, the method of Stendhal and E. M. Forster, he fails to establish for himself a sufficiently firm vantage-point from which to operate. This question of 'point-of-view' seems to me, in any analysis of Meredith, the fundamental one. What is his relationship to what he is describing? What is his relationship to his reader? On what is his observation, his judgment, his artistic sensibility, his *style*, based?

I think it is the expression of an intelligence which is remarkably acute, deep and far-ranging, but essentially abstract and lacking in real confidence, self-confidence, the artist's secure yet perilous poise. I think this is at bottom due to Meredith's isolation, his inability to identify himself with any social force or developing cultural tradition from which he might draw strength and the best kind of self-confidence. No British writer of his time – Dickens once dead – had so deep an understanding of the Victorian world and the way it was going. No contemporary novelist, not even George Eliot, got on to something so deep and promising and contemporary as Meredith's apprehension of what he, like Balzac before him, called 'egoism', the essence of nineteenth-century *bourgeois* man. No novel of its decade – the decade following *Our Mutual Friend* – says so much that is acute and penetrating about Victorian England as *Beauchamp's Career*. The trouble is that it says it – to such an extent – *abstractly*, rather than in the concrete terms of art. For the consequence of Meredith's failure to break through his social isolation is his taking refuge in a style in which a false rhetoric clothes an insecure irony.

The elements of this rhetoric – the juxtaposition of archaisms with colloquial speech; the heavy reiterated biblical phrases with their persistent 'cometh's' and 'goeth's'; the ridiculous inversions which would allow a sentence like 'Drove she ducklings to the water, every morning just at nine' to pass as prose; the tricks of Parliamentary oratory; the deliberate 'poetic' phrases; the coy confidences whispered *sotto voce* like the calculated indiscretions of Millamant's tea-table – what they amount to is a desperate attempt to cover up the actual insecurity of Meredith's own position: and they dominate the scene to the extent that he fails to find a standpoint which can give him real sustenance to back and fill out his real perceptions. Meredith is a vulgar writer precisely because he is afraid to be vulgar. Where Dickens, at his best, draws so effectively on the popular culture of his day – the fairy tales and nursery stories, the music-hall and melodrama, the popular songs and lampoons – and above all on the actual speech of the common people, Meredith falls back on a cultural *mélange* which he himself can only half respect.

The key-figure behind Meredith, for better and for worse, is undoubtedly Carlyle. It was from Carlyle, more than from anyone, that he gained his insight into the British world of his time – his sense of the corrupting power of the cash-nexus, of the social movement from the world of Sir Austin Feverel and Everard Romfrey to that of Manchester and of the consequences of this in human alienation and impoverished relationships.

The strength of Carlyle lies in his insights into *general* social and historical phenomena. He has a good deal of Hegel's sense of the nature and universality of process. The movement of things, the development of ideas, a sense of the revolutionary nature of reality: these perceptions impregnate his work. And he is shrewd too. He sees the tremendous significance of Chartism, the fundamental fraudulence of the business-men's enthusiasm for 'democracy'. But because he is so incorrigibly, in the philosophic sense, an idealist, his most potent insights are seldom disciplined by that concrete analysis which is the basis of the artist's perceptions. Of course, it is not difficult to see (with our rather smug hindsight) why Carlyle took refuge in heroes and rhetoric and romanticism in the pejorative sense and has to be seen, historically, as a forerunner of Nietzsche rather than of William Morris. It was extraordinarily difficult, in the first half of the nineteenth century, for the *bourgeois* intellectual, however shrewd and even revolutionary, to commit himself to an actual social movement, to become engaged in the realist's way in the down-to-earth grappling with concrete human problems. Carlyle's great contribution to the development of the novel was an indirect one – he helped men to see themselves as characters in history.

The Ordeal of Richard Feverel is even more closely connected with Carlyle than *Beauchamp's Career*. And whereas in the later novel, through its strong framework of political actuality, the problems Carlyle raises are elucidated, rendered more concrete, carried forward even (that last image of Beauchamp drowned in the Solent tells us a great deal about heroes and hero-worship), in *Feverel* the Carlylean cloudiness is mirrored rather than dispersed. Because in *Feverel* politics appears only on the sidelines (like the information that Austin Wentworth is a republican) the Romantic elements in both Carlyle and Meredith are given freer play. Sir Austin's 'system', which, more than anything, the book is 'about', is never really artistically defined. For that we have to wait for *The Egoist*. Here it is swamped in irony. And when, at the very end of the book, Lady Blandish grasps the full horror of it, the revelation is unsatisfactory, hysterical, abstract. All the positive forces of the novel depend on an objective definition, within the terms of art, of Richard's and Lucy's romantic love. But this never comes. The relationship is never 'placed'. It would be nice to take the novel as an extended comment on Carlyle's advice to the young to abandon Byron and take up Goethe. But in fact it is so full of the paraphernalia of Byronism that Goethe never really gets a look in. I think Meredith's *intention* in *Feverel* is fairly clear. As he himself put it: 'The moral is that no System of the sort succeeds with human nature, unless the originator has conceived it purely independent of personal passion.' In other words, 'To change anything you first have to be objective'. Meredith goes on (analysing the public response to his book): 'My fault has been that I have made the book so dull that it does not attract a second reading.' He ought to have said: 'My fault is that I have myself failed in creating an objective world of art and have stuffed it instead with Romantic verbiage.'[6]

This sounds unsympathetic. I do not mean it to be. Romanticism in its various forms and aspects and implications is the great critical problem of English nineteenth-century literature, and it is a problem precisely because the Romantic impulse contains at the same time all that is best and worst in the literature of the time. If Meredith – or Carlyle – had drunk less deep of the Romantic draught they would certainly not be the writers they are; but it is also doubtful whether they would have been writers at all.

Notes

1   *The Letters of George Meredith* (ed. C. L. Cline), 1970, Vol. I, p. 379, letter to Arthur G. Meredith.
2   *The Causes of Social Revolt* (1872).
3   *Aspects of the Novel* (1927), pp. 121–2.
4   *The Letters of George Meredith*, Vol. I, p. 485, letter to M. D. Conway.
5   The text is taken from the edition of 1897.
6   *The Letters of George Meredith*, Vol. I, p. 40, letter to Samuel Lucas.

What is Kim?

Everyone admires *Kim*, but among those who have written about the book there is little agreement. It wonderfully evokes British India – the sights and sounds and smells, the manifold peoples and cultures – there is no dispute about that. But to what end? With what meaning? How, above all, are we to take the reiterated question 'Who is Kim?' reaching its climax in the last pages of the book '"I am Kim. I am Kim. And what is Kim?" His soul repeated it again and again.' '*Thatt* is the question, as Shakespeare hath said.'

Mr J. I. M. Stewart says that:

Kipling came nearest to a successful novel in a book for young people – for we lose contact with *Kim* (1901) when we regard this story of an orphan white boy gone native, and using his native cloak of invisibility to become a peerless Secret Service agent, as other than essentially that.[1]

Mr Stewart's is, it must be admitted, aesthetically the safe line, for it allows us to respond to the colour and high spirits of the book – its remarkable virtuosity – without being faced with the need to take it seriously. But does it really fill the bill any more satisfactorily than the approach of Mr Edmund Wilson, which Mr Stewart is justifiably querying? *Kim*, argues Mr Wilson,[2] 'deals with the gradual dawning of consciousness that he is really a Sahib' and he finds it hard to respond altogether sympathetically to the book because of Kipling's failure to measure all the implications of what being a Sahib involves. The trouble with this argument, however plausible in relation to Kipling's outlook as a whole, is that, as far as *Kim* goes, it isn't quite true. Kim *is* conscious of being a Sahib, which in terms of British Indian lingo he indeed is, and his education at Lucknow and

with his Secret Service chiefs naturally enough increases such consciousness; but this is scarcely the central subject of the book, and,
looking at the novel as a whole, the remarkable thing is how little of
a Sahib Kim ends up as. In other words, Mr Wilson and Mr Stewart,
though in one sense standing at opposite poles critically, both fail to
come to terms with the climax and end of the book.

This is not altogether surprising for the end of *Kim* is certainly
very odd and I would not wish to suggest any watertight interpretation, a hundred per cent guaranteed. But whereas it is not easy to
know exactly how Kipling meant the end of the novel to be taken, it
is fairly easy to say what he did not, *could* not from the very nature of
the achieved book, intend. Mr Carrington, for instance, in his
valuable biography of Kipling, asserts

> Kim . . . has reached a stage of maturity and must take a decision. No
> longer a ragamuffin of the bazaars, but a beautiful godlike youth, he must
> choose between contemplation and action. Is he to follow the Lama or to
> return to the chains which enslave the Pathan and the Babu to their
> material duties? . . . Though it is not expressly stated, the reader is left
> with the assurance that Kim, like Mowgli and like the Brushwood Boy,
> will find reality in action, not in contemplation.[3]

I do not want to pre-judge the issue which I shall be discussing: but
surely this is an untenable argument. If Kipling intended to assure
us that Kim will find reality in action as opposed to contemplation,
why on earth did he not take steps to do so? If this is the issue and
this the choice, nothing would have been easier for Kipling than to
have made it clear. Kim has only to murmur a few words to the
Babu or to wake before Mahumud goes off and his commitment to
them and their Game (in so far as that is what is meant by 'action')
will be established. But the words never come. Mahmud and Hurree
assume he will come back to them. *We* can only permit ourselves
such an assumption if we ignore the whole weight of the final episodes of the book, whose movement in fact is in a contrary direction.

It is the oddness of the ending of the book[4] that reinforces the
temptation to see *Kim* as essentially not about Kim but about India.
There is a plausible, and indeed fruitful, case for such an emphasis
and Mr Edward Shanks made it when he wrote:

> If, as has been argued, it should be possible to say in a sentence what any
> real book is *about*, then it must be said that *Kim* is *about* the infinite and
> joyous variety of India for him who has the eyes to see it and the heart to
> rejoice in it.[5]

There is a great deal to be said for this approach. It is precisely this
sense of the teeming fullness and variegated colour of Indian life that
we most remember when we casually recall the book. India is spread
out before us, from Ceylon in the sea to the Himalayas that break
through the clouds, and the constant journeying of the main characters is like the movement of tiny figures across an enormous map.
Not that there is anything *general* about Kipling's picture of India.
The human figures are so strongly drawn and so idiosyncratic, their
language so rich and various, the colours of the landscape so sharp
and the tastes on the tongue so vivid, the sense of the past so pervasive, that there is no danger of a merely geographical – let alone
ethnological – survey. There is in fact a strong case for describing
Kim as being essentially about India the subcontinent rather than
about Kim the boy.

For the revelation of the richness and complexity of the Indian
scene Kipling has hit upon a series of remarkably effective ploys.
The most important, basic indeed to the whole project, is the idea of
revealing a whole society and culture through the eyes and experiences of not one, but two central figures, both of whom are at once
foreign and yet deeply involved. That Kim is not Indian is obvious
and every Western reader immediately grasps its implications. But
we do not perhaps recognise so consciously that Teshoo Lama is also
'pardesi' (a foreigner) speaking a language and practising a religion
which to the Indians is in some ways more unfamiliar than the British kinds. The Lama is, of course, Asian and in many respects more
at home in the Indian culture than an Englishman, but his strange-
ness is an important part of his role in the story. T. S. Eliot has
spoken perceptively of Kipling's

peculiar detachment and remoteness from all environment, a universal
foreignness which is the reverse side of his strong feeling for India, for the
Empire, for England and for Sussex, a remoteness as of an alarmingly intelligent visitor from another planet. He remains somehow alien and aloof
from all with which he identifies himself.[6]

This seems to me to express admirably the effect we get in *Kim*. It is
summed up best, perhaps, in the crucial last scene of all in which
Kim and Lama, the non-Indians, are left alone, deeply imbedded in
Indian things and nature, yet also isolated, the life of India going
on around them, without them, almost in spite of them. But the
point one wants to stress about this foreignness of Kim and the Lama

is that it gives Kipling, throughout the book, the perfect device for refracting the Indian scene, the perfect 'point of view' for his project; for these two 'experiencing agents' are at once inside and outside what they are experiencing and yet poles apart from one another, so that what they see and feel and respond to in the life around them is recorded in ways which set up for the reader the most revealing and valuable of tensions and insights.

This is one of the reasons why Kipling's own description of the book as 'picaresque' is, though one sees what he means, not very helpful in any attempt to define its quality. *Kim* is picaresque in the sense that its construction seems to be loose and episodic, that it consists of a string of situations rather than of one central 'dramatic' one, and that Kim himself has some of the characteristic attributes of the picaresque hero. But really the use of the word doesn't get us very far. Even the construction is subtler than one might at first suppose. Very few of the chapters end with the ending of an episode: on the contrary, Kipling's sense of continuity and juxtaposition are highly sophisticated. Again, the substitution of two for one single main figure at once undermines (as *Don Quixote* and *Joseph Andrews* long ago demonstrated) the essential simplicity of the picaresque method. And, perhaps most important of all, *Kim* is not in the end – or even, really, at the beginning – an essentially realistic (in the technical sense) account of the adventures of the main figure, or even of two main figures.

There is indeed an important element of truth in the view of Mr Stewart, that Kim has to be seen as a *Boys Own Paper* hero. Kim is a wonderfully attractive creature, but on the level of surface realism, one can scarcely take him quite seriously. If he is, as I believe, to be taken seriously on a level that is more important than surface realism, it is as well to recognise what we are doing.

Kim is a kind of idealised embodiment of what Kipling would have liked an inhabitant of British India to be: above all pettiness and below all theorising. (If one wishes to be biographical, one can say that he represents perhaps the best of the five-year-old Rudyard Kipling's potential selves.) This doesn't sound very complimentary, but it is in fact as good a basis for an artistic creation as any. Kim's progress may be on one level unbelievable (so is Perdita's) but in the important ways it is all right. For the basic imaginative conception of the Little Friend of the All the World corrresponds to a real human potential at this point in history and the tendency of ideal-

isation is in fact largely offset by the creation of the complementary
character of the Lama and the superb and utterly concrete reality of
the world which they explore.

Good picaresque literature – the *Lazarillo de Tormes* or, to stretch
a point, *Moll Flanders* – gets its effect from the straightforward
juxtaposition of an alien or unorthodox or at least irreverent and
down-to-earth consciousness upon a social reality which can only
marginally absorb it. This sets up a peculiar tension in which a simple but basic irony is brought into play and which historically tends
to work well because the irreverence of the picaresque hero in fact
embodies in a crude form some sort of human protest that will burst
out later into a respectable philosophy.

Kim, for most of Kipling's novel, has the underdog quality which
we associate with the genuine picaresque heroes and which comes
out in his unfailing resourcefulness. Like Lazarillo or the Artful
Dodger he knows his way around. What limits our response to Kipling's assurance that 'he had known all evil since he could speak' is
our sense that Kim himself until the very end tends to escape too
easily (partly because he is, after all, as a last resort a sahib) from the
consequences of the evil he encounters. He has the characteristic of
people in pornographic literature (I am not suggesting of course
that *Kim* is pornographic) that he does not have to stay till next
morning. Until, that is, he establishes a real, long-term relationship
with the Lama. All his other relationships, even with Mahbub,
whom he is genuinely fond of, are relationships of convenience.
That is why we cannot take him as seriously as, say, Huck Finn as a
picaresque hero. Yet we *do* take him seriously, on a somewhat different level.

How are we to define that level? Mr Kinkead-Weekes, in what
seems to me much the best consideration of *Kim*,[7] once or twice uses
the word 'emblematic.' Kim sitting on Zam-Zammah ('who hold
Zam-Zammah hold the Punjab') he describes as emblematic, and it
is the right word, indicating Kim's status as going beyond the
casually picaresque. Part of Kim's function in the book, as I have
suggested, is as an agent of discovery, the discovery of India to the
(presumed British) reader: Kipling's not infrequent use of the word
'we' to cover the inhabitants of British India is another facet of this
aspect of the book. But Kim, of course, is much more than a technical device: he begins, one might say, as the embodiment of a Kip-
lingesque ideal; but he finishes as a young man with a nervous

breakdown grappling with a real and difficult problem and one highly relevant to his world and time. Up to the point when, his 'training' finished, Kim goes to find Teshoo Lama in the temple of the Tirthankers in Benares his relation to reality is of a kind comparable to that of a Stalky or a Mowgli, though the reality he touches is far richer and more complex. Then, when he rejoins the Lama, he at first operates again in the same way, though on a rather more mature level. But the curing of the Jat's child is essentially the same kind of exploit as the steering of the Lama on to the train at Lahore, an exercise in superior technical know-how. Then comes the episode with the Mahratta on the train. For the first time Kim's operations as an agent in the Game and his function as the Lama's *chela* cut directly across one another. The Lama immediately notices this:

'Oh, *chela*, see how thou art overtaken! Thou didst cure the Kamboth's child solely to acquire merit. But thou didst put a spell on the Mahratta with prideful workings – I watched thee – and with side-long glances to bewilder an old old man and a foolish farmer: whence calamity and suspicion!'

Kim, with considerable self-control, does not argue but tries to pacify the old man with the ambiguous admission 'Where I have offended thee I have done wrong'; but the Lama is too intelligent to accept an apology which does not go to the roots of the problem:

'It is more, *chela*. Thou hast loosed an Act upon the world, and as a stone thrown into a pool so spread the consequences thou canst not tell how far.'[8]

From now on the conflict between the Lama's values and those embodied in the Game cannot be suppressed.

'Then all Doing is evil?' Kim replied, lying out under a big tree at the fork of the Doon road, watching the little ants run over his hand. 'To abstain from action is well – except to acquire merit.' 'At the Gates of Learning we were taught that to abstain from action was unbefitting a Sahib. And I am a Sahib.' 'Friend of all the World' – the Lama looked directly at Kim . . . 'To those who follow the Way there is neither black nor white, Hind nor Bhotiyal. We be all souls seeking escape . . .'

The conflict, always implicit, has never before been so uncompromisingly stated. The effect on Kim is to lead him to ask a question which may not at first seem quite relevant:

'I ate thy bread for three years – as thou knowest. [He is referring to the fact that the Lama has paid his school fees at Lucknow.] Holy One, whence came –?'

'There is much wealth, as men count it, in Bhotiyal,' the Lama returned with composure. 'In my own place I have the illusion of honour. I ask for that I need. I am not concerned with the account. That is for my monastery. Ai! The black high seats in the monastery, and the novices all in order!'[9]

And he goes on to reminisce about Tibet. We are not told whether Kim is satisfied by the answer. But it is interesting, and significant, that he should have asked the question at this particular moment.

I think it is clear that there has developed by this point in Kim's mind a clearer comprehension than before of the issues with which he is faced. His question about the source of the Lama's income is, in that context, highly appropriate, for what is emerging is a conflict between two approaches to life: an idealist approach, embodied in the Lama, which sees merit as lying in the rejection of action and the granting of entire precedence to the Idea; and the rather crude materialist approach of Kim, and the participants in the Game, for whom realism is essentially a shrewd awareness of the tactical activity necessary to cope with specific situations. In the earlier sections of the book this conflict, inherent from the very beginning, has largely taken the form of contrast. The Lama is unworldly, Kim precociously worldly. The Lama thinks a prostitute is a nun, Kim knows all about such things. The Lama is vulnerable, Kim tough and protective. Also, balancing the account, Kim is frightened of the cobra, the Lama serenely humane; Kim knowing, the Lama wise. Such contrasts are dramatically effective, injecting their own irony into the narrative; but their deeper implications are not followed up. At the first moment of crisis in their relationship – when Kim is found by the Regiment – the division in his life is glossed over by the Lama's recognition that 'Education is greatest blessing if of best sorts'. And during the next years Kim is able to lead two separate lives – school and holidays – which never touch, so that the Lama and the Game are kept in different compartments, with the connecting link that experience of the Road is relevant both to the Game and the Search. The period of education over, however, the conflict is bound, somehow or other, to be clarified and fought out.

Kim's question as to where the money came from for his education is, in fact, a very pertinent question. What he is seeking, not perhaps quite consciously, is a chink in the Lama's armour. Is the old man really so indifferent to Doing, to the operation of material reality, as he seems? Is he not perhaps playing some Game of his own? Isn't his indifference, perhaps, a bit of a fraud, a luxury which he can afford because he is, ultimately, materially secure? And Teshoo Lama's reply, simply invoking human need, is so unanswerable that it is not surprising that Kim drops the subject. For the reply does not reject the significance of money, of material activity (a rejection which would have played into the hands of the shrewd realist in Kim) but, rather, puts it in its place. Doing, the Lama's argument implies, is necessary: the question is, where does it lead?

The conflict, which first gains open expression during the episode with the Mahratta, dominates the remainder of the book. Kim manages, as has been remarked, to stage-manage the Lama's return to the Hills in a way which suits the interests of the Game. Once again the contradiction between what he is up to and what the Lama assumes he is doing is side-tracked or temporarily muted. The Lama is happy in the Hills, where the life and air are in harmony with his material needs and habits, and so he thinks less about his Search. But it is clear to the reader that, in dragging the old man into the very jaws of the Game, Kim is building up trouble for himself, and sure enough when the crisis comes it takes a form whose significance cannot be escaped. Superficially, in terms of the tactics of the Game, the events which follow the striking of the Lama have an outcome satisfactory enough. The old man, though badly shaken, survives. The nefarious plans of the Russians are thwarted. Kim can at the same time chalk up a success for himself as secret agent and demonstrate his loyalty and devotion to his Lama. But what has happened in fact makes further compromise impossible. A man cannot indefinitely serve two opposing masters. What the episode brings home to the Lama is not that his defences were inadequate but that material considerations, his love of the Hills, corrupted him and led him to forget the Search.

This is the significance of the return to the Plains, and Kim knows it. That is why Kim's crisis can no longer be put off: it is not simply that he has led the old man into danger, it is that he has led himself to an impasse. His rejection of the advances of the Woman of Shamlegh is relatively straightforward. His Sahib-consciousness helps him out there (though for the reader the episode does not strengthen confidence in the values of Sahibdom). But to the demands now put upon him by the total situation the jaunty self-confidence he can usually muster cannot be adequate. The documents he carries wrapped in oilskin and his sense of responsibility

for the Lama now weigh on him almost intolerably and the two
burdens pull his mind in opposite directions. When he finally gets
rid of the documents to Hurree Babu he literally does not know
whether the relief he feels comes from a sense of duty accomplished
or burden removed. Kim's crisis is physical, psychological, emotional, moral, all rolled into one. Kipling's sense of the intercon-
nection of all these elements is remarkably shrewd and deep.

The resolution of the impasse, which most readers clearly do not
regard as a resolution at all, seems to me beautifully achieved, and I
think Mr Kinkead-Weekes's emphasis on the rightness of Lockwood
Kipling's final illustration is an excellent piece of criticism. The
Pater seems to have understood his son's deeper purposes better than
many of his admirers, better perhaps than the author himself.

What Kipling achieves in these last pages – no doubt with the aid
of his daemon – is the cutting of a false knot, the clearing away of a
false antithesis. Thought and action have been at odds throughout
the book. Oversimplifying a little, the Lama has embodied thought,
the Idea: Kim has embodied action, Doing. The Search and the
Game have been presented – as indeed they are to their adherents –
as opposite poles: so that the Search (a concern with values) becomes
good but a bit irrelevant and the Game (practical politics) unscrupulous but necessary. And given such an antithesis in practice, since
there is no foregoing the claims of necessity, the Game is bound to
win, though a niche of respectful but ultimately ineffectual admiration will be reserved for the Lamas of this world. Then, with Kim's
breakdown and the Lama's discovery of the River, a double change
takes place.

The change in Kim can only take place when Hurree Babu has
taken away the documents, thus bringing to an end the uncomple-
ted adventure in the Hills. It is relief that this episode has been
completed, plus admiration for the complex courage of the fearful
Babu, that break through Kim's weakness and lethargy and lead to a
desire to find a solution of his inner crisis: 'I must get into the world
again'. At first he remains frustrated:

All that while he felt, though he could not put it into words, that his
soul was out of gear with its surroundings – a cog-wheel unconnected with
any machinery, just like the idle cog-wheel of a cheap Beheea sugar-crusher
laid by in a corner.

And his soul repeats again and again the cry 'I am Kim. I am Kim
and what is Kim?' until suddenly there is a resolution, physical

(through tears) and psychological 'and with an almost audible click he felt the wheels of his being lock up anew on the world without.'

This seems to me psychologically an extremely acute and convincing description of emergence from alienation, an emergence begun by a sudden *desire* to emerge, sparked off by an almost casual contact with relevant reality, and continuing through a process in which the physical and mental needs to re-establish contact are inseparably interwoven. Then, the moment of crisis over,

Things that rode meaningless on the eyeball an instant before slid into proper proportion. Roads were meant to be walked upon, houses to be lived in, cattle to be driven, fields to be tilled, and men and women to be talked to. They were all real and true — solidly planted upon the feet — perfectly comprehensible — clay of his clay, neither more nor less.[10]

And Kim, now lying flat upon the Earth, 'the hopeful dust that holds the seeds of all life' surrenders to her strength, relaxes and sleeps, awaking only after Mahbub, like Hurree, has gone back to the Game and only the Lama is there to help him back to life.

The book then ends with the Lama's account of his discovery of the River. Kim says nothing more except for a few typically down-to-earth comments on the Lama's narrative. The Game is not mentioned. His being a Sahib is not mentioned. The answer to the question 'What is Kim?' is given in terms that make no reference to either. Kim is a man in the world of men, neither more nor less. It is a real world, not an illusion (as the Lama's philosophy would have it), a world of Doing in which action is neither an irrelevance nor an end in itself but a necessary element in the relationship between men and nature, man and man. This is what Kim has come through to. He could not have reached this sense of unity without the help of the Lama, but it is not the Lama's philosophy that he now embraces; he could not have come through without the help of the adherents of the Game, but it is not the rules of the Game that he now submits to. And perhaps the key to the change that has come over Kim lies in the change in the way he formulates his ultimate question. Throughout his life, when critical moments have forced him to pose fundamental problems he has asked 'Who is Kim?' And the question has been accompanied always by a sense of being alone. Now the form of the question is changed from the individualist 'Who?' with its presumption of an answer in terms of some absolute or mystical 'identity', to the more fruitful 'What?' with its possibility of an answer which can begin to resolve the contradictions between the one and the others, between the reality and the idea, between the world of the Game and the world of Teshoo Lama. Kim has escaped from the false antithesis, the choice between action on the one hand and truth on the other, between an amoral materialism and an unworldly idealism. The new materialism to which he advances, and of which the emblem is his sense of identity with the earth and its processes, no longer excludes the human values encompassed in his relationships with the Lama.

No less important – and indeed complementary to the change in Kim – is the change which, in the very last pages of the book, takes place in the Lama. The old man achieves his object and discovers the River to which his Search has led him. But the act of discovery involves a reorientation as significant as Kim's. At the very instant of apparent fulfilment of his quest, when his Soul has escaped from the Wheel of Things and touched the Great Soul, he remembers Kim and, upon this, Soul withdraws itself from the Great Soul.

As the egg from the fish, as the fish from the water, as the water from the cloud, as the cloud from the thick air; so put forth, so leaped out, so drew away, so fumed up the soul of Teshoo Lama from the Great Soul.

'It is only then' as Mr Kinkead-Weekes admirably puts it 'that he sees the River which can cleanse him from a sin still with him; and when one has reached this point any old river will do.' Mr Kinkead-Weekes adds 'The "sin" can only be the element of selfishness in the search for the perfection of self by turning away from others'. That is one way of putting it: another way would be to say that the Lama at this point rids himself of idealism, the illusion that the world itself is an illusion and that any idea – call it the Great Soul or what you will – can have priority over material reality. He sees, in other words, that human relationships and spiritual values have their basis in material reality (this is the significance of the imagery of process through which the Lama expresses himself) and in this way, like Kim, cuts through the false antithesis between truth and action. It is thus that the resolution of the book takes place – not in terms of some new doctrine of salvation, religious or political, but in terms of the acceptance of reality by both Kim and the Lama, an acceptance which will inevitably affect their future actions. What those actions are to be would have involved, of course, another story and one which Kipling never wrote.

Notes

1 *Eight Modern Writers* (Vol. XII of *The Oxford History of English Literature*, 1964), p. 259.

2 'The Kipling that Nobody Read' in *Kipling's Mind and Art* (ed. A. Rutherford), 1964, p. 29.

3 Charles Carrington, *Rudyard Kipling* (1955), p. 362.

4 That Kipling was well aware of the oddness is shown by his own description. 'At last I reported *Kim* finished. "Did *it* stop, or you?" the Father asked. And when I told him that it was *It*, he said "Then it oughtn't to be too bad."' Kipling's conviction that it was his *daemon* rather than himself who wrote his books has its own significance and helps to explain why it is so often unsatisfactory to judge his work simply in terms of his known political opinions.

5 *Rudyard Kipling* (1940), p. 215.

6 *A Choice of Kipling's Verse* (1963), Preface, p. 23.

7 In *Kipling's Mind and Art*, pp. 216–34.

8 *Kim*, ch. XII.

9 *Ibid.*

10 *Ibid.*, ch. XV.

Sources and acknowledgements

The progressive tradition in bourgeois culture. Originally published in *Essays on Socialist Realism and the British Cultural Tradition* (London: Arena Publications, 1952). Reprinted in *Masses and Mainstream*, 7 (1954), pp. 9–20, and in *Radical Perspectives in the Arts*, ed. Lee Baxandall (Harmondsworth: Penguin, 1972).

The artist and politics. Originally published in *Marxism Today*, 3 (1959), pp. 139–45. This article attracted a number of responses, to which Arnold Kettle replied in a 'Discussion on the artist and politics', *Marxism Today*, 4 (1960), pp. 61–4.

'The Mental Traveller.' Originally published in *Arena*, I (1950), pp. 46–52.

From Hamlet to Lear. Originally published in *Shakespeare in a Changing World*, ed. Arnold Kettle (London: Lawrence & Wishart, 1964).

Bernard Shaw and the new spirit. Originally published in *Rebels and Their Causes: Essays in Honour of A. L. Morton*, ed. Maurice Cornforth (London: Lawrence & Wishart, 1978).

W. H. Auden: poetry and politics in the thirties. Originally published in *Culture and Crisis in Britain in the Thirties*, ed. Jon Clark, Margot Heinemann, David Margolies and Carole Snee (London: Lawrence & Wishart, 1979).

The precursors of Defoe: Puritanism and the rise of the novel. Originally published in *On the Novel: A Present for Walter Allen on his 60th Birthday from his Friends and Colleagues*, ed. B. S. Benedikz (London: Dent, 1971).

In defence of *Moll Flanders*. Originally published in *Of Books and Humankind: Essays and Poems Presented to Bonamy Dobrée*, ed. John Butt (London: Routledge, 1964).

Dickens and the popular tradition. Originally published in *Zeitschrift für Anglistik und Amerikanistik* (Berlin Ost), IX (1961), pp. 229–52. Reprinted in *The Carleton Miscellany*, 3 (1962), pp. 17–51, and in *Marxists on Literature: An Anthology*, ed. David Craig (Harmondsworth: Penguin, 1975).

Our Mutual Friend. Originally published in *Dickens and the Twentieth Century*, ed. John Gross and Gabriel Pearson (London: Routledge, 1962).

Beauchamp's Career. Originally published in *Meredith Now: Some Critical Essays*, ed. Ian Fletcher (London: Routledge, 1973).

Felix Holt the Radical. Originally published in *Critical Essays on George Eliot*, ed. Barbara Hardy (London: Routledge, 1970).

What is Kim? Originally published in *The Morality of Art: Essays Presented to G. Wilson Knight by his Colleagues and Friends*, ed. D. W. Jefferson (London: Routledge, 1969).

Index